CAR PC
HACKS™

Stolarz

O'REILLY®

Beijing · Cambridge · Farnham · Köln · Paris · Sebastopol · Taipei · Tokyo

Car PC Hacks™
by Damien Stolarz

Published by O'Reilly Media, Inc., 1005 Gravenstein Highway North,
Sebastopol, CA 95472.

O'Reilly books may be purchased for educational, business, or sales promotional use. Online editions are also available for most titles (*safari.oreilly.com*). For more information, contact our corporate/institutional sales department: (800) 998-9938 or *corporate@oreilly.com*.

Editor:	David Brickner	**Production Editor:**	Genevieve d'Entremont
Series Editor:	Rael Dornfest	**Cover Designer:**	Hanna Dyer
Executive Editor:	Dale Dougherty	**Interior Designer:**	David Futato

Printing History:

July 2005:　　　　First Edition.

 This book uses RepKover™, a durable and flexible lay-flat binding.

ISBN: 0-596-00871-6
[M]

Contents

Credits

About the Author

Damien Stolarz is an entrepreneur who has spent over half his life making computers talk to each other. He cofounded Static.com (now *http://www.akimbo.com*) in 1995, and in his long tenure as Chief Technology Officer he led the development of numerous technologies, including a direct-dial online service, networked multiplayer games, and peer-to-peer cost-reduction software for video streaming. In 2002, he left to start Robotarmy Corp. (*http://www.robotarmy.com*), a software consultancy and R&D house that develops large-scale media delivery software, amongst other secret projects. In 2004, Damien founded CarBot, Inc. (*http://www.carbotpc.com*), which designs and manufactures in-car entertainment computers and accompanying software. Damien is the author of *Mastering Internet Video* (Addison-Wesley). He holds a B.S. in Computer Science/Engineering from UCLA.

Damien loves email and is good about responding. You can reach him at *author@damienstolarz.com*, and you can find a link to his online journal at *http://www.damienstolarz.com*.

Contributors

The following people contributed to *Car PC Hacks*:

- Terran Brown [Hack #52] is a Project Manager at a leading international outsourcing company working with large Blue Chip customers. He has worked in the IT industry for eight years in various technical roles in wide-area networking and server support. His technical background led to his interest in car PC technology, and he is now one of the more recognized enthusiasts from the U.K. His web site is *http://www.letscommunicate.co.uk*.

- David Burban [Hack #60] is a high school junior in Los Angeles. He taught himself VB, but after a brief hiatus from programming, he matured on to Delphi. He now enjoys programming in Delphi in his spare time. Besides making NaviVoice and GammaControl, David Burban has also created software for showing car PC information on text LCD displays. His web site can be found at *http://www.whipflash.com/vamr/*.

- Lionel Felix [Hacks #4, #24, #29, #52, and #53] has worked in IT Systems Strategy for 10 years, designing and building enterprise networks and data centers. He has been tinkering with cars, car stereos, and computers since before he could drive or get online without adult supervision. He is currently consulting on various enterprise IT projects and providing IT executive coaching, and he continues to do terrible things to innocent vehicles and computers. He can be reached in his garage or at *ldfelix@carhacks.org*.

- Zoran Horvat (a.k.a. Zorro) [Hack #63] has more than 20 years of experience in the IT industry. He started developing software applications on the legendary Commodore C64. For 14 years he worked as a Software Engineer, Architect, and Project Manager. Now Zoran works as a freelancer, developing applications in C#, Visual Basic, C++, and Java, as well as web applications in DHTML. One of his favorite hobbies is in-car computing, and he developed PhoneControl.NET (*http://www.phonecontrol.net*) for linking mobile phones and car PCs. You can reach him at *PhoneControl@zoran-horvat.de*.

- Jirka Jirout [Hack #53] is an IT Manager at Metro Holland BV. He has been building electronic circuits and toys since he was 10 years old. He first learned to program on the ZX Spectrum and some obscure Eastern-bloc computers in the former Czechoslovakia, and eventually moved on to Windows PCs and then Macintoshes. His other hobbies are antique cars (especially the Tatra), photography, and building ship models. Jirka lives and works in the Netherlands with his wife and daughter.

- Kevin Lincecum (a.k.a. FrodoBaggins) [Hacks #64 and #75] started working with computers at age 10. He spent his time ripping apart hardware and software for kicks, and overworking his parents' phone lines on BBS systems (the precursors to the Internet). Having worked in the IT industry for nine years now, he has developed a love of programming, especially for car PCs. He is the developer of the popular frontend with the funny name, FrodoPlayer. All of his programs can be found online at *http://www.frodoplayer.com*. Kevin also asks that you visit his blog site at *http://www.teabaggins.com*, where you may find a slice of Frodo that many people don't get to see. And if you need him in a pinch, look no further than the MP3Car.com forums, where he spends a whole lot of his time keeping the "noobs" and veterans in line as an admin (when his wonderful wife Joanna will let him, and when his three cats, Marble, Sable, and Amy, give him any peace).

- David McGowan [Hack #73] received a B.B.A. in Management Information Systems and a minor in Computer Science from the University of Mississippi. When he is not working on CENTRAFUSE (*http://www.fluxmedia.net*), David can be found building appraisal-management systems for large lenders. Some of his other work includes a Java-based document management system, corporate intranet software, and a web-based appraisal delivery system. Recently David has spent most of his time writing in C#, but he is no stranger to Java, C++, or VB. When he's not programming, you can find David snowboarding in the Sierra Mountains or riding waves on the beach. You can contact him at *info@fluxmedia.net*.

- Paul Peavyhouse [Hack #65] has reluctantly enjoyed working at Microsoft since 1998, in the Real-Time Collaboration (RTC) and Conferencing fields. His CS experience came from creating the Night55 Vibe/Sonique MP3 player while failing out of Montana State University. It was here, while working on the MSU "Double Black Diamond" Solar Vehicle Project, that Paul learned enough electronics skills to be mistaken as the Unabomber by the authorities. His web site is *http://www.swooby.com/pv/*, and his Nissan 350Z car PC project can be seen at *http://www.swooby.com/z/navpc/*.

- Tor Pinney [Hacks #5 and #68] is a writer, traveler, cruising sailor, and entrepreneur. His book *Ready for Sea!* (Sheridan House) is an authoritative manual for outfitting modern sailboats for long-term voyaging and living aboard. Tor founded the world's first Internet-focused international yacht brokerage, Anchor Yacht & Ship Sales (*http://www.anchoryachts.com*), developing original techniques to list, promote, and sell yachts online around the world. Tor is presently traveling and writing full time. His web site is *http://www.tor.cc*.

- Jacob Riskin [Hacks #64 and #70] is an entrepreneur who cofounded and ran Static.com (now *http://www.akimbo.com*) as its CEO from 1995 to 2001. Jacob has over 14 years of experience in advanced programming design for online systems, and he codesigned Static's core technologies, including its P2P distributed file network, game synchronization toolbox, and client/server interface. Prior to founding Static in 1995, Jacob worked in the magazine publishing industry on a prominent video game magazine, *Gamefan*.

- Silvio Fiorito [Hack #49] spent six years working as a software engineer for various startups and large corporations in the Northern Virginia area during the height of the dot-com boom. After getting bored of writing code all day, Silvio decided to change pace and return to his studies just as the bubble burst. Along with impeccable timing, Silvio also has a love of tinkering with the latest and greatest in technology, keeping his car PC in a constant state of development. He is currently majoring in Information Security at George Mason University in Fairfax, Virginia. You can contact him at *silvio.fiorito@gmail.com*.

- Stéphane Monnier [Hack #74] is a thrill-seeking software developer based in Massongex, Switzerland. After retiring from his early career as a Swiss champion Go-Kart racer, he moved on to a career in high-voltage-control engineering. He is the author of Neocar Media Center (*http://www.neocarmediacenter.com*), one of the most popular car PC applications. He would like to thank Cyril (Gore), NMC's main debugger, as well as all the users from CarMedia.org and MP3Car.com who have helped with the application. He is most thankful that his girlfriend Joanna lets him code as much as he wants to. You can contact him at *netsuo@bluewin.ch*.

- J.P. Stewart [Hacks #67 and #68] is a Computer Engineer from Washington State with eight years of experience in writing custom online tools. He is currently working for an industry-leading software company building and breaking software. When not at work, he is usually busy either out taking pictures of the northwestern U.S., working on some current multimedia/home entertainment project, working on some other online tool for his web site (*http://www.jpstewart.org*), or working on software for his car PC.

- Adam Stolarz [Hack #72] did the photography for *Car PC Hacks*. A home-schooled high school student, he's also a skilled writer, a computer technologist, and a budding artist. He spends an inordinate amount of his own time and others' money on video games. He can be reached at *adam@carbotpc.com*.

- Jason Tokunaga [Hack #71] has a background in aerospace engineering but has made the jump to the sexier field of Project Management. He has worked in the software industry for the past six years, on projects ranging from distributed networking and streaming media delivery to enterprise-class applications. A die-hard video enthusiast, he's currently managing an unreasonable number of projects in the Web/IT division of a major studio. He has a degree in Mechanical Engineering from UC Berkeley.

Acknowledgments

Thanks to David Brickner, the editor of this book, who is even more laid-back than I am; Rael Dornfest, who originally took up my offer for the book and whose efficiency I admire; Jessamyn Read, who created all the diagrams; and my brother Adam Stolarz, who took the photos for the book under cruel and unusual deadlines.

Thanks to the production team at O'Reilly: Genevieve d'Entremont, Jessamyn Read, Keith Fahlgren, and Lydia Onofrei.

Thanks to Nat Wilson, who runs *http://www.mp3car.com* and knows so much about in-car computing that I trembled when I read his critiques. (Fortunately, it turns out I was on the right track most of the time.)

Thanks to Kevin "Frodo" Lincecum for writing great software and thus helping to create the market for car PCs.

Thanks to George Dean, a brilliant engineer and creator of the CarBot software architecture. I owe him a great debt of gratitude for making this book and CarBot possible.

Thanks to all the CarBot contributors, old and new: Mark Dixon, Jason Tokunaga, Matthew Wright, Zack Aaron, Jeremy Stolarz, Zack Gainsforth, Andrew DelGatto, Josh Bandur, Ashley Hoffman, Jim Baker, Chris Welch, Edwin Khang, Raffi Krikorian, Roger Killer, and Michael O'Reilly.

Thanks to Kalani Patterson and Michael Morena for their brave alpha testing of the prototype CarBot PCs.

Thanks to Robert Rucker, Aaron Matthews, and Alex Fox from Good Guys in my hometown of Canoga Park, who endured days and days of questions about car installations, customer preferences, and the 12-volt market in general. Special thanks to Robert, who did all the hard parts of my Mac Mini installation [Hack #54].

Thanks to the installers at Pacific Stereo in Woodland Hills, Jose Balz, Rene Beltran, and Jesse Alvarez, who gave my minivan more power, more treble, and better rearview visibility.

Thanks to Clint and Casey from Street Performers in Reseda, who did a fantastic job of modernizing my 1950 Nash Ambassador.

Thanks to Cliff Leeper and Joe Hegener from SyndicateAuto.com in San Diego for doing such a gorgeous install of Robert Baizer's CarBot.

Thanks to Lionel Felix for all his feedback as a reviewer and contributor, and for helping me get Carhacks.org running and keeping me rolling on the floor laughing. And speaking of comedy, I also have to thank Jeff Munsey, who did a thorough job of reviewing the manuscripts and cracking me up at the same time.

Thanks to Raffi Krikorian, who fixed so much of the imprecision in my exposition and taught me that voltage is more like a rock on a cliff than water in a hose.

Warm thanks to Tim O'Reilly, who has created a delightful playground for inventors and technology writers such as myself.

Thank you Dr. Darius Sankey for many years of kind guidance and support for my professional ventures.

And finally, thanks to my family, who is happy to have me back after my latest book-writing adventure.

Preface

The time for in-car computing has arrived. There are strong signs in every direction that personal computing technology will soon take over the car. It started with satellite radio, bringing streaming digital audio to the car. Then the iPod captured the digital audio player market and suddenly became a de-facto standard car audio component. MP3 players, in-car navigation systems, and touchscreens are now standard in many vehicles—and it won't stop there.

So why do people go through all the trouble of installing computers in their cars?

Choice is one reason. Today, you are locked into the navigation system that came with your car, if it even came with one—and the costs of upgrading to a new one are immense. Why shouldn't you be able to say, "I like the navigation system in the Infiniti, I think I'll get that for my Civic"? With an in-car computer, you can choose the implementation that you like the best.

Features are another reason. Once we get used to features (e.g., digital media such as digital video recorders and iPods) in one part of our lives, we want to be able to use them everywhere—including in our cars. Cutting-edge features that would otherwise require expensive hardware upgrades can often be acquired via a simple software download if you have a car PC.

Integration is vitally important as well. When you've got half a dozen different kinds of digital media sitting in the passenger seat of your car (mobile phone, camera, PDA, iPod, portable USB memory stick, CDs), you'd like them to be able to talk to each other. For example, many people stare wistfully at their digital audio devices, wishing that the MP3 audio would somehow leap out of them and into their car radios. Putting a computer in your car will allow all your gadgets to work with your vehicle.

Finally, forward compatibility is a huge problem for which a general-purpose computer is the only solution. A definitive standard for device communication in the car is unlikely to emerge anytime soon, but a PC can serve as a digital hub for all your devices. Consumer electronics and computing are inextricably linked; there are few devices a computer can't talk to in one way or another. An in-car computer can serve as digital glue for features, peripherals, and networks that haven't even been invented yet. With an in-car computer, you won't get left behind—and you won't have to buy a new car to get ahead.

Why Car PC Hacks?

The term *hacking* has a bad reputation in the press. They use it to refer to someone who breaks into systems or wreaks havoc with computers as their weapon. Among people who write code, though, the term *hack* refers to a "quick-and-dirty" solution to a problem, or a clever way to get something done. And the term *hacker* is taken very much as a compliment, referring to someone as being *creative*, having the technical chops to get things done. The Hacks series is an attempt to reclaim the word, document the good ways people are hacking, and pass the hacker ethic of creative participation on to the uninitiated. Seeing how others approach systems and problems is often the quickest way to learn about a new technology.

Traditionally, car guys don't know computers, and computer guys don't know cars. *Car PC Hacks* was written to bridge that gap. For computer hackers skilled in all things software and hardware, this book will fill you in on the wiring, power, and connector basics you need to get around a car. For mechanics and auto enthusiasts who can install speakers, amps, and stereos in their sleep but depend on their friends to fix their ailing computers, this book can show you the essential aspects of the computer/car interface in a language you understand. Once you've gotten the basics and realize how simple wiring computers into cars can be, *Car PC Hacks* shows you how to add sci-fi features to your car that will blow people away.

How to Use This Book

You can read this book from cover to cover if you like, but each hack stands on its own, so feel free to browse and jump to the different sections that interest you most. If there's a prerequisite you need to know about, a cross-reference will guide you to the right hack.

The first few chapters cover the basics of car wiring, showing how easy it is to hack your car and wire up speakers, radios, screens, and external devices and computers. They also show you how to make sure you have enough power in your car to power all your new devices.

The middle chapters get to the heart of the matter: wiring up a car PC. They cover the full range of options for installing, displaying, and controlling your car PC, and they provide several hacks on start-to-finish car PC installations.

The final chapters in the book introduce you to the many applications and features that become possible with a car PC. They provide full coverage of ways to access the Internet in your car, as well as introducing you to the most popular car PC programs used by thousands of people today.

How This Book Is Organized

Since this book is aimed at both "car guys" and "computer guys," it includes a lot of material for both audiences. Whether you are an end user just trying to figure out what program to run, or a software developer trying to figure out how to get your new creation into the dashboard, you'll find the information you need in these chapters.

Chapter 1, *Car Power Basics*

> This chapter goes over the basics of 12-volt power in the car. Its goal is to help you get rid of any myths you have about hacking into your car's electrical system and show you what you should look out for. It also shows you the similarities between computer and car power systems. When you're done with this chapter, you'll fear no outlet or wire.

Chapter 2, *Automotive Audio Entertainment*

> Your car PC isn't very entertaining if it isn't connected to your car's stereo system. This chapter's hacks show you how to get any device connected to a car's audio system, be it an iPod or a car PC. It also covers how to get the best sound over this connection and how to eliminate buzzes, hisses, and hums. Finally, it covers a few of the audio applications that only a car PC can deliver.

Chapter 3, *Automotive Video Entertainment*

> This chapter covers almost every option for getting video into your car. From touchscreens to rearview cameras to HDTV, every popular installation of in-car video is covered in detail. It also helps you understand the various video formats (car, home, and computer), how they differ, and how to get them into your car despite these differences. You're sure to come up with new ideas for your car after reading this chapter.

Chapter 4, *In-Car Computers*

> This chapter gets to the heart of the matter: installing a PC in your car. It covers choosing the hardware components that work best for car PCs, power supplies, and the other gadgets necessary to make your car PC work like it came with your car. It also covers operating system options and the trade-offs between them, including hints on how to speed up

boot time. The chapter ends with three detailed car PC installation case studies.

Chapter 5, *Car PC Interface Options*

The biggest challenge in car computing is safe operation for the driver. Keyboards and mice are useless in a vehicle, yet they are the primary forms of communication between humans and computers. This chapter covers the popular man/machine interfaces that *do* work in a car, such as touchscreens, remote controls, and even voice recognition. It also contains some hacks to force unruly desktop applications to behave in a vehicle.

Chapter 6, *Wireless Connectivity and in-Car Internet*

Wireless Internet and network connectivity are key ingredients in many of the cleverest hacks for car PCs. WiFi and 3G mobile phones make absurdly cool features possible. This chapter will help you figure out how to get your car online and how to transfer all of your audio and video media to your car seamlessly.

Chapter 7, *In-Car Applications*

To take advantage of the wide range of entertainment and productivity options available on your car PC, you need the right applications. This chapter highlights the leading car PC frontends and navigation programs for driver use. It also covers rear-seat entertainment options, such as video games and in-car theater. It even shows you how to link your car PC and the internal computers that make your car run.

Conventions Used in This Book

The following is a list of the typographical conventions used in this book:

Italics

Used for emphasis and new terms where they are defined, and to indicate URLs, filenames, filename extensions, and directory/folder names. For example, a path in the filesystem will appear as */Developer/Applications*.

`Constant width`

Used to show code examples, the contents of files, and console output, as well as the names of variables, commands, and other code excerpts.

`Constant width bold`

Used for commands to be typed by the user and to highlight portions of code.

Constant width italic

Used in code examples to show sample text to be replaced with your own values.

Color

Used to indicate a cross-reference within the text.

You should pay special attention to notes set apart from the text with the following icons:

This is a tip, suggestion, or general note. It contains useful supplementary information about the topic at hand.

This is a warning or note of caution, often indicating that things might not work out.

The thermometer icons, found next to each hack, indicate the relative complexity of the hack:

 beginner   moderate   expert

Using Code Examples

This book is here to help you get your job done. In general, you may use the code in this book in your programs and documentation. You do not need to contact us for permission unless you're reproducing a significant portion of the code. For example, writing a program that uses several chunks of code from this book does not require permission. Selling or distributing a CD-ROM of examples from O'Reilly books *does* require permission. Answering a question by citing this book and quoting example code does not require permission. Incorporating a significant amount of example code from this book into your product's documentation *does* require permission.

We appreciate, but do not require, attribution. An attribution usually includes the title, author, publisher, and ISBN. For example: "*Car PC Hacks* by Damien Stolarz. Copyright 2005 O'Reilly Media, Inc., 0-596-00871-6."

If you feel your use of code examples falls outside fair use or the permission given above, feel free to contact us at *permissions@oreilly.com*.

Safari Enabled

 When you see a Safari® Enabled icon on the cover of your favorite technology book, that means the book is available online through the O'Reilly Network Safari Bookshelf.

Safari offers a solution that's better than e-books. It's a virtual library that lets you easily search thousands of top tech books, cut and paste code samples, download chapters, and find quick answers when you need the most accurate, current information. Try it for free at *http://safari.oreilly.com*.

How to Contact Us

We have tested and verified the information in this book to the best of our ability, but you may find that features have changed (or even that we have made mistakes!). As a reader of this book, you can help us to improve future editions by sending us your feedback. Please let us know about any errors, inaccuracies, bugs, misleading or confusing statements, and typos that you find anywhere in this book.

Please also let us know what we can do to make this book more useful to you. We take your comments seriously and will try to incorporate reasonable suggestions into future editions. You can write to us at:

O'Reilly Media, Inc.
1005 Gravenstein Hwy N.
Sebastopol, CA 95472
(800) 998-9938 (in the U.S. or Canada)
(707) 829-0515 (international/local)
(707) 829-0104 (fax)

To ask technical questions or to comment on the book, send email to:

bookquestions@oreilly.com

The web site for *Car PC Hacks* lists examples, errata, and plans for future editions. You can find this page at:

http://www.oreilly.com/catalog/carpchks

For more information about this book and others, see the O'Reilly web site:

http://www.oreilly.com

Got a Hack?

To explore Hacks books online or to contribute a hack for future titles, visit:

http://hacks.oreilly.com

Car Power Basics
Hacks 1–11

Home electronics and car electronics are quite different. Homes are designed to power dozens of large appliances; cars are designed to power a handful of small electronic devices. Homes run on high voltages that could give you a heart attack; most of the electricity in a car won't even give you a shock.

This chapter is going to give you a rapid-fire, metaphor-rich tutorial on electronics, and automotive electronics in particular. It will go over key terms, such as voltage, amperage, and wattage, and give you a basic understanding of how to do arithmetic with these numbers. The goal is to get you up to speed quickly on car electronics, and show you the essential system upgrades that will help you hook up and power your in-car computers and accessories.

HACK #1 Understand Car Electrical Systems

Different electronic systems, such as those for houses, cars, and computers, use very different connectors, voltages, and power levels.

If you are familiar with only home or computer electronics, you will need a little bit of background before you start playing with the wires in your car. This hack will introduce you to automobile power. Because you will probably want to "bench test" your in-car computers in the house before installing them in your car, it will also show you how you can hack a computer power supply to power your in-car accessories indoors.

The first term you need to learn about is *voltage*, which is simply the amount of potential (work, force, energy, change) in an electrical flow. Different devices are designed around a certain level of electrical potential, which can be thought of as the amount of pressure propelling the electricity. The analogy most often used to explain voltage is water flow, where the pressure of the water coming out of a hose is like the voltage, which can be turned up and down by a valve or spigot. The same hose can release high-pressure water to clean a driveway, or a low-pressure flow to fill a water balloon.

Electricity, however, doesn't flow readily through the air like water does. Electricity travels well only through *conductors*, such as metal wires, and in order to flow it requires a return path (usually called the *ground*) going back to the source of the voltage. In our water metaphor, the ground would be represented by a drainpipe. (Of course, water conveniently doesn't require a returning drainpipe to flow.)

Another, slightly more accurate analogy for electricity is that of water pouring over a cliff. The cliff represents the positive (or +) end of a battery, and the electricity flows from the high cliff down to the ground (negative, or −). The higher the cliff, the higher the voltage. However, I'll continue to use the hose-pressure metaphor because of the corresponding analogy between wires and hoses.

Computer Voltages

Internally, computers run on several different voltages. The power supply, like the one seen in Figure 1-1, delivers all these voltages through the various colored wires that come out of it and connect to the motherboard. The black wires generally represent the ground, which allows the electricity to go back to the source and complete its round trip, or *circuit*.

The voltage going *into* the power supply comes from a wall outlet. This provides between 110V and 240V, depending on the country you are in. The computer power supply converts this high-voltage input into the various output voltages needed by the motherboard and computer peripheral devices. (To use a standard PC power supply in a car, you need to install an inverter to increase your car's 12V to 120V [Hack #11]).

The computer uses many different voltages for different chips and devices. Three voltages usually supplied by the power supply are 12V, 5V, and 3.3V. Many chips run on 5V; others run on 3.3V. Modern CPUs use even lower voltages, such as 2.2V or 1.8V, but the motherboard usually converts the higher voltages from the power supply to provide these lower voltages. The primary two voltages that come out of the power supply to power devices are 12V and 5V. 12V is good for powering motors such as those in hard drives, fans, and CD-ROM drives. 5V is good for powering the electronic circuit boards that these devices use. Figure 1-2 shows the four wires that peripheral connectors on standard computer power supplies have: 5V, 12V, and two ground wires.

Figure 1-1. An ATX power supply

Car Voltages

The electricity in your car comes from its battery. Though this large battery is referred to as a 12V battery, it's actually in the 13V range when fully charged and can dip down to 11V or lower if you leave a light on and discharge it. During engine cranking (starting the car) [Hack #45] voltage can dip down to 8V or lower, and if your PC power supply isn't designed to handle this it will hang or reboot your computer.

Computers are not very tolerant of voltage changes like this. For this reason, computer power supplies ensure that, no matter how the input voltage bounces around, the output remains stable. This is called *voltage regulation*. Automobiles, however, provide much sloppier, unregulated power. Automotive "12V" is more of an average than a precise voltage. Because of this, most devices built for cars have their own power supplies that also regulate the voltage.

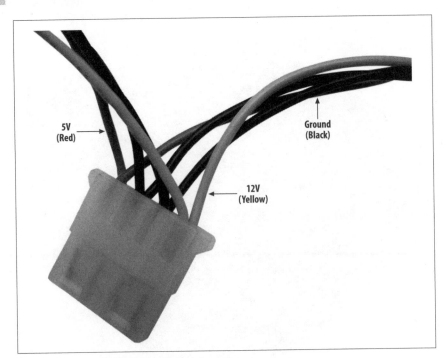

5V
(Red)

Ground
(Black)

12V
(Yellow)

Figure 1-2. Typical PC power supply wires

Traditionally, most third-party car electronic devices plug into the cigarette lighter socket (so named because its original purpose was to provide a method to light cigarettes). Even though most cars don't come with cigarette lighters anymore, the standard power outlet shown in Figure 1-3 remains and continues to be utilized.

> In cars, the entire metal body of the vehicle is usually connected in some way to the ground. Older cars run a single 12V wire to the cigarette lighter outlet center, and the outer shell of the outlet is then simply connected to the metal dashboard. Newer vehicles are made of plastic and vinyl, with some paint-coated metal thrown in, so they run both the ground and the 12V wire to the outlet.

The Key to Car Power: Off, Accessory, On/Ignition, and Crank

You probably don't think about it when you drive a car, but the position of the key switch determines where the electricity of the vehicle goes.

There are actually two kinds of power outlets in modern vehicles: *switched* and *unswitched*. Switched outlets are on only when your car key is in the

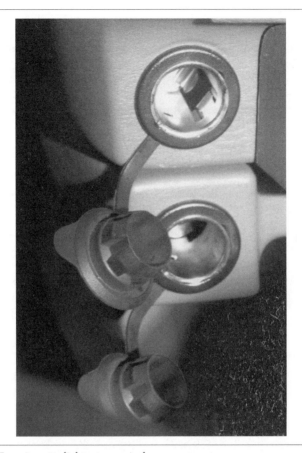

Figure 1-3. Two cigarette lighter power jacks

accessory or *on* positions. Naturally, when the car is on, any devices you have are on. When the key is in the accessory position, all of your accessories (such as the radio and any devices that are plugged in) are running. When the car is off, any switched power outlets are turned off, and usually the radio goes off too.

Unswitched outlets and hardwired accessories are always connected to the car's battery, whether the car is off or on. Car alarms are all wired this way, which is why they are designed to draw very little power. If you've ever left your lights on and come back to find that you can't start your car, you know why low power draw is important.

When you are cranking the engine to start the car, most accessories (including switched outlets) are turned off temporarily so that all the battery power can be devoted to starting the car. Fans, power windows and doors, radios, amplifiers, and most lights observe a "moment of silence" as the car starts. Because the battery must turn a heavy motor that cranks the entire engine, the voltage to all hardwired and unswitched devices usually sags during engine cranking, dropping from 12V to 9V or even lower. Thus, devices that must *always* remain on have to use very little power and endure wild variations in car voltage from time to time.

Discovering if Your Car Power Outlet Is Switched

Learning whether your power outlet (i.e., the cigarette lighter adapter) stays on when the car is off will help you determine whether you need to run additional power outlets for the devices you intend to use or install in your car.

To test your outlet, you need a device with a light and no battery, such as a cell phone charger with a light on it, or a small map light that plugs into a car power outlet. Plug in the device and observe it when you turn your car on and off. If the light or indicator is on only when the car is on, you have a switched outlet; if the device stays on no matter what, you have an unswitched outlet. It is generally a bad idea to leave devices plugged into an unswitched outlet.

The Hack: Making a 12V Power Supply for Indoors

If you're going to start hacking around with cars, you're going to want to bench test your in-car experiments and devices indoors. You may be working on your installation projects for several days, and you probably won't want to have your dashboard (or someone else's dashboard) torn open for that whole time. If you like to spend money, you can go buy a cool 12V power supply (such as Radio Shack part #22-504) with a nice car outlet on the front so you can do all of your testing out of the vehicle.

If you're a computer hacker, you probably have a few computer power supplies hanging around. Since these output 12V, it's simply a matter of making these power supplies operate with a switch to power a cigarette lighter jack.

If you have an old AT power supply (usually found in PC computers that run slower than about 200 MHz), you're set—just pull out that old Pentium 90 power supply, front-panel rocker switch and all. Figure 1-4 shows how you can splice, twist, or cleanly solder the car power socket to the black (ground) and yellow (12V) wires of the AT power supply that would normally go to a hard drive or CD-ROM drive. Make sure that the outer shell of the outlet connects to ground and that the bottom center of the outlet connects to 12V. Ignore the power supply's red (5V) wire; the car power socket doesn't use it. You can purchase a car power socket for a few bucks at Radio Shack (part #22-540).

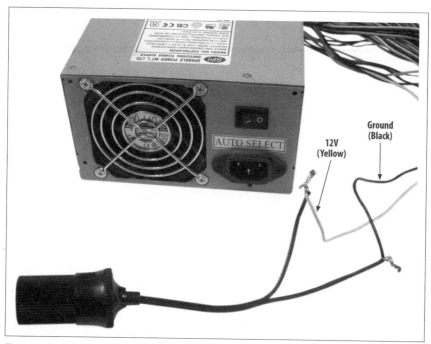

Figure 1-4. A PC power supply with an attached cigarette lighter powerjack

If you have a modern ATX power supply, it is designed to be controlled by software ("soft power") that switches it off and on or puts it to sleep and wakes it up. To override this behavior, you simply need to connect the green wire on the ATX connector to *any* black wire, as shown in Figure 1-5. Then, the power supply automatically outputs 12V when it is plugged into the wall. (This trick works best with a power supply that has its own switch.) If the ATX power supply does not have a switch at all, you can simply connect some sort of switch between the green wire and ground, and then you can turn the 12V off and on without having to unplug the power supply.

 ATX power supplies supply a maximum of around 20 amps for the 12V line. Keep this in mind when connecting devices; you'll damage or at least disable your power supply if you try to draw too much power.

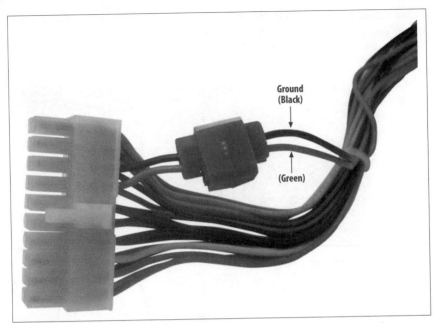

Figure 1-5. The splice you need to disable "soft power" on an ATX power supply

Prevent Electrical Fires

#2 Only you can prevent electrical fires (as the paraphrased saying goes), and fuses are an essential form of prevention.

In any electrical system, it's important to protect against miswiring that can result in device damage or even fires. This hack explains voltage, amperage, and power levels, and points out several of the safety features (i.e., fuses) of your automobile's electrical distribution system.

Amps

"Understand Car Electrical Systems" [Hack #1] defined voltage as the amount of potential or pressure behind electrical flow, and gave the analogy of a high- or low-pressure hose. To explain *current* in terms of water, we would be considering how many gallons of water went through the hose per hour. A very unscientific conceptual definition of electrical current (measured in *Amperes*, or *amps*—not to be confused with sound amplifiers!) is simply how many gallons of electrons pass through the wire per hour.

It's pretty simple: if you're trying to power a small device, such as a light in your car, you only have to give it a few teaspoons (*milliamps*, or *mA*) of electrons every hour. If you're trying to power your car radio, you need a cup of electrons every hour (*amps*, or *A*). If you're tooling around town in your electric car, that's where the gallons of electrons (*kiloamps*, or *KA*) come in.

To continue our simplified analogy here, the more amps you need for your device, the bigger your "hose" or wire should be. "Gauge Your Wires" [Hack #3] discusses the different sizes of wire and how thick they should be for a given application.

Fuses

Fuses are protective devices placed along the path of an electrical circuit. To *fuse* means, basically, to melt. Fuses melt to protect the circuit, wires, and devices when you put too much current (electrons per second, or amps) through them. You usually get too much current going through a wire because of a *short circuit*, which is when wires that shouldn't be touching touch. In a short circuit, the electricity that is supposed to go all the way to some device, such as a radio or light bulb, takes a direct path back to the battery. In other words, if the wire that is trying to bring 12V to the device gets loose and touches some metal in the car, the electricity tries to take a shortcut back to the battery through this metal (a "short" circuit, shown in Figure 1-6). Because this shorter circuit has no device to use the electricity, the energy simply heats up the wires, and if there is no circuit breaker or fuse, the wires will melt and possibly cause a fire.

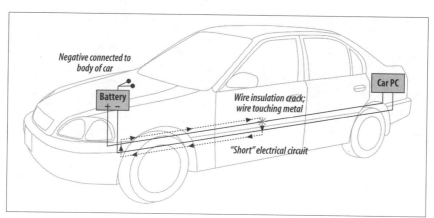

Figure 1-6. A short circuit

To protect against this situation, a fuse of a specific amp rating is put in the line between the battery and the device it powers, close to the battery itself. If a short circuit develops in the wiring or if the device malfunctions, the fuse simply melts once the amps get too high.

Automobile fuses come in several different varieties. There are small and large blade-edge fuses, small cylindrical fuses, and plastic fuses with metal strips. There are also fusible links, which look like wires but will melt like fuses at the rated current, as well as circuit breakers, which can be reset without replacement after the short circuit is repaired. If you're installing new fuses in the car, you can use either the very common blade-edge fuses or whichever ones your car already uses (so you can share the spares).

There is usually a location in the car where most of the fuses go, called the *fuse box*. It may be found under the hood, inside near the driver's ankles, in the glove compartment, in the trunk, between the dashboard and the door, or in some other location, depending on the car. As you can see in Figure 1-7, the fuse box contains a large number of fuses, each protecting a section of the car or a particular device, such as the radio, headlights, tail-lights, A/C unit, and so on. If the dashboard lights won't turn on even though the rest of the car seems fine, chances are the fuse has melted.

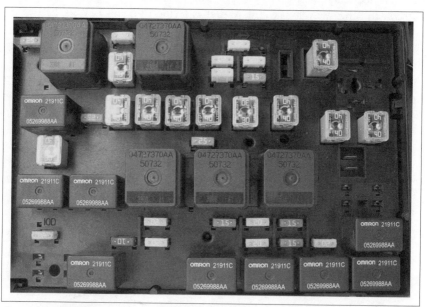

Figure 1-7. A fuse box

The manual that came with the car when it was purchased new, or a Haynes or Chilton's manual from any Pep Boys, should tell you the layout of the fuses in your car's fuse box and the proper amperage ratings of these fuses. Many cars have this diagram right next to the fuse box itself.

Fuses are rated for different amperages, and you should use a fuse just above the amperage that the device will draw. If a device is designed to draw 5A normally but can spike to 8A when it first starts (common for situations where a mechanical arm or switch activates at first, such as a CD loader or motor), it would be safe to use a 10A fuse for the device. If you used a 20A fuse and the device short-circuited internally, the 20A fuse would be very slow to "blow" or melt and would probably not save the device from further damage. The 10A fuse would start to melt as soon as the current went over the normal level, largely protecting the device and the wires that bring it power and possibly preventing a fire in your car.

> When a fuse melts, it's important to figure out why it did. If you were working on your radio while the car was on, you saw the red wire touch the metal frame, and now your radio doesn't turn on at all, you can be fairly certain that it was your fault. But if you've replaced the fuse for your taillights three times and it keeps blowing, chances are there's a short circuit you need to find and fix before you keep wasting fuses.

Protecting Your Devices with Fuses

Although the car has its own set of fuses, you may add devices that bypass the normal car power. Perhaps your power line goes straight to the battery, or your device connects, along with a lot of other devices, to a 20A fuse. You don't want a short circuit on your device to take out the fuse for all the gadgets in your trunk—you'd like to be able to tinker with your amplifier or car computer and know that you'll be able to conveniently replace the fuse right there if you accidentally cross wires.

You can insert a fuse anywhere you want using an *in-line* fuse connector (the "in-line" refers to the fact that you put the fuse wire *in a line* between your battery and the device it protects, as in Figure 1-8). It's generally better to put the fuse closer to the power source—that way, the length of the wire run is protected by the fuse.

> If you're connecting wires directly to the battery, your fuse should always be within a foot of the battery. This is because if there is a collision or the wire wears out and touches the body of the car, it could cause a fire. The closer the fuse is to the battery, the less unfused length of wire there is to cause trouble.

In-line fuses are available at hardware shops, car stereo shops, Pep Boys, and similar locations. To use them, simply choose the lowest fuse rating that will

Figure 1-8. An in-line fuse

still pass enough power to your device at its peak power usage, and then connect the fuse wire between the power source (i.e., the battery or wherever you are getting your 12V) and the device.

Here are some important tips for in-car wiring:

- Fuse the positive (red) +12V wire.
- Never run a wire to your device from the battery without a fuse.
- The positive charge uses red wire; the negative charge uses black. Invest in red/black sets of 16-, 14-, and 12-gauge braided wire. Avoid solid-core wire (the stuff that's hard to bend and keeps its shape), because it's not designed for automotive use.
- When grounding to the body, use a crimped-on washer post connector (which adds a circle to the end of the wire) and a metal screw to go into a small hole drilled in the body. If you use a metal screw with both a hexagonal nut and a Phillips-head top, you'll be able to tighten it with whatever tool you have handy.

If you need help on wiring, see "Connect Your Wires" **[Hack #4]**.

Gauge Your Wires

The general rule in car wiring is that the thicker the wire is, the better. However, thick wire is expensive, and financially it's worth learning how thick a wire you really need to bring power to all the devices you add to your car.

The width of wires is usually given in a unit called *gauge*. As with shotguns, a smaller number represents a bigger diameter. Continuing our electricity-as-water analogy, the wider your wire is, the wider a "pipe" the electricity has to go through. Thus, if you are trying to carry a lot of power to your trunk to power a small studio of TV screens, computers, and audio amplifiers, you will want to use a thick wire. But how thick?

Using a wire that is too thin can be a fire hazard: too much amperage will overheat the wire, potentially melting the insulation and lighting the carpet on fire. However, using a wire that is too thick can be a financial hazard: you will spend hundreds of dollars on wires alone and have no money left for gadgets.

Wire Sizes and Amp Ratings

Wire comes in several types, including *solid core*, which is just thick, bendable copper, and *stranded*, which consists of many smaller wires braided together. For automotive applications, stranded wire is more desirable than solid because it's more flexible, especially at colder temperatures.

The maximum amps a wire can carry safely depends on the gauge and length of the wire. You probably won't be running wire longer than about 6 meters (20 feet) in a vehicle, but it's good to know that the longer you run the wire, the thicker it should be, because some of the electricity gets lost along the way as heat.

Wire gauge differs in the U.S. and Europe. In the U.S. you will see the term *AWG*, for American Wire Gauge, which I will be using here. As mentioned before, gauge is a bit odd in that the larger the wire is, the *lower* its number is. (Europe uses a more sensible metric-system-based wire gauge scheme. I won't cover it here, but I will give you the metric equivalents of the AWG numbers so you can visualize how thick the wires are.)

If you are comfortable inside a computer, you are probably already familiar with several gauges of wire. The wire used to connect the reset/power buttons and front panel LEDs to the motherboard in most computers is between 24 and 22 gauge (about 0.5 mm in diameter). The wires that come out of a power supply to the ATX power connector on a motherboard are 18 gauge (about 1 mm in diameter), as are the yellow/black/red wires that go to peripherals.

To carry 12V around a vehicle, you will normally use 18-gauge and larger (i.e., smaller number) wires. The red or yellow 12V power cord in a dashboard going to the back of the radio might be 18 or 14 gauge (1–1.5 mm in diameter).

Wires get hot, and when you bundle them in groups, they get hotter. Thus, while 18-gauge wires are rated to carry 16A (according to the *AWG Handbook of Electronic Tables and Formulas*), this rating decreases tremendously when the wires are bundled and wrapped and run together in a plastic sheath under the carpeting.

There are many tables online (Google "wire gauge table"), most with somewhat conflicting data. Generally, you will use the gauges 12 (20 mm), 10 (25 mm), 8 (33 mm), and 4 (about 50 mm, or 0.5 cm). If you are powering a single device under 5A, 12- or 10-gauge wire can handle it. If you are going to power a full-sized computer, or several devices, use an 8- or 4-gauge wire. These are thick, heavy-duty cables that look like they should be powering a big motor. In fact, 4-gauge wires can be used to bring power to a winch, so they should certainly handle your in-car PC. 2-gauge wires (64 mm in diameter) are overkill, and if you go any thicker than 2 gauge, you're probably using the same size wire as the battery to the engine. If you need that many amps, you might consider adding another battery in the trunk **[Hack #10]**.

You should use the same gauge for the ground wire as you use for the 12V wire you run to your device, as the current path is only as thick as your thinnest link. Also, run the ground and 12V wires straight to the battery, with a fuse near the battery between the 12V wire and the positive battery terminal. Try not to tap off other connections if possible, unless you're powering a low-power device (not a computer or screen). This includes the chassis (car body)—even though it is connected to the negative battery terminal, this can add noise to your audio system or device.

The Hack: Powering Everything

A quick way to determine your power needs is to double the amperage you need to power, because when devices first turn on, they draw a lot more current. This "spike" in current needs to be accommodated. Thus, if you know your computer will run at 200 watts (200W / 12V = 16A), you should double that to 32A and add that to the amperage required by any other devices you are running (amplifiers, subwoofers, etc.) before you decide how thick a power line to run and what fuse to install.

8-gauge wire (about 33 mm in diameter) can easily carry 50A (600W) to the trunk, and 4-gauge wire (about 0.5 cm in diameter) can carry over 100A (1200W) to the trunk. A 2-gauge wire (64 mm) can carry upwards of 150A (1800W).

To tap directly into the battery, you need an additional wire tap for the battery terminals. Whether your battery has posts or screw-down connectors, it's as simple as purchasing an inexpensive extendable connector (Figure 1-9) that enables you to stack on a few connectors. A small power distribution block mounted next to the battery is even better if you have more than a few additional power lines to run. A power distribution block is a hub that receives power from the battery and splits it neatly into several fuse-protected *terminals* (places to connect a wire). There are many "show-quality" devices that are translucent and have big, pretty fuses. Your budget and appearance concerns will dictate how elaborate a power block you purchase. You can use one large fuse between the power and this block, and it can be used to turn off all power in an emergency or just act as a backup fuse for your system. Make sure the distribution block has a protective cover to prevent any short circuits.

Figure 1-9. An extendable post connector

If most of your devices are going to be in the rear of your vehicle, Figure 1-10 shows an excellent way to provide ample power for all your devices: running one very thick wire to a power distribution block in the trunk.

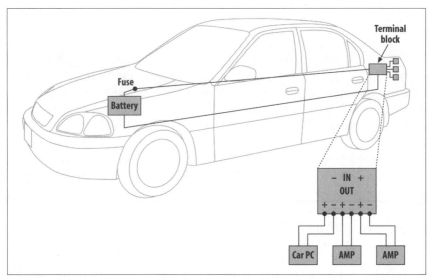

Figure 1-10. A power distribution block in a trunk

 Connect Your Wires

#4   There are several ways to do in-car wiring: quick-and-dirty, functional, or professional, depending on who's going to see it and how long you want it to last.

In the process of hacking computers and other devices into your car, you have to connect lots of wires. Unlike the inside of a computer, where all the wires are keyed and standardized, each car has its own set of connectors, and most of these are already in use. Except for cigarette lighter power outlets, which are really more for temporary connections, there is no standard "outlet" in the trunk of your car where you can seamlessly plug in your gadgets.

What happens instead is that new wires are run to the locations where devices are installed. They are usually run under the floor carpet, or inside the plastic baseboards or framing at the edges of the seats and carpets. When the wires poke out, professional audio shops usually surround them with plastic sheathing and zip-tie them down, as shown in Figure 1-11.

Connecting Wires

There are several ways to connect all your wires. Which method you choose depends on how permanent a solution you want, your budget and tools, and how important appearances are to you.

Figure 1-11. Tidy professional wiring

Twist and tape. The cheapest way to connect your wires is to twist them together and wrap electrical tape around them so they don't short out. This is the hallmark of an amateur, but it's my favored method when I am doing temporary installations or fixing or installing a radio while driving (er, not that I would do that).

The minimal tools required for this approach are:

- Hard fingernails (or sharp teeth) to strip wire insulation
- Electrical tape to insulate and protect the wires you twist together

You need to strip the plastic coating off the wire in order to expose the metal wire strands that you will be twisting together. You should strip up to an inch of insulation, as you want lots of exposed metal to make as strong a connection as possible. Then you simply take the two wires you are connecting and twist them together, clockwise or counterclockwise. You then cover the whole thing with copious amounts of electrical tape.

While this approach is extremely functional, it scores lowest on the scale of "gimped" to "crimped" to "pimped."

Solder and shrink. A much better, slower, but highly professional way to make permanent bonds between wires is to solder the connections.

The tools required for this approach are:

- Soldering iron
- Solder
- Heat gun (or hair dryer, or lighter)
- Plastic heat shrink
- Something to hold the wires still

The heat shrink is a plastic, cylindrical sleeve that you put over the soldered portion of the connection and then heat up. This causes the sleeve to shrink, cleanly covering the soldered area and making it look like one tidy contiguous wire. Make sure you cut the heat shrink long enough to cover the solder bond and reach both wire insulations, and that you slip it over one of the wires to be bonded *before* you connect them. Also, keep the heat shrink far down one of the wires, away from where you're soldering—the heat of the solder could preshrink your heat shrink and make it hard to work with. Figure 1-12 shows one step from this process.

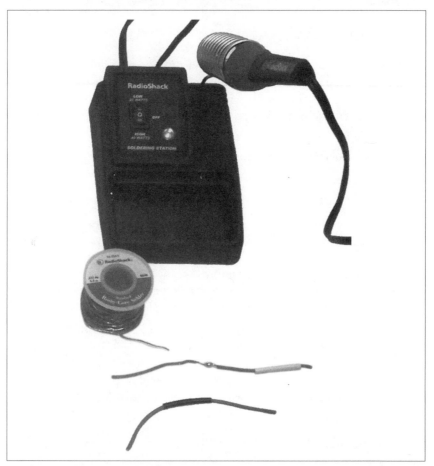

Figure 1-12. The solder-and-shrink method

While this is no mini-course on soldering, the basic concepts here are that, being careful not to burn your hands, you place the two wires together, *heat them up*, and then put the solder on the wires. It will flow between all the wires (if they're braided) and make a nice solid bond.

Then, after you've let the solder bond cool, you slide the heat shrink over the solder bond and heat it up quickly with the heat gun/hair dryer. One hack that people use in a pinch (with good porous heat shrink, not shiny smooth stuff) is simply to hold the heat shrink in the flame of a lighter. The heat shrink will shrivel into place if you heat it quickly and evenly—it's a skill similar to roasting marshmallows over a fire.

Crimp and save. There are a variety of very handy crimping approaches to wire bonding, and these are excellent in any situation where you are trying to tap into an existing ground or 12V wire that already goes somewhere and that you don't want to cut. We'll look at three kinds of wire crimps here.

The tools required for this approach are:

- Crimping tool (or vise grips or pliers)
- Wire crimps
- Electrical tape

One way to crimp wires together is to use a "piggyback" crimper (Figure 1-13, left). This small plastic and metal clamp can be put on one continuous wire, and another parallel wire can be bonded to it. You simply place both wires in the clip and crush it down. The metal in the crimp will slice through the insulation on both wires and connect them.

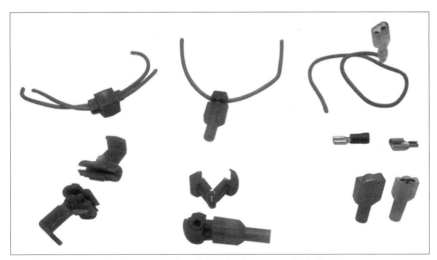

Figure 1-13. A piggyback crimper, female blade plug tap, and blade plugs

Another excellent crimp connector is a female blade plug tap (Figure 1-13, middle). This connector crimps onto an existing continuous wire and forms a T outlet that a male blade connector can tap into. This is excellent, say, if you've found 12V and ground wires in the trunk of your Dad's Lexus that you want to use to plug in some device, but you want to be as inconspicuous as possible in case he decides to take the car back to the dealer after you've blown several fuses.

Male and female blade plugs (Figure 1-13, right) are classic crimp connectors. When professionally installed, they are good because they can be plugged and unplugged multiple times. This is important when a device is going to be uninstalled from time to time. However, the crimping tools you get with most handyman kits for these plugs tend to make such weak crimps that the ends pull off the wire on the first or second unplugging. Still, these are useful connectors, and some of them even come with their own plastic shielding, so you don't have to use electrical tape to insulate them.

—Damien Stolarz and Lionel Felix

Calculate Your Car's Battery Life

HACK #5

To make sure you don't kill your car battery, learn how to do quick-and-dirty estimates of power drain for in-car devices.

There are a number of ways to compare battery characteristics. One of the main measurements of power storage capacity is amp-hours, which roughly means the number of hours for which your battery can put out a certain number of amps. However, interpreting exactly what this number means is tricky.

If you've ever seen the movie Apollo 13, you may remember the scene where the scientists and astronauts are calculating how much power they have left, and trying to come up with an escape plan that doesn't use too much of the spacecraft's limited power. Automotive electronics is often like that. Everything is fine while the engine is on and you're still generating electricity. But once your car is off and you're running on batteries, you have to count every electron, or you'll find yourself in the parking lot holding out jumper cables and begging for a jump start.

The reason you want to know how many watts a device is using is so you can determine how long you can run it in your car, with the engine off, without killing the battery.

Basic Car Hacking Toolkit

You will need several tools and supplies while hacking your car PC. This is just a quick list that should cover a wide variety of needs:

Cordless drill, drill bits, and assorted driver heads
> A cordless drill is a must-have for a professional installation. A powerful drill with strong torque will make quick work of pilot holes, fasteners, screws, and long bolts. Drill bits are good for pilot holes, which keep plastic from distorting and weakening and let you fasten large-diameter grounding screws to interior body panels. Most hardware stores carry assorted driver kits that include Phillips, Torx, flathead, hex, and a few other types of driver. When one wears out, replace it. Old driver heads strip fasteners.

Reamer
> A little-known gem that's good to have, this makes little holes bigger. It's good for plastic where you want to sink a switch, run a cable, and so on. It's better than using a drill bit to make big circles.

Interior panel tool
> This looks like a miniature garden tool. It's perfect for getting the majority of your car's interior panels loose without breaking the fasteners. Although your dealership will have replacement fasteners, they will charge you a lot for them.

Wire-stripping tool/crimper
> When facing a spaghetti bundle of wire to install, a quality Klein Tools or Craftsman stripper will save you hours. Strip only enough to make it into the end of a crimp, or around a terminal post. Exposed wire poses a grounding hazard.

Razor knife
> Useful for cutting electrical tape, splicing into the middle of a wire, and opening blister-packed components. Always cut *away* from your body/ fingers.

Side-cutting wire cutter (a.k.a. dikes)
> A clean cut makes for an easy strip and quick and neat work.

Work light and mirror
> Cars, being small, will tend to have spaces where your head won't quite fit, making you work blind. Get a small mirror that can be propped in place when a direct view isn't possible. Things that are hidden and necessitate mirrors tend to also be in dark places. Have a few different lighting options available, from direct beams to caged bulbs. Hot bulbs burn carpet/skin and should not be left unattended.

—continued—

Multimeter
> Checking continuity, voltage, and amperage is critical before throwing the big switch. Multimeters also make it much simpler to find a bad crimp.

Car-specific tools/bits
> Your car may contain special fasteners, Torx bits, hex heads, c-clips, and other various maddening things that come loose only with a special tool. It may be wise to go to the dealership to find out what tools you need, and then go somewhere else and buy them cheaper. Better yet, borrow it if you only need it once.

Crimps
> Pick up a variety pack for a good starter kit. It should contain blade ends, washer ends, butt crimps, splicers, and other ways to crimp and connect wires. Add to that kit as you need.

Big clips
> Most hardware stores will have some assortment of clips. These make it very simple to solder together wires when you happen to not have a third or fourth arm handy.

Soldering irons and solder
> These will make the solder and shrink approach to connecting wires easier.

Odds and sods
> Electrical tape, an assortment of sheet metal screws, washers, double-sided foam tape, zip ties, self-adhesive Velcro strips, a hacksaw, gorilla glue/epoxy, a ruler/straight edge, a grease pencil/permanent marker, eye protection, and a good old loud shop radio.

The Difference Between Amps and Watts

In the house, you use watts for your power-consumption math. You know that the 40-watt light bulb is the dim one you use in the small lamp, and the 100-watt light bulb is the bright one for the porch. You may also know that you upgraded your computer power supply from the gimpy 250-watt unit it came with to one that supplies 650 watts, perhaps even with glowing purple lights and an array of variable-speed fans. These numbers make sense because the power bill comes in kilowatt-hours, and you know that if you run your 100-watt light bulb for 10 hours, you've used 1 kilowatt-hour.

Watts are used to measure power, and to get wattage, you simply multiply the voltage times the amperage. So what's our non-scientific definition of a *watt*? A watt is simply the number of gallons of electrons that flow at a given pressure. If you have a 12V battery and you flow 1A of current, you're applying 12 watts of power. If you have a 1.5V battery and you flow 1A of current, you're applying 1.5 watts of power. You've still moved the same number of electrons, but the 12V electrons had a lot more pressure behind them and thus had a lot more power. This is also why you don't want to plug 12V into your 1.5V device; you don't want to use a fire hose to wash your car, either.

While individual devices such as hard drives and CD-ROM drives list their current draw in amps, general calculations are done in watts. This is because in a computer, you have 120V coming into the power supply, and all manner of 5V, 12V, 3.3V, and other voltages flowing within the computer. Batteries, however, are usually rated in amp-hours—i.e., they tell you how long this battery could put out that many amps. Thus, you have an incentive to figure out how many *amps*, not *watts*, your device is drawing.

In general, to calculate watts (power), you multiply the voltage that a device is using by the current it is drawing. The formula is power (watts) = voltage (volts) × current (amps).

If you have a laptop computer, turn it over and see if it tells you the voltage and amperage draw. My laptop says on the bottom that it runs at 24.5V and that it uses a maximum of 2.64A. This means that it runs at 64.68W, or about 70W. This makes sense to me; I know that old desktop computers used 150W and 200W power supplies and that modern units have 350W and higher power supplies.

Fortunately, in a car, everything runs at about 12V. Thus, you can move between amps and watts easily and think in whichever unit suits you. If you know a device uses 60W, then you know it will draw 5A at 12V. If you know a device is using about 2A at 12V, you know it's drawing 24W. Divide or multiply by 12—the conversion is simple enough.

Note that these are rough calculations; we'll ignore the fact that the voltage from the battery could be 13.8V instead of 12V, or that you might be using power converters that raise or lower the voltage and lose power in the process.

Battery Capacity

A typical battery is designed to output some level of current for a certain length of time. This is measured in amp-hours (Ah). In our ongoing water analogy, this would equate to how many "gallons per hour" or "gallons per day" of electrons the battery could put out. (There are other measures of battery capacity as well; see "Upgrade Your Car Battery" [Hack #6]).

An average car battery has an amp-hour rating of about 50 Ah. But does this mean it can put out 50A for an hour, or that it can put out 1A for 50 hours? The interesting thing about batteries is that the faster you try to pull out the electrons, the less it can provide. If you had a battery rated at 50 Ah, you could put out far more than 50 hours if you drew only 1A. For instance, if you ran all your interior lights (together, they might add up to 1A) on a 50-Ah battery, you could easily go 50 hours (about 2 days) or more. A good battery might last as long as a week.

However, if you hooked up some item that drew 50A, it would be pulling $50A \times 12V = 600W$. This would be like powering 10 normal indoor light bulbs, and it would kill your battery in just a few hours or less.

To be more precise, battery vendors designate the number of hours over which their amp-hour ratings apply—usually 20 hours. By specifying "50 Ah @ 20 hours," they are saying that you get 50 Ah if you drain the battery over 20 hours. That works out to about 2.5A per hour (50 Ah / 20 hours = 2.5A). In other words, if you draw 2.5A, you should get exactly 20 hours of life out of a fully charged 50-Ah battery. If you draw only 1A, you should get *more* than 20 hours, but it's hard to say how much more—perhaps 40+ hours. If you draw 5A, you will get *less* than 20 hours, and probably less than 10 hours because you're draining it above its specification.

So, if you know a battery has a specific Ah rating, just divide it by 20 to get the amperage at which you could run your devices for 20 hours. By keeping your device amperage under the value you get, you should be able to get your 20 hours or more of power.

When you get to the end of the 20 hours, the battery is not completely drained. However, it will have dropped below 11 volts, and it is for all intents and purposes "discharged," in the sense that the voltage is too low to start your car or power your device. The battery most likely also will be damaged and will have a shorter life span, as conventional car-starting batteries are not designed for deep discharge.

The Hack: Calculating Battery Drain

If you know that your in-car computer or device has a 70W power supply, you know that the device could be using up to 6A (70W / 12V = 6A). But just as you're not using all 350W of your desktop power supply, you're probably not using the full 70W available to this device—your device might actually be drawing only 2A. How do you figure it out?

Method one: Power arithmetic. You can do some rough back-of-the-envelope calculations to determine how many amps or watts your devices will draw.

Most devices, such as hard drives, list their amps on the top of the case—both their peak draw (when you first turn them on) and their normal draw when they are powered. You can do some simple calculations to find out how many watts they draw. As an example, many hard drives draw around

500 mA (0.5A) of current normally, and run on 12V. If you need to know how many watts, just multiply these figures: these hard drives draw about 6W normally.

If you can figure out the draw for each device in your system, you can add them up to get the total. A Pentium 4 might draw 60–100W; a mobile Pentium chip might draw 20–30W. (I got these results by Googling "cpu wattage.")

If you knew you had a motherboard, a hard drive, and a mobile Pentium, you could estimate that the total wattage drawn would be in the 36W range. Divide that by the 12V power supply of the car, and you would expect a current draw of 3A. Based on our earlier calculations, which determined that a 50-Ah car battery can provide 2.5A for 20 hours, you would expect to get less than 20 hours for these devices on a 50-Ah car battery.

Method two: Amp meter. If you have a multimeter with an *amp meter* feature (sometimes called *ammeter*; most have them), you can figure out your current draw just by hooking up the meter in between your battery and your devices (as shown in Figure 1-14). You'll be able to see exactly what the draw is, and then figure out how long you can power that device on your battery.

Figure 1-14. A multimeter connected between a power supply and device

In our example, the computer is drawing around 2A. Our 50-Ah car battery could probably power this device for more than a day.

Testing Drain

Although these techniques give us some idea of the current drain, we still don't know how long the battery will last when the computer is hibernating and drawing only, say, 200 mA (0.2A) of current. The best way to do this is simply to connect it up and see how long it goes.

If you're concerned about running out of power and getting stranded, you may want to look at "Add a Second Car Battery" [Hack #10].

—Damien Stolarz and Tor Pinney

HACK #6 Upgrade Your Car Battery

If you want to add a lot of electrical devices to your vehicle and still be able to start it up and drive it, you may need to upgrade your car battery.

There are two primary competing purposes for the battery in a vehicle:

1. To provide a very high-amperage output for several seconds to start the car, then allow the engine to generate any further needed electricity.

2. To provide a medium- to low-amperage output for many hours when the vehicle is off, to power devices such as car alarms or the station pre-set memory in car radios.

To meet these two different needs, two types of batteries are used in automotive applications: conventional lead-acid and deep-cycle.

If you are familiar with laptop or mobile phone batteries using nickel cadmium, nickel-metal hydride, or lithium ion, you know that they are designed to be completely discharged and recharged many times. Conventional automobile batteries use *lead-acid* and are designed to put out a large current (to start the car) for a short time, and then be recharged after only a shallow discharge. If you completely discharge your automobile battery (say, by leaving all the lights on for several weeks) you are likely to severely limit the life of the battery.

Recreational vehicles (RVs) often have two batteries—one *starting battery* with its good starting characteristics, and one *deep-cycle* battery designed to put out a lower amperage for a long time and to survive deep discharge.

In addition to the starting and deep-cycle qualifiers, a few other measurements are used to compare batteries:

Cranking amps (CAs)

This is the maximum output amperage the battery can sustain for 30 seconds (i.e., to start the car). A good battery can put out 1 kiloamp (1000A) for about 30 seconds before the voltage starts to sag. Since cold weather makes batteries very tired, another necessary comparison is *cold cranking amps* (CCAs), which are how many amps the battery can sustain for 30 seconds in cold weather. This number will be lower than the CAs—for instance, in the 800A range. Bigger engines (with more cylinders) and diesel engines require higher CAs or CCAs to start in warm or cold weather (respectively). In warm climates, CCAs don't matter much; in cold climates, this becomes an important measurement— don't underrate your battery if you want your car to start in the winter. The two measurements aren't quite interchangeable, but they're roughly proportional; a high-CCA battery is generally a high-CA battery, and CCAs are always lower than CAs.

Reserve capacity (RC) and amp-hours (Ah)

Both of these terms describe how long a battery can put out a lower number of amps. *Reserve capacity* describes how many minutes the battery can put out 25A before the voltage goes too low. *Amp-hours* are defined for much lower currents, and usually specify how many amps the battery can put out for 20 hours before the voltage drops.

Convenient Power Connectors

One benefit of a battery upgrade is that you can get one with a dual-post configuration. Some vehicles have posts on top of the battery, and the battery connectors bolt around these posts. Some batteries have sockets on the side that you screw battery connectors onto. If you purchase a battery that has both, like the one in Figure 1-15, you can use the unused set to cleanly run thick wires to the trunk of your vehicle. For more on how to hook these up, see "Gauge Your Wires" [Hack #3].

The Hack: Installing a Deep-Cycle Battery

If you are installing many gadgets in your vehicle, you will be most impacted by the amp-hours the battery provides. Most likely, you will be tapping the battery for only 5–10A, or perhaps more amps if you run your stereo at full blast for a long time while the car is off.

As mentioned earlier, a deep-cycle battery is designed for applications where there is a long time between vehicle starts, or where the battery does a lot of work while the vehicle is off (i.e., when it's not being charged). The latter situation is what we're trying to address.

Figure 1-15. A car battery with both kinds of connectors (posts and sockets)

Although deep-cycle batteries are not as good at starting, this is where the CCA and CA ratings come in. If you overcompensate with the cranking amps, you should be able to install a deep-cycle battery and have it consistently start your car, while still being resilient to the constant device draw of all your gadgets.

In your search for a suitable deep-cycle battery, you will probably encounter hybrid deep-cycle and starting batteries, or possibly marine batteries. Marine batteries are designed to deal with months of not starting and still put out a starting current; they also are designed to deal with the vibration and rocking that occurs on a boat. These features are unlikely to be of benefit to you if you have decent suspension on your car, don't go offroading, and drive your car frequently. However, a hybrid might be a good way to split the difference if you're in a cold climate and are concerned that a normal deep-cycle battery won't have enough power to start your car in freezing weather.

Optima (*http://www.optimabatteries.com*) makes a series of battery upgrades that are extremely popular in competition cars. Their Yellow Top series, in particular, is designed to take heat, vibration, and deep discharges with minimal capacity loss (see Figure 1-15).

When you purchase your new battery, get the largest unit that will fit in the space you have and that has greater CCAs and CAs than your existing battery (assuming your existing battery is the correct one for the vehicle and successfully starts your car). Any auto shop should be able to look up your vehicle in its database and tell you what shape and kind of battery you need.

Swapping your starting battery for a deep-cycle battery will give your car a lot more electrical staying power with the simplest installation. But if you really need to run devices for a while when your car is off and you don't want to ever risk needing a jump start, you should consider a dual-battery setup [Hack #10].

HACK #7 Add New Power Connectors Throughout Your Car

Modern devices such as laptops, cell phones, and video cameras often have 12V power adapters so they can be used, or charged, from a car's cigarette lighter outlet. If you have more devices than outlets, you can easily add more power connectors.

Some modern vehicles come with switched and unswitched 12V outlets throughout the car. If your vehicle is not so equipped, you can easily and cleanly install 12V power outlets wherever you have a plastic panel.

Let's say you're going on a trip. You and your friend/spouse both have cell phones, but they're from different manufacturers, so you have different car chargers. You've also brought along your laptop, so the kids/passengers can watch DVDs on the way, and your iPod adapter, so you can recharge it while you're playing tunes. You have a cold box that stays cool when it's plugged into the cigarette lighter adapter, and to top it all off, you've got your video camera plugged into a power inverter [Hack #11] (you were scatterbrained and forgot to charge it, and you're hoping to recharge it on the way so you can use it tonight).

How can you make it possible to use all of these devices simultaneously? Well, the first approach is to get one of those triple-decker one-outlet-to-three splitters, which look strange and take up a good deal of dashboard space. But if your car only has the cigarette lighter power socket that really *holds* a cigarette lighter, and points awkwardly up from an open ashtray (as in older Mercedes), then what you really need to do is install more outlets.

Your friends/family surely won't mind while you implement this hack in just a few hours. You'll be on the road in no time, and all your devices will have the power they need, where they need it.

Planning Your Wiring

The first step is simply to draw a quick sketch of where you want the outlets. The cleanest installation will be where you can find a nice flat plastic,
vinyl, or other panel with a few inches of depth behind it.

Depending on whether you want to separate the wires into different fuses or
put them all together, you may be able to handle all your outlets with one
long pair of wires running from front to back. Pick a continuous path for the
wires to flow through the car, hopefully with a minimum of pulling up carpets or pulling down headliners.

The advice in "Gauge Your Wires" [Hack #3] applies here—you want to pick a
wire thickness that can handle all your devices. If you figure that each gadget draws perhaps 2A, and you plan to add 5 outlets, then a 15A or 20A fuse
should be enough to handle them (and their spiking current demands when
you first plug them in or turn them on), and you should have wire that can
handle all this (perhaps 12 gauge or 10 gauge).

You can purchase car adapter outlets from Radio Shack, Pep Boys, and even
Wal-Mart. The auto stores are likely to be cheaper and have more accessories.
You want to find outlets that are designed for tidy installation in a pre-drilled
hole, and if you're lucky you will find something in stock that you can use.

If not, your best bet is the dealer—any dealer. Most new cars have an option
for these power outlets, and a little rubber cap that says "12V." These units
are designed to flush mount in a hole in the plastic. You can just go to a
dealer and say "I need a 12V power outlet insert," and mumble when they
ask you what car it's for. The part should probably cost around $10–15.

If you're still trying to leave town on schedule, you may want to just grab an
external adapter from Pep Boys and go. Later, when you have time, you can
do the clean installation described in the next section.

Drilling Holes

The satisfying part of this installation is when you drill the holes. Remove
each panel where you've decided you want an outlet, together with all its little screws and clips. Be careful not to lose them, as there's nothing that
screams "lousy install" like a panel that never quite fits again. Once you've
taken off the panel and verified that there's enough room behind the panel
for the outlet, you can then draw a circle the size of your outlet on the panel
and start drilling.

Plastic is very forgiving, so if you don't have a lot of drill bits—especially the
large (approximately 1" diameter) needed for this install—you can use any
wide metal blade with the same inner diameter to bore out your hole. Of

course, your best bet is an exactly sized drill bit for the outlet (or a reamer); you'll find that the bits used to cut holes for doorknobs work well for this.

Switched or Unswitched Outlets?

Assuming you've remembered to purchase two reels (black and either yellow or red) of 10- or 12-gauge wire and an in-line fuse assembly at Pep Boys or the hardware store, you can now tap off the power. If you want unswitched outlets (which are always on, whether the car is on or not), you can simply run your two wires to the battery terminals, tapping off the power there. You should put a fuse right near the battery, at the beginning of the 12V wire.

If you want switched outlets that have power only when the car key is in the on or accessory positions, you'll need to locate a wire that has 12V only when the car is on. The color of this wire varies from car to car. Also, in this case, you don't need to use a fuse—and you may want to match the diameter of the wire you find to tap off of. (It's pointless and possibly misleading to use a thicker gauge of wire to connect to a 10A fused accessory wire.) If, however, you plan to upgrade later, running thicker wire won't hurt—as long as you don't later look at the thick wire and think "Okay, looks thick enough for my power drill," fire up the drill, and melt the accessory wires it's attached to.

You'll find switched 12V wires in Figure 1-16, in the dashboard, behind the radio, and behind the ignition switch itself. Your best bet in this case is to get a Chilton's or other car manual for your vehicle so you know exactly what you're hooking up to and sharing power with and can choose a red accessory wire that has a nice big 15A or 20A fuse on it.

 You don't want to blow a fuse and suddenly have no driving lights, so make sure you stick to wires that are for accessories, not for main car functions.

Installing the Power Outlets

Once you have attached your fused wire to the car's battery, or connected to a wisely chosen accessory wire, you can run your cables under the car's carpet or under and along the floor edge plastic or metal framing to your first outlet.

 Make sure that your battery is disconnected while running the wires, or at least that the wires are disconnected. If the wire shorts with the body of the car, it can make a nice, slow, smoldering fire, or at least ruin all the wires in your dash by melting them together.

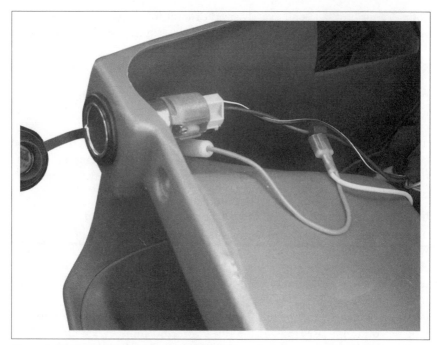

Figure 1-16. Switched 12V wires conveniently located in the center console

You should connect the red or yellow wire to the middle post of the power outlet, and the black ground wire to the frame or sleeve of the outlet. Depending on the back of the outlet, you will need to either splice a few wires, or use a blade-edge connector to fit into whatever factory power connector came with your expensive dealership-provided power outlet.

You can now "daisy-chain" your power outlets. To run power to the next outlet, simply run the red/yellow and black wires from the first outlet to the next, and so on. Make sure that you wire things well and use copious amounts of electrical tape as needed, to ensure that there are no exposed wires that could short with the body of the vehicle and create electrical fires.

In the time it took to do this hack, you probably could have recharged your video camera in the house; but you've now solved your power needs for *future* trips, and your car now has an outlet for every passenger. The few hours you delayed in leaving for your trip will be more than made up by the mobile entertainment you can now enjoy on the way.

Use a Huge Capacitor to Sustain Power

A large capacitor is often used to maintain bass amplifier response, and can address other problems as well—including voltage sags when the car is started.

One of the many goals of aftermarket car audio systems is to create a rever-beration that exceeds the boundary of the car, shaking other nearby cars and buildings. Car audio enthusiasts have been using 1-farad capacitors for years to make sure their cars go *Boom! Boom!* without brownouts or voltage sags.

Bass response is the ability of the subwoofer to reproduce the low-frequency bass sounds in music with fidelity. One of the problems with subwoofers is that they need a lot of electrical energy to move the large speaker to repro-duce the low-frequency bass sound waves. When the bass beat kicks hard, the speaker should instantly slam in response—but often, the car's battery and electrical system can't put out enough power to ensure an instant response.

I can explain this with another water analogy. Sometimes in houses with old plumbing, you lose water pressure in the shower whenever someone flushes the toilet or turns on the washing machine. Plenty of water is coming to the house via the mains; that's not the problem. The problem is that the plumb-ing can't maintain the pressure when too many demands are made on it.

Understanding Capacitors

Capacitors are one of the solutions to the problem of sagging voltage (electri-cal pressure). Capacitors are devices that store up electricity, like a tempo-rary battery (think "capacity"). One of the uses of a capacitor is to help keep voltage at a constant level.

Returning to the water pressure problem, imagine you had an extra device hooked to your plumbing, which I'll totally randomly call a capacitor. This extra device consists of a reservoir that holds perhaps 30 gallons of water. Whenever someone makes too many demands on the water system, the capacitor steps in and supplies the extra water.

So, if you're taking a shower, and then somebody flushes the toilet and washes their hands, the capacitor has enough water to keep the pipes full for a little while and keep the pressure up. If, however, someone turns on the washing machine and someone else starts watering the lawn, the reservoir will probably run dry after a while, and the capacitor won't be able to main-tain a comfortable shower pressure for the duration.

With apologies to both the plumbing and electrical professions, this is roughly how an electrical capacitor works. Normally, the car is putting out upwards of 13V (remember, "12V" is just what it's called; the battery actually runs higher). When the bass amplifier demands massive current, the voltage of a normal electrical system might "sag" to 12 or 11 volts. If the car was driving at night, you might actually see the headlights dimming to the beat.

With a large capacitor installed, however, the vehicle maintains the 13V that the battery is putting out. Since the beats are of short duration, the capacitor keeps the voltage up; the battery or engine puts out the current, and the audio system effectively delivers a "block-rocking beat."

Car PC Capacitor Use

Sustaining audio output is not the only benefit of using a capacitor. Of interest to in-car computing is the capacitor's ability to maintain voltage when, for instance, you're starting the car. When a car is started, for a few seconds the vehicle pulls almost all the battery power for cranking the engine. During this time, devices that are connected to the car battery have to endure a voltage that drops to much lower than 12V—possibly even 7V or lower, depending on the state of the battery. If the car starts right up the voltage can come back up, but it's often too late for the car computer that began to boot when you first turned the key and then died when you started cranking.

With a large capacitor and a good battery, it's possible that your computer can survive car-starting without a reboot. But that isn't the primary purpose of a fat capacitor, and buying an appropriate power supply that lets your computer survive engine cranking [Hack #45] is cheaper. Probably.

Capacitors come in several shapes and sizes. The most recognizable are the little black cans you see on a motherboard. Whenever you see a small cluster of capacitors like the one in Figure 1-17 rising up from a computer motherboard, they are often near a power source, keeping the voltage constant. You see them a lot in power supplies as well.

Capacitors are rated in *farads*, and the small capacitors inside electronics are in the microfarad range. You can think of farads as mega-gallons of electrons.

Audio capacitors like the one in Figure 1-18, in comparison, are huge. They can be a foot long and as thick around as a small fire extinguisher. They come in 1-farad (1F) or higher capacities. Even though this sounds like a small number, it's not. Farads are just big units.

The capacitor enhances the battery and is installed *in parallel* with the battery. Usually, the capacitor is installed near the audio equipment it is supporting (i.e., in the trunk) and near the power distribution block or amplifiers.

Figure 1-17. Several microfarad capacitors (courtesy of Chris Gare)

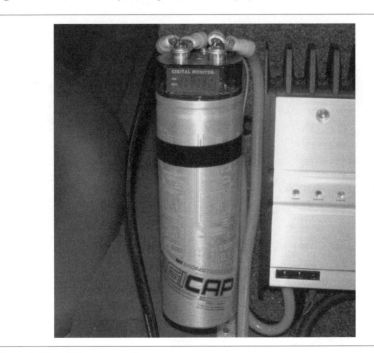

Figure 1-18. A 1-farad capacitor

The 12V line from the battery (red/switched or yellow/unswitched) goes to the + side of the capacitor, and the ground (usually black) wire from the battery ground goes to the − side of the capacitor.

1F capacitors for audio use come with their own mounting brackets and many of them are designed to look cool. They're easy to install and are essential for maintaining voltage levels in demanding car electrical systems.

Upgrade Your Car's Alternator

It's possible to install so many electronic devices in your car that the battery continues to discharge even when the engine is running. Upgrading to a high-output alternator ensures that there's enough power to feed all the devices while keeping the battery charged.

An *alternator* is a device in modern automobiles that acts as the voltage generator for the engine (Figure 1-19). While the battery does the job of getting the engine started, once the car is running off fuel it technically doesn't need a battery anymore. You could even disconnect the battery while a car was running, and it would probably continue to run (this applies to older cars without a lot of electronics; newer cars would throw a fit because the battery keeps the voltage levels stable). If you've ever gotten a jump start and then driven around with a "dead" battery, you understand this feature.

Figure 1-19. An alternator in a car

Once the engine is started, it's actually the alternator's job to supply the electrical power for the whole car. As an electrical generator the alternator is very efficient, but its voltage tends to fluctuate. The car's battery acts to smooth out the voltage and keep it at around 13–14V. In the process, the car's battery gets recharged.

A normal alternator might be designed to put out 100A. This might seem like a lot, but once you start adding high-power devices with hungry CPUs, you could easily exceed this level. Once that happens, the car will act as if the alternator has stopped working—the battery will have to make up the difference between what the alternator is putting out and what the car's entertainment system is demanding. The battery can thus become completely discharged, and for conventional batteries, this essentially makes them "dead." If you don't realize that the real problem is that you've exceeded your alternator's capacity, you might think that your battery is dead and upgrade it to a new top-of-the line battery, only to kill that one, too.

The solution to this problem is to upgrade the alternator. You will probably want an auto shop to do the installation unless you are handy with a wrench and know how to set the right tension on a belt. Luckily, installing an alternator is almost always a simple (i.e., inexpensive) job. The alternator is usually right on top of the engine and easily accessible.

If you ever get "dying battery" or "dying alternator" symptoms such as dim headlights or difficulty starting, even though you know the battery and alternator are good, upgrading the alternator may be the solution. Also, if you've calculated your power requirements and they clearly exceed the 100A your alternator probably puts out (perhaps because you've installed your Alienware gaming machine in the trunk), you should definitely upgrade the alternator.

If you plan to upgrade your alternator, be sure you read "Add a Second Car Battery" [Hack #10] before you buy, because if you are planning on adding a second battery you may want to get a dual-output alternator that charges both batteries independently.

Add a Second Car Battery

#10

Adding a second car battery is a great way to get lots of standby power when the vehicle is off. You can upgrade your car so that it has the same power setup as a recreational vehicle, with one battery for starting and running the engine and another for powering devices.

Adding a second battery doesn't really increase the number of devices you can power while the car is on—for that you need to upgrade your alternator [Hack #9]. What a second battery does do is more than double your power storage capacity, increasing the time for which your devices can run when the engine is off and ensuring that your primary battery always has the power to start your car.

To illustrate the information in this hack, I'm going to appeal to your intuitive understanding of batteries. If you look at the label on AAA, AA, C, and D batteries, you'll discover that they all supply 1.5 volts. But you would expect that a D is better than a AAA somehow, if only because it's bigger. What you may not know is that the main difference between the two types of batteries is the length of time each battery can put out 1.5V, and how many amps they can sustain. That's why devices that need to put out power for a long time, such as flashlights or boomboxes, use D batteries, while remote controls and pagers only need AA or AAA batteries.

You may or may not also know that you can wire a pair of batteries in parallel. The combination will output the same voltage, but for longer. For example, if you take 4 AA batteries and wire them in parallel (tops to tops and bottoms to bottoms, with wires daisy chained between them), they'll probably be able to put out more sustained power than a single D battery, but only at the same 1.5V that a single battery delivers.

What you wouldn't want to do is put a D battery in parallel with a AAA battery. After the AAA battery was discharged, the D battery would still be putting out voltage, and the AAA battery would be sucking it up—not the desired effect. The general rule is that you put batteries in parallel only when they are the same kind and age. Even then, if one of the batteries goes bad it can take the other ones down with it, so don't leave a dead battery mixed in with good ones.

If car batteries are connected in parallel, the more-charged one will always be trying to jump-start the less-charged one. So, although you could simply wire a second car battery in parallel with the first, there are better and safer ways to implement a two-battery system.

Battery Isolators

One excellent way to implement a two-battery system is with a *battery isolator*. These devices range from less than $50 to several hundred dollars, depending on the sophistication and features. Ideally, the job of a battery isolator is to combine the power of the two batteries for everything from powering devices to starting the car, while making sure that a fault in one battery can't kill the system. In essence, it becomes a redundant array of batteries—all the benefits of a backup battery, with none of the drawbacks. And depending on whether starting power or device power is more important to you, an isolator can make sure that devices deplete only the secondary battery, always leaving the primary battery charged to start the car.

In practice, the isolator uses a bit of the power itself (*diode isolators* will drop alternator output by about 1 volt, have large heat sinks, and are somewhat inefficient). It's not that easy to keep two different batteries fully charged, united in power, but divided in risk. Isolators come in several kinds, from simple switches that flip from one battery to another, to complex microelectronic circuits that actively monitor the charge levels on both batteries, charge them appropriately using alternator power, and use both of them to power devices and start the vehicle.

Because of the large currents needed to charge a battery, any second battery setup will need to run thick (4-gauge or so) wires from the alternator/front battery back to the second battery, unless the second battery is also being mounted near the engine. Exactly how to do this will be in the installation instructions that come with the battery isolator.

Dual-Output Alternators

If you want a very simple isolated system, you may be able to achieve it with a dual-output alternator. These are designed to charge two separate batteries independently. You can install your second battery to be charged by the secondary output of the alternator, and wire most of your devices to this second battery. When the engine is running, the vehicle will power the devices. When the engine is off, the second battery will power the devices, leaving the primary starting battery untouched and always charged and ready to start the car.

Conventional Versus Deep-Cycle Batteries

In "Upgrade Your Car Battery" [Hack #6] I discussed the two basic types of car batteries. In RVs, the usual approach is to have *both* kinds of batteries, each doing what they do best. A conventional, high-cranking-amps, lead-acid battery is connected to the ignition, lights, and basic car electronics. A second, big, deep-cycle battery (or several) is charged by the engine as well, but when the engine is off these batteries power devices such as refrigerators, TVs, computers, and so on.

There's never any risk of killing the starter battery by powering nonessential accessories, and if the deep-cycle battery goes dead, no harm is done—the engine can just charge it back up on the next drive, if it's long enough. However, keep in mind that the stock alternator isn't designed to charge batteries from a deep discharge on a regular basis, so you may want to upgrade it as well [Hack #9].

This arrangement depends on a good battery isolation circuit, and the same system can be installed in any vehicle with room to put an extra battery.

Battery Fumes

An important consideration when installing and using a secondary battery is the potential for battery fumes (a.k.a. poison gas). These fumes are created when a battery is being recharged. While many batteries today are "sealed" lead-acid, it's difficult to completely seal a battery. RVs and work trucks have both their batteries vented to the outside, either in the engine compartment or on the sides of the vehicle. If you are installing a second battery in a hatchback, or even in a trunk that can allow gases into the passenger compartment, ensure that the battery you are installing is designed for this, or provide appropriate ventilation for it by building an enclosed battery box that vents to the outside of the vehicle.

> Battery fumes are explosive and toxic, so a DIYer building a battery box should make sure that it vents to the outside. These gases are generated only when the battery is being charged. Consequently, deep-cycle batteries recovering from a deep discharge will produce more fumes then a starting battery recovering from an engine start.

Many battery makers recognize this dual-battery application and will tell you whether their batteries are safe near passenger compartments. As a practical note of experience, I've owned an Audi, a VW Bug, and a Mercedes, all of which had batteries under the back seat from the factory, so don't be paranoid—just vent appropriately.

Put Home Power Outlets in Your Car

#11 If you need to power a device that doesn't come with a car adapter, or if you want to run a top-of-the-line PC that consumes 300 watts, you will need to use a device called an inverter to convert your vehicle's 12V to the 120V or 220V found indoors.

"Understand Car Electrical Systems" [Hack #1] showed how you can convert the high-voltage power from a wall outlet into the 12V and other voltages needed by computers. If you need to power an in-home device in the car, however, the reverse can be done, using a device called an *inverter*.

What Inverters Do

American household voltages have been standardized at around 120V, and power in Europe generally runs at 220V. While vehicles and batteries use something called *direct current*, indoor voltages are *alternating current*. Direct current (DC) is simple: 12V on one wire, 0V on the other, and the current goes around in a loop from the 12V wire through the device and back to the 0V ground wire. Alternating current (AC) has a wavy pattern: the main two wires in AC trade off being at ±60V (in North America), back and forth, 60 times per second. (In Europe, the voltage waves ±110V, 50 times per second). The third "ground" wire in AC voltage usually connects to a metal pole sticking into the ground, and it actually acts as a failsafe return path for current if there should be a power surge, short circuit, or lightning strike. So, inverters have to do two things: they have to increase the 12V 10 to 20 times, and then they have to convert the simple DC voltage to the more complex back-and-forth AC current.

Inverters use a certain amount of the power coming into them just to convert the voltage—about 20% of the wattage is lost in translation. Thus, if your computer needs 100W to run, the inverter will draw 125W from the battery/alternator in order to supply it. In practice, you should probably have an inverter rated for *twice* what your devices demand. In my experience, when you first turn on devices (such as computers or power supplies for laptops) they create a big power surge, which can flip the circuit breaker built into your inverter. Then, even though the device settles down to its rated power draw, well within the inverter's rating, the inverter will have freaked out and shut down everything. The only caveat is that too powerful an inverter will waste power (on fans and heat) and give you less running time when the car is off—but you shouldn't be using an inverter if you're trying to maximize battery time.

Choosing an Inverter

Inverters come in various sizes and generally look like heat sinks, as you can see in Figure 1-20. They are usually packaged in colored aluminum and have a 12V plug on one side and several outlets on the other side. They often include an easy-to-replace fuse on the outside.

The key to comparing inverters is their wattage, because each inverter is designed to power devices only up to a given wattage. (I discussed how to convert amps to watts in "Calculate Your Car's Battery Life" [Hack #5].)

A small inverter might be able to handle 50W, or just over 4A (50W / 12V). That means it could power a few cell phone chargers, or perhaps a laptop power converter. Larger inverters might be rated for 200W, 300W, 500W, or even 1200W. The higher the wattage rating is, the more likely it is that the unit can supply power for hungry devices such as dual-processor computers, 21" flat-screen monitors, or power tools.

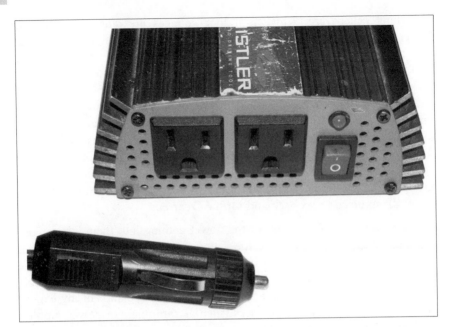

Figure 1-20. An inverter

If you are using a smaller inverter, you are likely to quickly exceed its power, so you have to make sure you overcompensate. Also bear in mind that almost all devices have a current spike when they are first turned on or plugged in, so if you are using a small inverter at its wattage limit, you may need to power on your devices one at a time so as not to trip the circuit breaker or fuse built into the inverter.

Powering High-Amperage Inverters

Beware of having eyes bigger than your sockets—when you see a power outlet in your car, it's very tempting to start hooking up power strips and extension cords and treating it just like wall power, but most wall outlets can easily supply thousands of watts, whereas only the biggest inverters come close to that.

If your vehicle is off and you don't have a dual-battery system [Hack #10], you're probably not going to be able to start your car for long if you use a huge inverter. Sustaining 1200W requires 1200W / 12V = 100A. As discussed in the previous hack, conventional batteries might be able to put out 25A for 2 hours, but a 100A draw is like cranking your car to start it—something batteries are designed to do for only about 30 seconds. If you're running a huge inverter without a huge secondary battery, you're going to need to leave the engine idling while you run your devices.

This car-as-generator approach is the same one taken by bigger work trucks and pickups. When they need to power high-voltage AC power tools, they have an inverter professionally installed in the truck and have power outlets right on the back of the vehicle. In RVs there are power outlets as well, and these run off either the power of the engine, a bank of batteries charged by the engine, or a separate, more efficient generator that runs off the gas (or even another fuel, such as propane or diesel).

The Hack: Wall Outlets in Your Car

If you really want to do a high-quality installation of power outlets, make sure that all your power supply issues are taken care of: that you have a strong enough battery to power these outlets for a while (or a secondary battery that can be completely discharged), or that you power the outlets only when the car is on.

If you have a very strong inverter but only a single battery, you probably want to make sure the inverter only powers on with the engine. First, to make sure that you won't drain your battery while driving, read "Upgrade Your Car's Alternator" [Hack #9]. Then, because you need to run a thick cable to supply 100W or more to the inverter, read "Gauge Your Wires" [Hack #3].

If you need a very high-current switched output (so that the inverter is on only when the car is on), you are going to need to use another device to turn the current on or off. The reason is that the switched wires that run from the accessory or on positions of the ignition are not going to be thick 4-gauge or 2-gauge wires. Thus, you are going to need to use a device called a *starter relay* (see Figure 1-21) to activate the 100A current on the power wires when the thin accessory wire goes on.

The automotive relay is a simple switch. It has four terminals (wire posts): IN, OUT, 12V, and ground. You can even see from the size of the terminals which posts activate the switch and which posts carry the heavy relay current.

You can mount the relay in the trunk or the front of the vehicle; it's probably easier to mount it in the trunk if that's where you're mounting the inverter. Because other devices (such as amplifiers) will want access to the unswitched high-amperage 12V, you should supply them first and then route the power into this relay, and then to your inverter.

At this point, your inverter will turn on when the car key is in the accessory position or when the vehicle is on. If you want to make sure that it is on only when the engine is actually on, you will need to consult your vehicle's manual or an installer, who can find a switched 12V connection that's on only when the car is on.

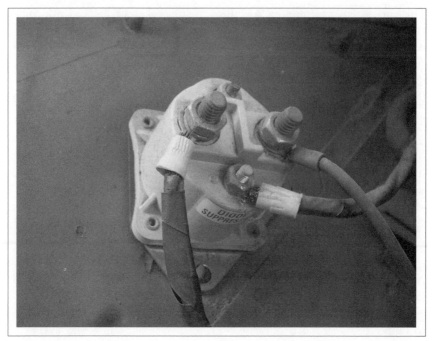

Figure 1-21. A starter relay

Using a power strip is possible with a high-output inverter, and thickly insulated extension cords are pretty safe as long as you don't run them underneath the carpets or hide them in such a way that they might short out on the metal of the vehicle.

If you want the electrical outlets cleanly exposed for easy access or prominent display, your best solution is to install the inverter right behind the panel where you want the outlets. With this setup, you aren't snaking these higher-voltage 120V wires dangerously around your vehicle.

Hacking High Voltages Safely

You may not have known this, but 12V of DC power is not likely to shock you. You can test this by touching the poles of your battery, one with each hand. You most likely won't get a shock; if your hands are wet you might feel a tingle.

Wall outlet high-voltage AC is another thing altogether. Do the same trick with AC, and your body will jerk back and you'll hurt for a while. You might get a small heart attack, or you might get "frozen" onto the wires and not be able to let go.

It's not a good idea to run AC power through the walls of your car. If you short out the power against the body of the car, you could damage the vehicle, shock yourself, and possibly create an electrical fire.

The goal of this hack is to install actual power outlets in the walls of your car, just like those in your house. However, realize that you're now dealing with high AC wall voltage. You do not want to run high-voltage AC wiring any distance in a car. Besides being very unsafe, it may not be legal unless installed by a licensed electrician (who may laugh at you when asked to install it). The best solution is to safely mount the inverter so that its power outlets are flush mounted with the walls of the vehicle.

Running 12V wires around the car is pretty harmless, because if the wires short circuit they will ultimately just blow a fuse. However, the high-voltage output from the inverter is the same voltage you have in your house, and just as you wouldn't run extension cords under the carpet in your home, you shouldn't do this in a vehicle.

If you really want to put a wall outlet inside your vehicle, make sure that the power is run safely, according to the electrical codes and regulations that RVs must comply to. You can look at a copy of the National Electrical Code (NFPA 70) at a technical library or buy NFPA 70 at *http://webstore.ansi.org*.

AC power should go through insulated wires, inside more insulated metal conduit, and should run in such a way that there's no chance for the high-power wires to come into contact with *anything*. In short, make sure anything you install is both *safe and legal* before you have to explain to the insurance adjuster why your 120V wire shorted with your gas tank, detonating your vehicle like a pipe bomb after only a small fender bender during rush hour.

One additional but less threatening aspect of AC current is that it can create interference with audio systems. Take care to keep high-voltage AC lines shielded and apart from audio cables to reduce interference. FM reception can be degraded while using an inverter because of the interference, so if your radio starts getting bad reception, your recently installed inverter may be the culprit.

CHAPTER TWO

Automotive Audio Entertainment
Hacks 12–22

Audio entertainment has long been the steadfast companion of the driver. Since the first tube radios were introduced, the latest audio technologies have always found their way into vehicles—and the recent success of sub-scription satellite radio and portable music players shows that people will adopt almost any new technology that satisfies their need for audio choices.

This chapter focuses on ways to get the latest audio-entertainment technolo-gies into your car, whether it was originally equipped for them or not. While auto manufacturers are slowly seeing the light on satellite radio and MP3, it may be a while longer before they begin equipping vehicles for general-purpose computers, MP3 players, and portable hard drives. Still, with some basic understanding of your car's audio system and a few simple tools, you can hack the latest audio technology into your vehicle's sound system.

HACK #12 Get a Headful About Your Car Audio

The centerpiece of your car's entertainment system is the car radio. You should know how it interacts with your car's speakers and other electronics before you yank it out.

Almost every car ships with a radio. Most car radios also include a tape deck or a CD player, and some current vehicles still come equipped with both. Many new car radios are also capable of controlling a multi-disc CD changer or connecting to a satellite radio. Because the car radio is really a master control for all sorts of electronic entertainment devices, it is often called a *head unit*.

Head Units

General Motors, BMW, Honda, Saab, Ford, and car company you can think of, all manufacture different head units for their vehicles, and they often use different units depending upon the year and vehicle model. Each car company has its own proprietary interface for CD changers, and there are no real standards. Figure 2-1 shows a simple OEM (original equipment manufacturer) head unit.

Figure 2-1. A CD and tape player head unit

There's rarely an opportunity to upgrade the head unit for a better one from the dealer who sold you the car, but the vast majority of cars can accept aftermarket head units. These range in price from under $50 for a simple model to upwards of $2000 for a fold-out touchscreen that can interface with DVD players, CD changers, and satellite radios, and that includes navigation capabilities.

Although many new cars are starting to make aftermarket stereo installation more difficult by "featuring" swooping dashboards that require nonrectangular head units sold only by the car's manufacturer, there actually are some size standards for car stereos.

Single-height stereos, which are used by most car manufacturers, correspond to a size called *DIN* (which stands for Deutsches Institut für Normung, a.k.a. the German Institute for Standards, who established the standard). DIN is about 2" high and 7" wide. Chrysler and a few other manufacturers produce radios that are twice that height and fit a size called *double DIN.* You can purchase inexpensive plastic adapter molds that allow you to install a single-DIN radio (the more common size for aftermarket radios) in a double-DIN hole. Most double-DIN holes are just large enough to fit a 6" diagonal screen, which presents interesting hacking possibilities (see Chapter 3).

More and more head units are becoming tangled into functions of the vehicle itself, making their replacement difficult. For instance, in many cars, the electronics in the head unit integrate with things such as seatbelts, brake sensors, alarms, navigation systems, or even airbags. Fortunately, aftermarket adapters exist to replace or substitute the missing functionality when a factory head unit is removed. Before you pull out your complex modern head unit, Google your make and model of car and see if there will be any side effects.

Amplifiers

Most OEM and mid-range aftermarket head units have four amplified outputs, which go directly to the front and rear lefthand and righthand speakers, as well as RCA outputs that can be routed to an external amplifier to power additional speakers, subwoofers, and so on. One of the main reasons to upgrade a head unit is to upgrade the audio amplifier. Most factory head units have a small, built-in amplifier that powers the four to eight speakers in the vehicle. In order to get high volumes without distortion, or to power larger or better speakers or a subwoofer, the quality of the amplifier needs to be increased.

One way to increase audio quality is to remove the task of amplification from the head unit altogether and go to a multi-piece system consisting of a head unit, which produces the sound to be amplified and runs through RCA connectors, and several amplifiers, which produce the high-powered signals that go to each of the speakers.

External amplifiers generally power two to four channels each (see Figure 2-2) A *channel* is sound that is supposed to come from a particular location, such as front left, front right, or center. If you are going to power six speakers and a subwoofer, you will need two or three different stereo amplifiers.

Cabling

The quality of your speaker cabling directly affects the quality of your music. Long unshielded cables are subject to distortion, picking up hum and noise and adding this to your audio with unpleasant results. If you are familiar with computers, you understand the importance of decent-quality cabling

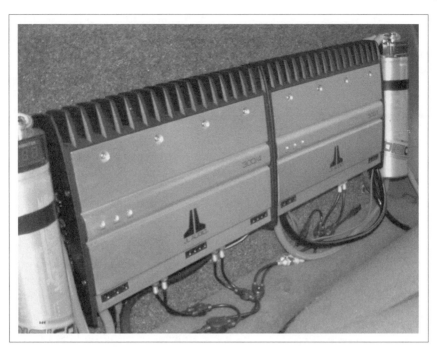

Figure 2-2. Multi-channel amplifiers

and the data loss that can occur when cheap or flaky cables are used. The same principles apply in car audio, but you may experience tremendous sticker shock when you realize that your installer is charging you hundreds of dollars just for the cabling.

A lot of the cost of cabling comes from the look of it and the brand name. You can certainly get just as good a result buying a bulk quantity of high-quality cable and running it yourself as you can paying for a brand name and a professional installation. However, as with making and running your own network cables, the question is whether you want to risk being a victim of your own quality control (or lack thereof).

The Hack: Remove Your Head Unit

If you are installing a PC in your car, chances are high that you'll need to pull out the head unit for one reason or another. Perhaps you're just pulling it out temporarily to run some wires back to your computer. Perhaps you're going to upgrade it with a better model [Hack #13]. Or perhaps you're tearing out the whole center dash unit so that you can fabricate a fiberglass enclosure for your new 7" LCD touchscreen. In any event, there are a couple of things you should know.

Because car stereos are a high-theft item, manufacturers don't make it *too* easy to pull out a radio; nonetheless, it is often simply a matter of unscrewing enough Phillips-head screws. To give dashboards a seamless look, most screws are located either behind panels or toward the bottom, near the carpet.

Many vendors require you to use a specific tool to remove the radio itself. While these "special tools" aren't strictly necessary if you pry with enough force, they are necessary if you don't want to bend, scratch, or break your dashboard. The basic, inexpensive tools you need to disassemble any car stereo are, in rough order of importance:

- A Chilton's, Haynes, or factory manual for your car
- *http://www.google.com*
- An acquaintance at a local car stereo installation shop

The last item will serve you best when you need a specialized $300 tool to pull out your BMW's stereo. Simply drive it over to the stereo shop and provide proof that you own the car (if necessary)—your installer friend from the shop shouldn't mind popping out the radio for you so you can continue your hacks.

Once any necessary proprietary tools are applied, the head unit usually disconnects easily. It is only connected to a few things: a wiring harness, which brings power to the unit and sends audio out to the speakers or external amplifiers; possibly a bus connector (for external devices such as CD changers); and an antenna connector. Antenna connectors are fairly standard; they come in only a few different sizes and are all approximately the same shape (Figure 2-3).

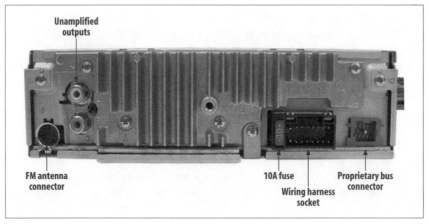

Figure 2-3. Connectors on a head unit

Even if you have one of the new super-complicated systems, complete with OnStar, factory touchscreen navigation, or other goodies, you can open up your dashboard and see what's going on behind it. The wires are normally keyed so that there's only one way to plug them back in, so you can almost always safely disassemble the unit and be able to put it back together again without connecting the wires incorrectly.

HACK #13 Install a New Head Unit

After you've pulled out your head unit, you may want a few tips on putting in a new one.

Most technophiles' needs will exceed the capabilities of their factory car stereos very quickly. First, they'll want to play some computer-based audio format, such as MP3, and they'll have to use a tape adapter to get it into the stereo. Then they'll start wanting to load up MP3s on a CD, and they'll be frustrated that the built-in stereo won't play them. Even if it does, they'll expect the works—intuitive navigation, album art display, and track names. They may also want to install satellite radio in addition to the CD changer. With a three-to-five-year development cycle for new products, auto manufacturers usually can't keep up. That's where the aftermarket comes in.

If you're looking to hook up an in-car computer to your factory stereo, there are definitely ways to do it, but it's often easier to just upgrade to an aftermarket stereo with auxiliary inputs, or even a fold-out video screen. And as you may want to upgrade your sound in the process, adding an external amplifier [Hack #15] is a very standard and beneficial upgrade. But if you're just replacing the head unit, in many cases it is simply a matter of splicing together the correct wires.

Standard Head Unit Wiring

A bundle of wires grouped together in a car is called a *harness*. All radios with built-in amplifiers have pretty much the same wires going from their specific harness to the car, with a different plastic end connector.

Your conventional factory and aftermarket head units usually have the following wires (see Figure 2-4):

- Front left speaker (two wires, + and –)
- Front right speaker (two wires, + and –)
- Rear left speaker (two wires, + and –)
- Rear right speaker (two wires, + and –)
- +12V switched power (usually red)
- Ground (0V, usually black)

- +12V standby power (usually yellow)
- +12V cable out (indicates radio on; goes to amps and retractable antennas)

Since these wires are usually present in any car, installing another head unit is often as simple as buying the right adapter to link your new head unit to the corresponding wires of your car. You can even just cut off the connector and splice the wires individually (this solution costs less but is more permanent). The metal chassis on most head units will also be connected to ground. Figure 2-4 shows cut and labeled wires that are ready to be spliced.

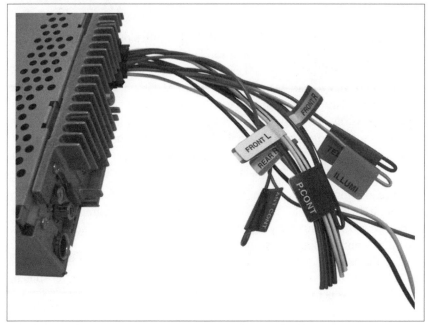

Figure 2-4. Labeled head unit wires ready for splicing

Adapters for Mounting

Some dashboards have single-height DIN slots for car stereos; other vehicles, such as Chrysler/Dodge/Plymouth cars, use a double-height DIN slot. For a clean install of a single-DIN device in a double-DIN dashboard, you should purchase a universal adapter. This plastic mold fits in the double-DIN slot and accepts a single-DIN device.

If you are installing an aftermarket head unit into a vehicle with a space-age-looking dash, you will have to look online or ask your local installer if they can order an appropriate *faceplate adapter*. These plastic adapters are made for some popular cars that have strange head unit mountings. If no adapter exists, though, all is not lost: good stereo shops can fabricate a mount using fiberglass, ABS plastic, or other materials, paint it, and install it for a custom but seamless fit. Pretty much anything can be installed into anything if you have the installer custom-fabricate a method of mounting it.

Proprietary Bus Connectors

Recent-model factory head units and higher-end aftermarket head units come equipped with special "buses." Just like USB ports or other standard computer connectors, these vendor-standard buses allow a family of devices to communicate both analog and digital data. CD changers, satellite radios, and other devices connect to the head unit through this bus. In a factory head unit, there might also be some other wires that connect to alarm systems or other parts of the vehicle's electronics.

If you have any of these devices installed, such as a factory CD changer, changing your head unit will most certainly disable it. You generally have to match any add-on equipment to the head unit.

If you are installing a new head unit to make it easier to use external audio sources, take a look at "Get Computer Audio into Your Head Unit" [Hack #14] to ensure that the head unit you want to replace it with has an input adapter for your computer or device. Also make sure that you really have to replace your head unit—it's possible that you can get an auxiliary-input adapter to make your (modern) factory head unit do what you want.

Caveats

Make sure you study up on the car stereo for your car's year, make, and model, either on Google or by studying the shop manuals or asking the dealer. Specifically, you need to know if there are any strange interconnections between your head unit and other necessary car functions. If the head unit goes too far beyond the basic wires listed earlier, stop and get knowledgeable assistance for your specific vehicle.

Some head units are required to be installed for the car alarm to work. If you replace these, you still have to keep the head unit stashed somewhere (for example, under a seat). Some head units integrate closely with features such as OnStar that hook into the car's computer, the airbag system, and so on. In these cases, it may be difficult to find an adapter that preserves the factory safety features, and you may be essentially stuck with your factory head unit. So know before you go, lest you find that the jaws of life never arrive to pry you out of your car because you snipped two wires you didn't recognize, which disabled your OnStar, which prevented it from reporting that your airbag had deployed.

Get Computer Audio into Your Head Unit

#14 Aftermarket CD changers and DVD players have become very popular of late, as have MiniDisk players, MP3 players, and legions of other small audio devices. To use these devices in a car, however, you'll need to smuggle the audio into your (usually closed) head unit.

The concept of getting audio *into* the car stereo is almost completely foreign to automobile manufacturers, who tend to run years behind state of the art when it comes to audio technology. And the concept is familiar but threatening to aftermarket manufacturers, who want to lock you into buying *their* CD changers and *their* navigation units, not allow easy use of your own laptop or MP3 player.

Fortunately, there are several ways that you can get audio into your head unit.

Tape Adapters

A tape adapter (Figure 2-5) looks like a cassette tape with a wire coming out of it and a mini headphone plug (2.5 mm) on the end. The headphone jack plugs into your external audio device. Tape adapters have a magnetic output device that converts the sound coming in the wire into magnetic signals like those on a normal cassette tape.

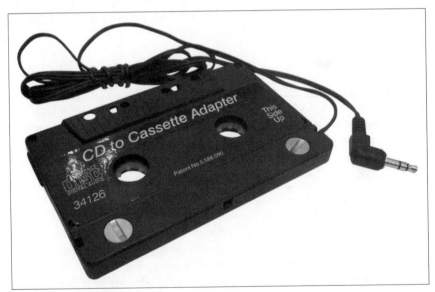

Figure 2-5. A tape deck adapter

Tape adapters are the cheapest solution for audio input; they can be purchased for $10–20 and they plug in and work right away. They are the quickest way to get your computer or MP3 player's audio into the car's head unit, and they work quite reliably.

However, from an audio perspective, tape adapters are a pretty low-fidelity solution. For one thing, the audio signal goes through multiple translations—from the source, through a wire, through a magnetic head, read back by a tape head, then amplified—and it loses a bit of quality in each step. Additionally, the spindles that move the tape are rotating for no reason, and these scraping rotors and their motors generate both electrical and audible noise. ("Reduce Your Audio System's Noise" [Hack #17] has a tip on how to partially solve this problem.) Finally, cassette playback was never that clean to begin with. Even the highest-end tape deck with Dolby noise reduction never rivaled the clean sound of CDs—tape decks always have a bit of noise and hiss.

FM Modulators

If you ever connected a video game system to a television in the mid 1980s, you are familiar with the concept of *FM modulators*. An FM modulator takes an input signal (audio or video) and rebroadcasts it on a particular station frequency. A relatively nonintrusive way to get a head unit to play external audio is to simply broadcast it on some frequency that isn't used in your area. VCRs do this all the time—if your TV doesn't have auxiliary input (the yellow, white, and red RCA connectors), your VCR simply broadcasts its signal on channel 3 or 4. You set your TV to that channel, and voilà, you have video.

FM modulators of all kinds usually have a range of frequencies, either at the low or high end of the frequency band, so that you can adjust them to some station that isn't being broadcast in your area. For instance, your adapter might have a switch to choose between 88.1MHz, 88.3MHz, 88.5MHz, and 88.7MHz. Another adapter might have the choices 106.7MHz, 106.9MHz, and 107.1MHz.

The sound quality of FM modulation can vary a lot, depending on the quality of the FM receiver and the quality of the FM modulator (and the amount of local interference by other broadcasters). Some small portable FM modulators, such as the iRoq or other similar units for iPods (see Figure 2-6), are battery operated, have a small range, and simply need to be positioned near the FM receiver head unit.

Other FM modulators, such as those built into aftermarket CD changers, splice directly into the antenna connector for the car. This allows a stronger FM signal that can override a competing signal from the airwaves and allow your external audio to work consistently. If you often drive on long-distance

Figure 2-6. The iTrip FM modulator

trips and don't want to have to keep changing the station every time another competing station pops into range, a more permanent FM modulator such as this is probably your best bet.

The sound fidelity range of FM is limited and is only about two-thirds the range that a CD can faithfully reproduce. As a result, FM modulation is never the best for audio fidelity. (Though MP3s may add audio glitches, they can produce sounds all the way up to the 22,500-KHz range; FM only goes up to about 14,000 KHz.)

Auxiliary-in Adapters

Almost all modern head units, factory or aftermarket, can control some sort of CD changer. While there are hundreds of different CD changer models, each of these boils down to a similar interface: button presses are sent to a CD changer, and audio comes back from the CD changer.

This same interface can often also be used as a simple auxiliary-in (AUX-in) adapter, as shown in Figure 2-7. A whole industry exists around building replacement CD changers for factory and aftermarket head units, and these same vendors provide AUX-in adapters as well.

Some of the AUX-in adapters even have multiple inputs with a switch. If your head unit already has a factory CD changer attached to it, these switching

Figure 2-7. An AUX-in adapter for a Volkswagon

head units will allow you to toggle between the CD changer and several other inputs.

The sound quality of AUX-in can vary somewhat, because the expected sound input volume level of the AUX adapter isn't necessarily the same from head unit to head unit. But it is usually far better than tape adapters or FM modulation.

Aftermarket Head Units

If you can't find the right adapter for your factory head unit, or you want to upgrade your stereo anyway, the simplest way to get auxiliary input is to buy an aftermarket head unit that includes an AUX-in plug. Most of the mid- to high-end units have them these days, because they are already being used to integrate DVD players and video game systems. I've used Pioneer head units, and while the mid-range units don't come with AUX-in plugs on the back, they are compatible with an adapter I know I can purchase cheaply. Higher-end units usually have a pair of RCA jacks for AUX-in built in.

Digital Inputs

While not common yet, some high-end stereo systems are designed to provide full six-channel surround sound for DVD playback in the vehicle. Instead of running six individual wires, you can use digital optical sound links to move the audio around. If you are considering using one of these systems in conjunction with an in-car computer, you may be able to use the optical digital output of the computer (nonintuitively named *S/PDIF*) to send your audio straight into the head unit.

As home entertainment systems are redesigned to fit the mobile entertainment market, more and more "digital" features will show up in vehicles. The gradual convergence of PCs and audio/video entertainment makes such high-end systems easy to integrate with an in-car computer.

Adjusting Input Volume

The main problem with any analog audio input solution is one of balancing the volume of the audio source with the expected input volume of the adapter. A factory CD changer always outputs its audio to the head unit at a constant volume, and the head unit then amplifies it to the volume selected by the user.

When a computer or other device is connected to a head unit through any of these analog methods, audio distortion can result from mismatched volume. If the computer volume is too low, the head unit volume has to be turned higher. This will add hiss and digital noise. And when you switch back to normal radio, your speakers are likely to blast your ears off because your head unit's volume is turned up too high. Conversely, if the computer volume is too high, the head unit volume has to be turned down. This can result in *clipping*, where input volume is so high that the higher-frequency sounds are "cut off" and don't come through, resulting in distorted audio even at low volumes.

One solution to this problem is to balance your computer or other device's volume to the right level through trial and error, but the ideal solution is to get unamplified output from your computer or device. The iPod, for instance, actually has two audio outputs: an amplified, volume-adjustable headphone output on top, and a single-volume output that comes out of the bottom dock connector. Similarly, some PC sound cards have both a headphone out and an amplified out for connection to speakers. If you're using a computer, always use the unamplified or lightly amplified output; if you're using another device, use a fixed-volume output (if one exists).

The term *line-level* describes a certain voltage between 0.5V and about 4V. Ideally, line-level is the kind of output you would like. Another term you will encounter is *preamplified*, which is the kind of signal you want for an auxiliary input. A preamplified signal is several volts, but is not designed to actually power speakers or headphones. It's a strong, clean signal, with no distortion. The best signal is from a device or sound card that outputs a preamplified line-level signal of around 4 volts.

Choosing Your Adapter

Tape adapters are cheap and easy to install, but they are the least clean installation (an unsightly wire hangs out of your tape player). They also require you to have a tape player in the first place. They are all similar in sound quality; the only difference I have seen is in the quality of the cable that runs to them. You can buy a Sony model in almost any electronics store, and these sound better than generics.

FM modulators are very consistent in their operation and work in almost in any vehicle. They range from cheap $30 battery-powered adapters to perhaps $80 for an installed hideaway version. A reputable installer has told me that there are differences between FM modulators, and that brand-name units from Clarion and other manufacturers probably do a better job than cheaper models. I've personally had poor luck with the iRoq and other portable, battery-powered FM broadcasters. In some cars, however, the iRoq works well, and I know people who swear by it.

Auxiliary-in adapters, when they work right, are the best-sounding analog connections. When installed and working correctly, these give you the highest quality sound possible, as good as you would get from a factory CD changer or other integrated device. They range in price from $25 to over $100. If you are doing a permanent installation of a computer in a recent (5– 10 years old) vehicle that has a CD changer option, chances are one of a variety of vendors makes an AUX-in adapter for your vehicle.

The biggest names in aftermarket AUX-in adapters are:

- *http://www.peripheralelectronics.com*
- *http://www.PIE.net*
- *http://www.soundgate.com*
- *http://www.blitzsafe.com*
- *http://www.pac-audio.com*

Although this book is about in-car computers, it's hard to ignore the dominating presence of the iPod as an in-car audio device. iPods sound best with AUX-in adapters, and each of the manufacturers listed above also makes special iPod adapters that allow control of the iPod via the head unit [Hack #18].

If you have upgraded or are going to upgrade your car to a high-end head unit with digital inputs, you're far ahead of the game. Your computer can integrate with such a unit as easily as with a DVD player or other high-end entertainment device, with extremely high quality and fidelity.

The digital (optical or coaxial S/PDIF) inputs available on some of the newest car amplifiers will provide the cleanest audio solution, but you may not be able to control the audio volume easily from your stereo head unit. These products start at several hundred dollars and go up depending on the make of the amplifier and whether it comes as part of a multipart stereo system.

Have you considered using a Mac Mini **[Hack #54]** as your iPod adapter? Then you can have not just your Mini, but the iTunes Music Store in the car as well!

Multiplexing Your Inputs

As a final note, you may have a whole handful of devices that you need to connect in addition to your computer. To switch between various input sources, you can use a three-way audio or audio and video switch **[Hack #35]**. The switches are just like those you might use on your TV set to switch between video games, DVDs, and TV. You can choose between, say, your DVD player, your portable MP3 player, or your in-car computer. If you mount these switches in your center console or glove compartment, you can easily access them without hanging a bunch of wires across your dashboard.

Amp Up Your Computer Audio
#15

Connect your PC or other audio device directly to an amplifier, bypassing the head unit altogether.

If you have an external amplifier in your vehicle, you may not have to adapt your head unit to get audio from external devices to play through your vehicle's speakers. Although the head unit/auxiliary-in approach in "Get Computer Audio into Your Head Unit" **[Hack #14]** gives you the ability to control the volume of all devices from the head unit, you can connect computers and portable devices with their own volume controls directly to the RCA inputs of your amplifier, bypassing the head unit altogether.

Amplifier Inputs

Amplifiers come in two-channel (stereo) and four-channel varieties, with a corresponding number of RCA inputs. You can see an amp and these inputs in Figure 2-8. Some amplifiers also have a set of "high inputs" that can take the output of a cheap head unit's built-in amplifier, convert it down to a lower level, and then reamplify it with the strength and audio fidelity of the amplifier. There are also separate *line-level converters* that can achieve the same function, for when your head unit doesn't have RCA outputs.

If you install a separate amplifier for all your speakers, as in Figure 2-9, you can improve the sound quality and add additional options for inputting audio from sources other than the head unit.

Figure 2-8. An amp and its RCA inputs

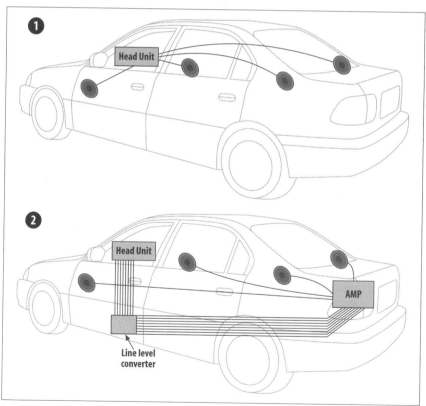

Figure 2-9. Adding an amp to the sound path

One of the features of a head unit is a front-to-back audio balancing feature called *fade*. If you use the pair of RCA outputs of many lower-end head units, such as with a two-channel amplifier, you will have to split this stereo signal into four channels for the front and rear lefthand and righthand speakers, and you will lose the fade feature.

Bypassing Your Head Unit

The nice thing about a computer is that it has line-level (0.5–4V) mini-jack outputs, which can be readily adapted to RCA inputs with a simple cable. This means that the computer can act like a head unit of sorts. There are several approaches to using this audio signal.

RCA switch box. In an approach similar to the one suggested in the section "Multiplexing Your Inputs" in "Get Computer Audio into Your Head Unit" [Hack #14], you can use an RCA switch box (audio only or audio/video) to connect multiple input devices directly into the RCA inputs on your head unit, as shown in Figure 2-10. The benefit of this approach is that you put the switch box in your center console, and it allows you to rapidly change between your head unit, your PC, and perhaps a portable audio device that you plug into the center console compartment.

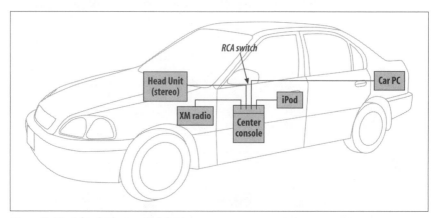

Figure 2-10. A hooked-up switch box

The drawback of this approach is that you have only fairly clumsy control over the volume of your devices. Since the amplifier does not have its own volume control, it depends on the volume coming into it. While the head unit will work fine, PCs and portable devices usually have an amplified, non-line-level output, and if you forget to set the volume very low on the device itself, or accidentally raise it too high, you could blow out your speakers (or your ears).

> Amplified audio devices such as MP3 players and computers, when connected to a car amplifier, can produce too high a volume for the amp. Either ensure that your PC's or audio device's volume is set and will stay low, or use a line-level converter to ensure that the sound is set lower. Painful and potentially serious damage to hearing and/or equipment could otherwise result.

PC pass-through. Another interesting and potentially very useful approach is to pass the head unit audio *through* the PC and connect the PC to the amplifier, as in Figure 2-11. In this way, you're using the computer as your mixer and head unit. If you can get a sound card that gives you preamplified line-level outputs, this is the safest approach, as it will not increase the volume to unsafe levels.

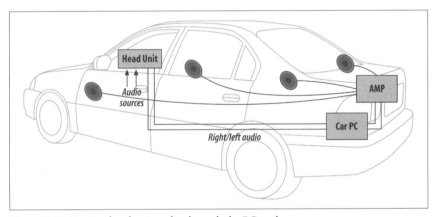

Figure 2-11. Passing head unit audio through the PC to the amp

Some PC sound cards even have a pass-through feature, where the input line is connected to the output line when the computer is off—in this case, the head unit (radio, CD player) audio is passed directly to the amplifier. Other computers require the computer to be on, but allow you to set the pass-through audio in software.

The interesting aspect of *this* approach to software developers reading this book is that you can implement some TiVo-like features—such as the ability to pause live radio—from the head unit. As it passes through the computer, anything you play on the head unit can be recorded, ripped to MP3, processed with Winamp audio processor plug-ins, and so on. (In fact, that's one of the things we're currently working on at my company.)

Eliminating the head unit. Replacing your head unit altogether is the most adventurous approach. As your car computer takes on more responsibility for feeding you audio, you can simply reclaim the space in your dash and install a screen for your car computer there instead. Figure 2-12 shows how you'd hook it up to the amp.

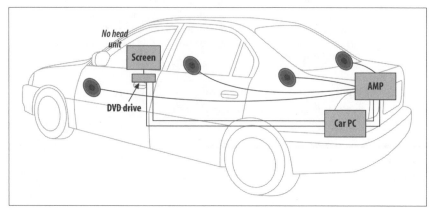

Figure 2-12. Using your PC as a head unit connected to the amp

Obviously, this approach requires that you run software that controls all of your audio needs while you are driving, including selecting devices, adjusting volume, and so on. In essence, you are using a general-purpose computer to implement a head unit in software. Fortunately, there are a handful of applications out there (and more appearing every day) that control many aspects of car audio via a touchscreen. In Chapter 7, you'll find many hacks explaining these frontends in depth.

Make a Very Cheap AUX-in
HACK #16

If your budget is highly constrained or you're out in the wilderness, there's still a way to install an auxiliary input to your tape deck.

Let's say you're preparing for a long drive home from your grandparents' ranch in the country. Your car is old—it runs well and has surprisingly good A/C for its age, but the cassette player just started eating tapes and you don't want to drive a thousand miles without music.

You brought your laptop, and with amazing foresight you also brought your car power adapter for the laptop. You want to listen to the music stored on your laptop, but road noise makes its tinny speakers inaudible while you're driving. You'd like to output the audio through your car speakers, but how? The obvious solution, to use a tape adapter, isn't an option, because your grandparents live in a small town that stopped growing in the 1970s—there isn't a store where you can buy the tape adapter you need.

Still, if you're enterprising, and lucky, you may be able to hack your way out of this technological void. Here's how the hack might go.

First, you have to yank the deck out of your car to take it apart. You improvise some pliers, and pull the head unit out of your vehicle. Using a steak knife as a makeshift screwdriver, you open the unit, pulling off the top cover. You notice that there are two spots inside the tape deck where you see wires that might let in some audio. The actual wires running from the magnetic head that reads the tapes look like they could be spliced, and you have a pair of cheap headphones at hand, so you decide to sacrifice your headphones and connect them to the tape deck, using the twist-and-tape method of connection [Hack #4].

You cut the earpieces off your headphones to expose the wires. You then splice the red (right channel), white (left channel), and black or copper ground wires from your cheap headphones to the corresponding colors in the tape deck, as illustrated in Figure 2-13. You can usually identify the ground wire, even if it's not black, as a braided wire that surrounds the white and red headphone wires.

Figure 2-13. Audio input wires spliced into the tape deck

That done, you need to shove in one of your pre-eaten tapes so that the tape deck thinks there's a tape to amplify. Turn the volume on your laptop all the way down to the lowest squeak, plug in the headphone wires sticking out next to the tape, and voilà—the sound is amazingly passable. You get on the road and feel MacGyver-ish pride, knowing that you could probably survive on a post-apocalyptic earth with your techno-improvisational skill.

Reduce Your Audio System's Noise

There are ways to reduce or eliminate the buzzing and high-frequency noise that the engine adds to your in-car audio.

Despite the fact that we spend so much of our time listening to music in our cars, the automobile is a fairly hostile environment for someone seeking audio perfection. The alternator of the car and the electrical pulses from the spark plugs both create oscillating electronic currents in the audio signal. Really, any moving electrical part can create magnetic waves that show up in electrical wires as audible noise. This is why cables are shielded.

The power from the 12V car battery that powers your car computer fluctuates from 12–14V and includes many other little electrical oscillations from the car. While the battery can still successfully power your computer, the little fluctuations pass through the computer and show up in the analog audio signal that it puts out. At other times, the car's electrical noise is picked up directly by audio wires that act as a sort of antenna. This *line noise* can mess up the audio on its way from the computer to the head unit or the speakers.

Just as there are many potential causes for line noise, there are a number of ways to reduce the noise in a car computer setup. We'll look at those now.

Install Better Wires

You can spend hundreds of dollars on high-quality speaker wire and RCA cables alone. However, the importance of using quality wires is not to be underestimated. Cheap, thin, long RCA cables are like antennas that can pick up noise all along the path they travel through the car. Upgrading to thick, shielded cabling can reduce unwanted noise in the audio signal.

Monster Cable (*http://www.monstercable.com*) is one of the leading manufacturers of well-shielded cable. They're expensive, but if you use cheap cables the labor of re-running wires and diagnosing hums and buzzes will work out to be more costly in the long run. Just as with computers, using high-quality cables will save you a lot of head-scratching time in the end.

Some cable and interconnect manufacturers will brag about how their wire is hand-made by Swiss engineers and cold-rolled in zero-oxygen chambers, allowing for a superior signal-to-noise ratio. Although all cable is not created equal, you can get superior interconnects without spending a fortune. You don't want to use the super-thin 20" RCA cable you bought at the 99-cent store, but the mid-line Monster Cable Phoenix Gold wires and cables will cover most bases. For places where RF interference will be an issue, seek more heavily shielded cables, or possibly go with a coaxial RCA cable. These provide more shielding from interference, but the cables are very stiff, making tight bends difficult or impossible, and most coax is either black or white, which limits your color-coding options. Canare (*http://www.canare.com*) is a leading manufacturer of coaxial cable. They make the cables and connectors that TV and radio stations use for broadcast, which will probably be sufficient overkill for your car.

Install Shorter Wires

Long cables waste space and have to be coiled and shoved out of the way in the trunk. Using a 25-foot cable when a 15-foot cable will do also adds more length to the cable to pick up more noise from electromagnetic fields around the car. Well-shielded or not, too much cable is a bad thing. Use the correct length of cable, as short as you can get away with. If you invest in a few tools and some raw materials, you can make your own interconnects. The advantage of this is that they will be the right length, which makes for clean installs. Also, most raw cable is better quality than you would find in an off-the-shelf premade cable.

Use a Better Power Supply

The power supply itself, which should be regulating the input voltage, can be a source of noise. Many small in-car computers use a DC-to-DC power supply, instead of the AC-to-DC power supply used in desktop PCs (i.e., an ATX power supply). While these DC-to-DC power supplies regulate the 5V signal, some of them also pass the car 12–14V right through on the 12V line. This also passes along the noise to any device in the computer (e.g., the motherboard) that uses the 12V supply.

A manufacturer called Opus Solutions, Inc. (*http://www.opussolutions.com*) makes an excellent high-wattage power supply for in-car use [Hack #42]. Not only does it have features for turning the computer on and off with the car, but it regulates the voltage as well and helps eliminate noise from the whole computer.

Upgrade the Sound Card

While this is more in the realm of computers than automotive audio, it's well known in the computer world that the sound card alone can add a good deal of noise, due to the electrical and magnetic fields inside a PC case. If the audio built into the motherboard is cheap or has a built-in amplifier that adds noise to the signal, you should get a new sound card with an output line that doesn't try to amplify the signal to improve the sound quality.

Because sound cards that plug into the computer can pick up noise from the case, an external USB sound "card" may be a better bet. Some of these external sound adapters output 5.1 six-channel DVD sound, or even digital sound over optical cables. The USB sound card runs sound digitally through a USB cable over the USB protocol, allowing long runs of cable that are immune to analog interference. The noisy step, which is the digital to analog conversion, is then done as far away from the computer as possible, and as close as possible to the head unit or amplifier it is connecting to. The sound card can be linked with short (less than 3 feet), shielded, high-quality RCA cables, virtually eliminating the chance of interference between the computer and the amplifier.

Some of the newest six-channel amplifiers (designed for 5.1 surround sound) have an optical or coaxial digital input—all six channels of sound go right from the sound card to the amplifier. For sound cards that have 5.1 digital output, this is a surefire way to eliminate interference problems from the computer to the amplifier—but it won't solve buzzes that are already in the computer due to noisy input power.

Eliminate Short Circuits

Every speaker has two wires, a send wire and a return wire, that connect to the amplifier. If either of these wires shorts (touches) the chassis or any metal part of the vehicle, you will still get sound, but you'll also get any buzzes running through the metal of the vehicle. Remember, in a modern vehicle, the metal of the car is eventually linked to the negative battery cable as a grounding measure. In this case, when you accelerate, you will probably be able to hear the revving of the engine as a "bzzzzzzz!" prominently featured along with your audio entertainment.

If you have this problem, try unplugging all the speakers (either from the amplifier or from the head unit if the amplifier is built in) and then plug them in one at a time, to see when the buzz appears. You shouldn't have to drive the car to test the speakers—just idling and revving the engine should reproduce the problem. If one of them does buzz, it might be that that speaker is shorting with the metal body of the car.

In fact, any device (not just speakers) that contacts the body of the car or ground wires may pick up unwanted signals. If metal parts of the computer (such as its case) are touching the body of the car, this could carry noise as well. Try isolating (through nonconductive insulators such as rubber, plastic, or vinyl) the computer or other device from the body of the car to see if this improves things. You can purchase little rubber feet for less than $1 at Home Depot. The more jelly-like the insulation is, the better, as this also provides vibration damping for the computer.

Another way that ground shorting can occur is if the black ground wire is connected to the body of the vehicle near the device, instead of running all the way back to the negative battery cable. To solve this, make sure the ground is truly connected directly to the battery, such as through a power distribution block, as described in "Gauge Your Wires" [Hack #3].

Use Electronic Noise Filters

Electronic noise filters are small devices that go in-line between the power and the device. They remove fluctuations from the power signal and transmit a cleaner 12–14V. This can help the device (radio, amplifier, computer, CD changer, etc.) output a cleaner audio signal. SoundGate (*http://www.soundgate.com/products/filters*) makes several noise filters.

Eliminate Ground Loops

Ground loops are flows of current caused by different voltage levels in different parts of the car, due to resistance from long wires or the body of the car. When devices on opposite ends of the vehicle are both connected to ground (i.e., the negative battery terminal), one of them is actually very close to the battery, and one is far away. This distance between, say, the head unit and the amplifier can cause hisses and clicking noises in the system.

One way to solve this problem is to make sure that all the devices are connected to a common ground—that is, to the same ground wire or to several ground wires that directly connect. Don't just screw down to the body of the car (a common and easy approach) or whatever black ground wire is handy in the trunk. Instead, make sure that good, thick wires connect the negative terminal to all the audio-related devices.

Use an Audio Isolator/Decoupler

Audio decouplers can also be used to solve ground loops. Audio isolators make sure that only the audio signal gets cleanly through, without the ground loop noise, by completely isolating the voltages between the two devices. SoundGate makes units for this purpose (see *http://www.soundgate.com/products/isolators-filters/filters.htm*).

Use Better Connectors

Computers tend to have mini-jacks (2.5 mm) coming out of their sound cards. Higher-end sound cards have RCA outputs, which not only stay plugged in better but have more metal contact, and thus less signal resistance. If there are no other options than to use a mini-jack, purchase one with the right length, an angled head, and a thick, shielded cable. Smaller wires are more susceptible to interference, and a straight head makes it easier for the plug to pull out unintentionally.

Gold-plated, professionally mounted plug connectors can do a far better job than poorly soldered, cheap connectors that lack adequate shielding. Preformed connectors are also more tolerant of frequent plugging and unplugging without breaking off.

Use Better Power Inverters

Power inverters that convert DC 12V to AC 120/220V do not always do a perfect job of emulating wall current—the waveform may not be exactly what the computer's or device's power supply expects. The power supply output may also have unexpected signals, which could cause the device to perform a bit out of specification and create hums or additional noises.

A different power inverter, or a different computer power supply that can deal with a "modified sine wave" power inverter, may solve this problem. Exeltech (*http://www.exeltech.com*) makes the best inverters with true sine waves, designed to provide power for more sensitive applications such as audio.

Segregate Cabling

A simple way to minimize the amount of power signal interference with the audio lines is to run them as far apart as possible. You can run the power lines down the passenger side of the car and the audio cables down the driver's side, for instance, and then run them to your car PC in the trunk without crossing.

Add Shielding

High-end computer cases actually have two layers of metal surrounding the computer motherboard. This tight metal cage around the computer components actually helps block stray electrical signals, both incoming and outgoing. To maintain this protection, it is even important that all expansion card slots are covered with metal brackets.

Reduce Tape Adapter Noise

If you use a tape adapter, there's another possible source of noise. Turn your car key to the accessory position, insert a tape adapter tape, and listen. You will hear, either faintly or loudly, a rotating, scraping noise. This is the sound of the tape rotators uselessly spinning within your stationary tape adapter, and the corresponding amplification of this noise through the sound system.

When I used to drive a 1983 Cutlass Sierra, I could hear this noise even when driving—an annoying cyclical scrape amplified by my nice sound system and laid on top of whatever I was listening to, in addition to the noise emanating from the tape player itself.

One day, the old tape player was noisier than normal, and it was clear that the rotating gears were stuck on the tape adapter. I could hear a loud "click click click click" as the gears kept sticking. Finally, the noise subsided—the tape player had broken.

When I put in a normal tape, nothing happened. No sound, just the quietest buzz as the tape player tried to amplify the nonmoving piece of tape that the head happened to be on. But when I used the tape adapter, the sound was quiet and perfect (well, as much as a 1983 sound system can be perfect). The unfortunate event of my tape player breaking ended up showing me that I didn't need the tape rotators to actually spin in order to use a tape adapter. In fact, the sound quality had never been so good.

If you have pretty much stopped using tapes for audio and are using your MP3 player or computer exclusively in an older car, you don't really need the noise generated by the spinning tape player. And if you don't mind a little constructive destruction, you can purposefully "break" your own tape player in order to reduce noise when using your tape adapter. (Of course, this means that you won't actually be able to play tapes anymore.)

The real trick to this hack is getting in and either unplugging the motor or disconnecting the rubber band or gear that goes from the motor to make the tape spin. Some units will let you unplug the motor; in the unit I used in "Reduce Your Audio System's Noise" [Hack #17], however, the tape deck "knew" when the motor wasn't connected and wouldn't play, so I had to disable the spinning mechanically. Experiment and see.

The braided outer wire of well-insulated coaxial cables is another example of a metal "cage" that protects against electrical interference. In any wire or metal device through which current flows, magnetic fields are formed. Tight metal cages can absorb and block these stray signals.

This general principle of shielding can be applied to fully debugging a car computer's buzz problem. If you're certain that you've eliminated all the

noise flowing into the computer through the power input, that you've isolated the computer case from the car chassis, and that you've grounded your
computer directly to the battery, the source of the noise could be a shielding
problem. Many cheaper car PC case manufacturers don't bother to properly
insulate their cases from either dust or electromagnetic interference. If the
case has open card slots, shut them with metal shields. Sometimes case manufacturers use a tinfoil-like metal shielding in order to pass electromagnetic
interference tests. If your case isn't almost airtight, try to get another case
that is a fully enclosed metal shell, properly designed to shield against interference (e.g., a small desktop PC case from a leading manufacturer).

Control Your iPod with Your Car Stereo Knobs
HACK #18
Apple's iPod can now integrate directly with a number of factory and
aftermarket head units.

Apple's iPod portable audio player is quickly becoming the de facto jukebox standard for cars. Until just recently, however, the state of the art for
iPod/vehicle integration was cigarette lighter power and a tape adapter. Give
some points for style, though—the plastic and wires of these adapters were
white.

This situation improved dramatically when Apple released the first interface
that allowed iPods to be controlled by the CD changer controls of several
BMW models, as well as the Mini (the car, not the iPod). With the iPod
BMW adapter, the iPod emulates a CD changer when you plug it into a special adapter stealthily hidden away in the glove compartment. You can create
five playlists in iTunes that can be selected by the CD changer buttons 1–5;
button 6 selects additional playlists in sequence. (Visit *http://www.apple.com/
ipod/bmw/* for more information.)

On the heels of Apple's announcement, everybody got into the game. Pacific
Accessory Corporation (*http://www.pac-audio.com*) released the Swiss Army
knife of iPod adapters, the AUX-POD. This device can interface with the factory head units of dozens of different car makes and models. The first generation of adapters are relatively simple in operation; they allow you to click
"next song" and possibly to select playlists with the factory controls, and
they terminate in a simple wire that you connect to the bottom of your iPod.
PAC's newer adapters are designed to use the full text-display capabilities of
modern satellite-radio-ready head units.

The major aftermarket vendors have responded and added more features to
take advantage of their high-tech head units. Alpine's KCA-420i (*http://
www.alpine.com*) upped the ante by displaying the full song title and album
name and adding search features, and Pioneer has announced a unit with

comparable features. In fact, just about every major stereo manufacturer is adding iPod integration into some part of their product line.

The beginning of 2005 saw dozens of third-party vendors cashing in on the market dominance of the iPod and releasing iPod adapters for cars. A number of competitive second-generation models with search and track-name-display features are in the works, and the iPod adapter arms race is escalating, with battles underway to make the most sophisticated iPod head unit adapter.

Tune Your PC for Radio Reception

HACK #19

With the right receiver, your PC can take over the radio function of a car's head unit.

Receiving radio broadcasts via home PCs has always been somewhat of a novelty option. Every generation of PC has had its tuner cards or external USB receivers. But as radios already do a great job of receiving broadcasts, it's only the added features—such as remote control and timed recording—that make PC radios valuable. Now you can take advantage of these features with your car PC, too.

PC Radios

There are two basic kinds of PC radios: external radios connecting to USB or serial ports, and PCI cards with FM tuners on board. Almost all of these cards output analog audio via a pair of cables and use the USB or PCI connection only for tuning the station. There's no real point in sending audio over a digital connection, because the broadcasts are analog to begin with. Instead, the audio goes into the CD-in, line-in, or microphone input of the computer's sound card.

Every computer radio comes with software that allows you to control the tuner, select different channels, and display which channel you are on. None of these applications, however, are designed for in-car use; they are generally quickly-thrown-together Windows programs that do a rudimentary job of tuning and may or may not offer extra features such as timed recording, pause, and so on.

Problems with PC Radios

Radio is one of the most difficult responsibilities for the PC to take over. For one thing, head unit radios are very mature and sophisticated, and they are designed to clearly receive broadcasts while moving at highway speeds. PC radio cards and USB receivers, on the other hand, usually use the cheapest radio chip available and are designed to sit still on a desk or in a window. This means that the signal quality of these devices is not as high as it could be.

Another problem with PC radios is that they do not adhere to a standardized programming interface. Each new unit from a different manufacturer has its own method of changing stations, and these aren't usually part of a published API. Luckily, the interfaces usually get reverse-engineered by the Linux community to produce open source drivers and documentation, but this does mean that in-car GUI software has to be re-coded to control each different FM receiver.

Finally, most of the PC card and external radios do not pick up AM signals. While not that important for the desk-bound target market of the devices, lack of AM radio is a showstopper for many drivers.

The Hack: Getting Radio to Your Car PC

In 1999 D-Link came out with an excellent FM radio tuner, the DSB-R100, that was easily controlled by USB. There are now many third-party applications that can control that unit, because it's been around so long. You can still buy them on eBay and in car computer forums such as *http://www.mp3car.com*. A company called Radio Time (*http://www.radiotime.com*) bundles an almost identical unit with their subscription service, and Griffin Technology makes the Radio Shark (*http://www.griffintechnology.com/products/radioshark*), which works on Macintosh computers but may have third-party drivers for Linux by now. A number of PCI TV Tuner cards also include FM tuners. Hauppauge (*http://www.hauppauge.com*) makes several different inexpensive PCI and USB TV and FM tuners.

Whatever radio tuner hardware you find, it's probably going to be supported by Radiator (*http://www.flesko.cz*), a freeware program for tuning and recording radio from any PC radio device. In fact, you can find a rather complete list of the radio tuner hardware available for PCs at the Radiator web site. Radiator is probably the best program for car PC use—it's supported by car PC frontends such as CENTRAFUSE [Hack #73] and FrodoPlayer [Hack #75].

If you must have AM your options are limited, but you will find that there are more expensive *scanner* units (costing several hundred dollars) that pick up AM, FM, and a variety of other signals, such as police and emergency frequencies, and are controllable by USB. You can have it all—just not on a shoestring budget.

Once you have chosen an FM tuner, you need to route the antenna from your car to the antenna input of the device, or your reception is going to be pitiful. For this you need an antenna splitter that allows you to tap into the antenna while still letting it go to your head unit. The most useful of these splitters are called *scanner splitters* (Figure 2-14), because they're designed to split the antenna signal out to a scanner. These usually have a standard BNC connector on the end.

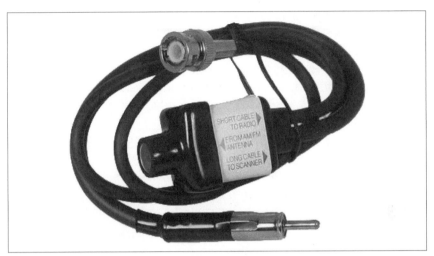

Figure 2-14. A scanner splitter for an antenna and its connector cables (courtesy of http://www.walcottcb.com)

Once you have this antenna connection, it needs to be adapted to the antenna input of your tuner. Tuners usually accept either a U.S. television coaxial male connector (Type F) or, less usually, an RCA-type input. Radio Shack carries a BNC-to-coax adapter, as well as RCA, BNC, and coax adapters.

If you don't want to buy all of these adapters, or you are getting rid of your head unit altogether [Hack #15], you should be able to just splice and solder the correct connector onto your radio—simply take a piece of coaxial cable (for television), and solder it to a simple FM splitter. You don't want to start cutting up the cable that runs your antenna to your car stereo; it's always cheaper and easier to destroy a $10 part in the process of hacking than to explain to the dealer why you need a new antenna wire run through the body of your car.

Once you get this antenna linked into your receiver, you should get better reception than you ever did with the receiver in the house. Your car PC now has the potential to replace your head unit's radio, especially if you take advantage of the car PC frontend software that we cover in Chapter 7, such as FrodoPlayer.

PC XM Radio

The success of subscription satellite radio in the U.S. is either strong evidence of consumer interest in audio entertainment, or strong evidence that traditional radio sucks. In either case, satellite radio services such as XM and Sirius are getting more popular every day, and most new car head units are satellite-ready.

For a while, the hardware cost for satellite radio was very high, and you could easily spend almost $400 to upgrade to satellite radio. In the last year tuner hardware prices have plummeted, and the basic XM receiver (called XM Direct) now costs less than $50, and can be used with any XM-ready stereo head unit.

What's more, with a simple cable you can build for about $15, you can turn your own car PC into an XM-ready head unit! You can find a schematic for the appropriate cable at *http://www.i-hacked.com/content/view/56/94/* (or just Google for "XM Direct PC Cable"). Using these inexpensive cables, most of the car PC frontends (see Chapter 7) include the ability to tune XM radio.

If you don't want to build, you can buy premade homebrew cables for about $25 on the forums at *http://www.mp3car.com*, or you can buy hardware and software from TimeTrax (*http://www.timetraxtech.com*). Their software not only connects the XM Direct receiver to your computer, but also allows you to do scheduled recordings [Hack #20].

Record Radio Shows
#20

A variety of software programs enable your computer to make scheduled recordings of radio programs.

TiVo has grown in popularity over the past few years, and personal video recorders (PVRs) are proliferating as a must-have feature for set-top boxes. Naturally, consumers of audio content want the same features, and many PC programs have been developed to meet this demand.

The real key to a functional personal media recorder (PMR) is the database. It's quite easy to plug a radio into a sound card, tune it to a station, and record, but what makes the process more user friendly is to have the computer tune the channel automatically and provide the end user with a menu of choices. Also, as the success of *TV Guide* tells us, the information on what is playing is as valuable as the recording itself.

TiVo-Like Functionality for Radio

While there are a bunch of programs that find and record online radio stations, few of them control the radio to change the station, and almost none of them offer any sort of radio program listing. However, one subscription service, Radio Time (*http://www.radiotime.com*), does it all, and will provide you with an inexpensive radio tuner that looks conspicuously like the D-Link DSB-R100.

As Radio Time has to pay licensing fees for their database of program listings, they pass that cost on to the consumer in the form of a subscription service. For around $40 a year, you get access to their database of the programs in your area, and they will sell you the FM receiver hardware as well.

To use their system, you simply enter a Zip Code, and you get a list of radio stations in that area. The stations are displayed in a web interface and include many of the program search features you'd expect (by station, category, genre, etc.).

To use this interface on the road you must have mobile Internet access (discussed in Chapter 6), but programs you record, once set, record at their scheduled times regardless of connectivity. The service recommends broadband Internet access, because it can record a wide variety of Internet radio stations as well.

The real problem with timed recordings in the vehicle is not the Internet access—the problem is that when your car is off, your computer is off, and thus your timed radio recordings will not record.

There are a couple of solutions to this dilemma. One is to simply do your timed recordings on your desktop PC, which always has power, and then transfer the resulting MP3s to your car PC [Hack #64].

Another approach is to use a car computer that wakes up on a schedule. Many PCs have a timed wakeup feature, but even these deep "sleep" modes draw too much current and will kill your car's battery over time. Some solutions to this problem are discussed in "Boot Your Car Computer on a Schedule" [Hack #47].

HACK #21 Listen to Email, Weblogs, and RSS Feeds on the Road

Have your email, blogs, and RSS feeds read to you using computer text-to-speech voice synthesis. It's safer than reading while driving.

Computers have had primitive speech synthesis capabilities since the early 1980s (you may remember the awkward computer voice of the Speak & Spell), but only recently have computers gotten powerful enough to produce speech that sounds, well, natural. While the alt-rock band Radiohead pioneered the use of speech synthesis in a song on their album *OK Computer*, this hack shows off some products that you can use to have your email read back to you or keep up with blogs while you're on the road.

Reading Email

To get the email messages into your car PC to begin with, you need to either carry them to your computer via a portable storage device or follow the hacks in Chapter 6 to enable your computer for Internet access.

One option for reading your mail is to use a product such as ByteCool's CoolSpeech (*http://www.bytecool.com*), which fetches email from a POP3 email account and reads it to you. The program relies on the built-in voices available on your computer, and you can purchase additional, higher-quality voices from their web site that work with Microsoft's Speech API (SAPI). You don't have to worry that the emails will get deleted from the mail server; the email feature in CoolSpeech is read-only and leaves the messages in place so that you can download them later with your regular email client.

Another approach is to simply convert the emails or text documents to MP3 on your desktop computer, and then carry the MP3s to your car computer via a portable drive. You can Google "email TTS MP3" (or similar key-words) to find a variety of programs to do this, such as Visual Text To Speech MP3 (*http://www.visual-mp3.com/text-to-speech/*).

In fact, most text-to-speech programs (*http://www.microsoft.com/speech*) come with some sort of helper application you can use to quickly convert text to speech and save it to a WAV file, which can then be easily ripped to an MP3 by another program. For more on this approach, check out Hack #62 in *TiVo Hacks*, by Raffi Krikorian (O'Reilly), which you can find online at *http://hacks.oreilly.com/pub/h/549*.

> When I listen to email, I use a program that was developed by my own company, the CarBot Player [Hack #59] (*http://www.carbotpc.com/software*). It reads emails in sequence and acts just like a CD player, so you can click the next track and previous track buttons to cycle through your emails as if they were tracks on a CD.

Reading RSS Feeds and Weblogs

Since I love to keep up with snippets of news but hate the time sink of actu-ally going to Slashdot, I've rigged up a couple of RSS feeds to email news to me. *RSS* (Real Simple Syndication) is a protocol used by thousands of news-oriented web sites to deliver real-time text summaries of news stories.

Using Aaron Palmquist's *rss2email* program (*http://www.aaronsw.com/2002/rss2email/*), I set up NPR main news feeds and Slashdot headlines to for-ward to my secret car-only spam-free email account, which I then retrieve on my way home from work using my in-car WiFi connection [Hack #62].

The actual scripts run on my home computer (a Mac), so I always have a full set of world news and geek news headlines, conveniently read to me as new emails. *rss2email* is designed to run on Linux/Mac OS X, but since it doesn't have to run on the car computer itself, you just need a Mac or a Linux box running somewhere. (On Windows, all the blog-aggregator programs I could find only worked with mail servers based on the IMAP or Exchange server protocols, and thus wouldn't work with the more prevalent POP3 protocol email readers that support mobile text-to-speech.)

The real challenge of using these programs on the road is that they still require a keyboard to get the email readback started. Safely controlling all these disparate apps is covered in "Car-Enable Clunky Applications" [Hack #58].

Find Out What Was Playing on the Radio
#22
If you know what time you were listening to the radio, you can find out what song you were listening to using a web service.

"Record Radio Shows" [Hack #20] highlighted a subscription-based web application that provides a program guide for upcoming terrestrial (and Internet) radio. However, with a different web service you can answer the question "What was that song?" for a day *after* the program ran.

Yes, Inc. (*http://www.yes.com*) licenses song-by-song playlist information and provides it for the U.S. radio market. Using the drop-downs on the Yes.com main page, you can select a city, a local station, and then any airtime in the last 24 hours. The site then displays the five songs or programs that played nearest that time, giving you the option to purchase the tracks from either Amazon.com or eBay (Figure 2-15).

To use this service, you simply need to know what station you were listening to, and at what time.

Hacking the Hack

If you have a car PC running, you can use this approach to bookmark songs you hear on your car radio. Simply add an application to your PC that notes the time, and whenever you hear a song you like, click that application. In Linux, it is trivial to tie a button to a shell script to do this. For example, the following command will append the time and date to a text file:

```
# date >>yestimes.txt
```

A similar device could be easily whipped up for Windows—for example, a Visual Basic application with one button that appends the time and date to a logfile.

Find Out What Was Playing on the Radio

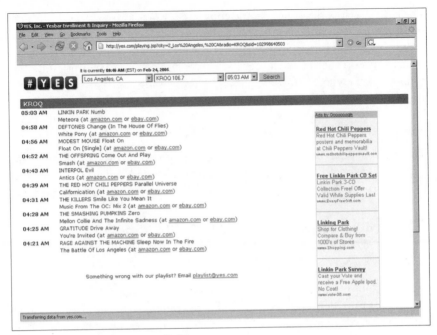

Figure 2-15. Yes.com's program listing page

An even better solution is to add such a button to an open source radio controller application. Then you can note not only the time but also the station that is playing, simplifying the process of identifying that song in the future.

If you are really adventurous, through creative screen-scraping, you can get the track names of the songs playing on the radio in real time (assuming you have a mobile Internet connection). Example 2-1 contains a Python script that can access Yes.net information (courtesy of Raffi Krikorian).

Example 2-1. Screen scraping script for Yes.net

```
#!/usr/bin/env python2.3

## \file YesNet.py
## \brief a simple object to access Yes.net information

import re
import urllib2

optionvaluere = re.compile( 'value=\"(.*?)\".*?\>(.*?)\<\/' )
cityre = re.compile( 'name=city.*?\>\s*(.*?)\s*\<\/select', re.S )
cityurlre = re.compile( '\s' )
radiore = re.compile( 'name=radio.*?\>\s*(.*?)\s*\<\/select', re.S )
sidre = re.compile( 'name=sid.*?\>\s*(.*?)\s*\<\/select', re.S )
```

Example 2-1. Screen scraping script for Yes.net (continued)

```
playingre = \
        re.compile( '\<td\scolspan=\"2\"\>.*?\n\s*(.*?)' +
                    '\s*?\n\s*(.*?)\s*?\n', re.S )

class YesNet:
    def __init__( self ):
        """setup our data structures"""
        self.citymap = self.getcities( )
        self.radiomap = {}

    def getcities( self ):
        """pull the list of cities that we can query for.

        this is a helper function used in the initialization. it's
        mostly so that we can create a mapping between city names and
        the internal name that yes.net uses.

        \return a mapping of city names
        """
        yesurl = urllib2.urlopen( 'http://www.yes.net/home_bar.jsp' )
        cities = \
                optionvaluere.\
                findall( cityre.search( yesurl.read( ) ).group( 1 ) )
        citymap = {}
        for city in cities:
            citymap[city[1]] = cityurlre.sub( '%20', city[0] )
        return citymap

    def listcities( self ):
        """a function that will list the cities that yes.net knows about

        this returns the human-readable version of the cities that
        yes.net knows about

        \return a list of city names
        """
        return self.citymap.keys( )

    def getstations( self, city ):
        """given a city name, get the stations that yes.net knows about

        this takes a human version of the city name, looks up the
        appropriate yes.net internal version, queries for that, then
        returns a list of station names. we also have to cache this
        so we can do fast lookup on whether a radio station is valid.

        \param city the human-readable version of the city name
        \return a list of the stations in that city
        """
        if city not in self.citymap:
            return []
```

Example 2-1. Screen scraping script for Yes.net (continued)

```python
        urlcity = self.citymap[ city ]
        yesurl = \
                urllib2.urlopen( 'http://www.yes.net/home_bar.jsp?city=%s'%
                            ( urlcity ) )
        stations = optionvaluere.findall( radiore.\
                                          search( yesurl.read( ) ).group( 1 ) )
        stationlist = []
        for station in stations:
            stationlist.append( station[0] )
        self.radiomap[ city ] = stationlist
        return stationlist

    def getlastplayed( self, city, station ):
        """given a city name and a station name, get the last played

        this takes the human-readable city name and the station name,
        and queries yes.net. from yes.net, it attempts to retrieve
        the list of the last few songs played and returns them in a
        list

        \param city the human-readable version of the city name
        \param station the station name
        \return the list of what was played
        """
        if city not in self.citymap:
            return []
        if city not in self.radiomap:
            self.getstations( city )
        if station not in self.radiomap[ city ]:
            return []
        yesurl = \
                urllib2. \
                urlopen( 'http://www.yes.net/home_bar.jsp?city=%s&radio=%s'% \
                        ( self.citymap[ city ], station ) )
        sid = \
            optionvaluere. \
            search( sidre.search( yesurl.read( ) ).group( 1 ) ).group( 1 )
        yesurl = \
                urllib2. \
                urlopen( 'http://www.yes.net/playing.jsp?' +
                        'city=%s&radio=%s&sid=%s'%
                        ( self.citymap[ city ], station, sid ) )
        playingmatch = playingre.search( yesurl.read( ) )
        return [ playingmatch.group( 1 ), playingmatch.group( 2 ) ]
```

CHAPTER THREE

Automotive Video Entertainment
Hacks 23–40

The miniaturization of LCD-panel technology has made it possible to put a video screen almost anywhere. The first-class airline feature of personalized video entertainment has quickly become a cattle-class requirement. Now all savvy parents install multiple screens in their SUVs to keep the kids from fighting. It's a video world, and the number of things you can feed to a screen is vast: movies, TV shows, surveillance feeds, navigation aids, rear-view cameras, video games, and video conferences, to name a few.

Computers have become the "Swiss Army knife" of video manipulation. It makes sense to have a single machine solve all your video needs—storage, playback, and editing—especially in an environment where power and space are often limited. And a computer does far more than just imitate the video appliances it replaces—it usually goes beyond their capabilities. Instead of a DVD player, you can have a video jukebox. Instead of just viewing the images captured by a rear-view camera, you can have your computer record the license plate of the car tailgating you. Instead of just telling you where to go, a computer-based navigation system can tell you everywhere your car has ever gone. And instead of having to choose which video game system to install in your car, you can have your computer emulate all of them.

In this chapter, we focus on getting video displays into the car by various means, so that you'll be able to view the output of your in-car PC. I'll briefly introduce the several video-connector technologies you'll encounter in the process, and then go over a number of conventional and novel methods for mounting a screen in the car.

Understand Video Connectors

#23   If you can connect a VCR or game console to your television, you can connect a video screen in your car.

Televisions have been finding their way into cars since the early 1980s, when miniature 12V-powered TV sets appeared on the market. Picture tubes were long and unwieldy, though, and the small space available in a car made them impractical for rear-seat entertainment. Tiny LCD flat-screen TVs were initially installed in airplanes for in-flight entertainment, but once they started coming down in price they began migrating from the airplane to the car.

While larger LCD screens are designed to connect to computers, most small LCD screens are configured to connect to VCRs and DVD players, and thus have the same kinds of inputs as a television. The screens used for factory navigation systems use yet another method of connection.

Figure 3-1 shows the four basic connectors you will be dealing with when you connect screens in your car:

Composite
> These are the ubiquitous yellow RCA-type plugs and jacks that you see on VCRs and video game consoles. They are the most widely used video connector and work pretty well at carrying standard television and video signals. However, they were not originally intended to carry high-resolution computer signals, and their color is a bit washed-out. You often find composite cables bundled with two other RCA cables, where yellow is the video and the red and white cables carry the stereo audio. Most flat monitors for cars have a composite video input.

S-Video
> These are your basic upgrade from composite. They look sort of like PC keyboard plugs but have only four pins. Because they have four wires instead of two, they are able to separate the brightness and color signals and send them separately. This results in a brighter and sharper picture. S-Video cables should be used whenever possible. S-Video can be downgraded to composite with a simple, cheap adapter. Some higher-end in-car screens have S-Video inputs.

RGB
> These connectors provide a sharper and higher-quality image than composite and S-Video television connectors but do not provide the high resolutions that computer connectors provide. RGB has separate wires for red, green, and blue (hence RGB), as well as one or two synchronization wires. The factory screens in most vehicles that have built-in navigation

systems use RGB connections, making the text more readable than with composite or S-Video connectors.

VGA

These are the traditional 15-pin connectors found on the back of any computer. These connectors separately transmit red, green, and blue signals along with several other signals to synchronize the monitor to the many resolutions that a computer can produce. Flat-screen computer monitors and touchscreens for both indoor and automotive use have VGA connectors.

Figure 3-1. From left to right, composite, S-Video, RGB, and VGA connectors

Choosing Your Connector

Every modern PC has a VGA output, and any computer designed to connect to a television has a composite or S-Video output. The choice of how to connect a screen to your in-car computer depends on how you intend to use the screen (for video or text) and your budget.

The cheapest screens are composite, and you can get headrest screens of this type for less than $150 at your local Wal-Mart. These screens usually have a much lower resolution than conventional TVs—perhaps only around 400×200 pixels—but they're still perfectly adequate for watching movies.

Most of the screens you see in retail stores have composite video connectors and are designed to connect to in-car DVD players, not computers. Thus, they have bright screens and are ideal for viewing films or playing video games. If you want to do actual work on your computer, such as running an office application, you'll need a VGA connector and a high-resolution display. Otherwise, the text may be blurry and illegible.

Small flat-screen monitors with VGA connectors can *multisync*, meaning they can adjust to whatever resolution you send to them. However, unlike conventional monitors, they have a *native resolution*, a precise number of horizontal and vertical dots that they can actually display. These screens look their sharpest only when the computer's output matches the native resolution.

Powering and Feeding Your Screen

The screens described in this chapter have several things in common. Almost all the screens have multiple inputs—they can switch between several composite video sources, or even VGA. Many of them have built-in speakers, and some have headphone jacks or even wireless headphone connections. And all of them run on 12V. The screens with built-in speakers that face away from the viewer are essentially useless for most audio applications, but they can be used for the speech on a navigation system. Built-in headphone jacks are a convenient solution for private listening.

Whatever screen you choose to install, you need to run at least two wires to it: one to feed it power and another to feed it a video signal. You can snake these wires to the video and the power source, be it in the trunk, under a seat, or behind the dashboard. Running these connections under the carpeting is a great way to keep them concealed. Depending on your vehicle, you may have to unscrew floorboards or other items to loosen and lift up the carpeting. If you have multiple audio and video sources [Hack #35], you'll need to run wires from each source to the screen, which usually has two or three inputs.

You'll also need to run a wire to a source of 12V power. Screens usually take less than 1 amp of power (for instance, the Lilliput 7" touchscreen takes about 550 mA), so they can run off any available accessory-switched 12V line. It's a good idea to power the screens only when the car key is in the accessory or on positions [Hack #4], or they could slowly kill the battery when your car is off (the Lilliput draws 16 mA in standby).

Cables that carry video can be susceptible to RF interference. If you are going to spend a little extra on something, make it the cables. Shielded video cables will help eliminate cross-talk interference (wire-to-wire electrical interference), engine whine, or interference from strong wireless antennas. It's best to run your audio/video and power cables on opposite sides of the car, if possible. Flexible, shielded conduit can be used to protect wires against moisture, friction, and interference. Avoid putting cables in places where they may be pinched by a door, crushed by feet, or submerged. It's good to do the same for power connections, as 12V car power does not play well with water.

The following hacks describe the unique installation steps and features of particular screens. Once you get the wire down to the floor, you'll know what to do if you read "Connect Your Wires" [Hack #4].

Choose Your Screens

#24

Choosing the right screen or screens for your vehicle depends on the available space in the vehicle and the intended applications.

There are a variety of screens that can be installed in your vehicle. In a large RV or a boat, you can get away with just installing a cheap, small television set. But in a car, you are usually limited to flat screens. There are also many places to install screens in a vehicle, and once you start installing them you may not be able to stop.

In-car flat screens vary widely in quality. Based on *LCD* (liquid crystal display) and the better *TFT* (thin film transistor) technologies, these screens can cost from less than $100 to over $1,000, depending on size and viewing angle (that is, how good the picture looks when viewed from above or from the side).

Both wide screens and conventional screens are available for the car. Wide screens usually have an *aspect ratio* (i.e., horizontal to vertical ratio) of around 16:9, and just like wide-screen high-definition televisions (HDTVs), they are designed to show movies. As a result, the common 7" touchscreens have an oddball resolution of 800×480 pixels. Conventional screens have a 4:3 aspect ratio, like traditional televisions, computer monitors, and video game consoles. Most video games will look a bit stretched on a 16:9 screen. You should choose a screen based on what you will use it for the most—if it's for DVD or computer use, go ahead and get a wide screen. If it's for older console games and standard-definition TV shows, you may want to stick to a 4:3 ratio.

Another consideration is how much customization you want to do. A good car installation shop will have a skilled fabricator who can make any screen you buy look like it was factory installed, as long as you have room to install it. If you are installing it yourself and do not have the necessary creative skills or tools available, you should get a screen that installs easily and seamlessly.

Some newer screens developed for mobile audio/video will come with an anti-glare ultraviolet coating, similar to what is used for instrument clusters and other displays in the car. These coatings will make it much easier to see the screen during daylight hours (particularly at dawn and dusk). Make sure you ask about how well the screen works in bright conditions before you make your purchase.

Off-the-Shelf Screen Options

Portable 12V televisions have been around since the mid 1980s. Originally used for watching TV while camping, they evolved into larger versions that install in RVs and boats. Nowadays they can come with VHS tape or DVD players built in.

Portable flat-screen DVD players are widely and cheaply available. They aren't particularly designed for in-car integration—they usually flip open like laptops, and most of them don't take external video input—but depending on your hacker skills, you may be able to convert many of them into cheap in-car screens.

Headrest screens were first seen in airplane in-flight entertainment systems, and then they migrated to cars. Now, you can purchase them for less than $100. If you don't want to cut your headrest, you can even buy replacement headrests with screens preinstalled. You can purchase these in 4:3 or 16:9 aspect ratios, and in low and high resolutions. Many of them have multiple video inputs, so you can choose between, say, a DVD player and a video game console. The higher-end integrated units come with wired or even wireless headphones, so that the screens' users can have their own private audio-visual experiences without bothering other passengers. Headrest screens are great if there are multiple video entertainment options to choose from. They are always visible, however, and may attract thieves (window tinting can help).

Fold-down screens range in size from 5" diagonal to the size of in-home screens. Cheap PC screens can even be adapted to fold down in a vehicle [Hack #30]. They are usually installed just behind the driver and passenger on the ceiling, so that the one or more rows of backseat passengers can all see the screen. Most factory-installed DVD playback systems involve a single ceiling-mounted fold-down flat screen. Because they hide away into the overhead console, they are less obvious and potentially less prone to theft.

Sun visor screens can be as large as headrest screens and usually come preinstalled in a replacement sun visor with a mirror and light. The video cable to these screens can be cleanly routed down the front pillars of the vehicle for a seamless look. These hide away well and are good for providing customized video entertainment for the front passenger; however, the viewing angle is a bit high.

Rearview mirror screens are designed to assist you in backing up, which is why they are usually sold along with a camera designed to be mounted on the rear of your vehicle. These are typically small 4:3 screens installed to the left of the rearview mirror. While they are a bit small for actually watching movies, they can quickly show the driver what his passengers are watching. They are also excellent for showing the currently playing song and track info, album art, or similar information to the driver.

Motorized fold-out screens are the most stealthy and slickest installation, but they have their problems. All high-end head units now have an option for a fold-out 7" screen, usually with navigation and DVD options as well as touch-screen menu controls. These are some of the most expensive screens, because they are integrated into a head unit that also receives radio stations, controls other devices such as satellite radio, and plays CDs and DVDs. They usually also come with an auxiliary input option allowing you to connect external video (i.e., a computer), but not at high VGA resolution. Also, the touch-screen interfaces of these screens do not send the keypresses to the computer, so they are ineffective for in-car computer control. "Install a VGA Touch-screen in Your Dashboard" [Hack #26] has more information on this subject.

There are actually two types of foldout screens: motorized screens and their cheaper sibling, the spring-assist monitor. As is the case in most things, the more moving parts there are, the more potential there is for breakdowns. A motorized screen not under a warranty will require expensive repair if and when the mechanism fails. A nonmotorized, spring-assisted unit will save you money both in the purchase price and down the road. The trade-off is the lack of automation and having to push/pull things to turn them on and off.

Factory Screens

Built-in center console screens with factory navigation features come in many mid- to high-end vehicles. The benefit of these screens is that they are seamlessly integrated with the interior of the vehicle. The drawback is that they are often slaves to their factory-designated functions, and in the U.S., because of various laws against in-car movie viewing, none of them display DVDs without assistance. A number of aftermarket companies have designed adapters for certain models of car that allow external devices to be attached to factory screens [Hack #32], and a Google search on your particular car can also help you find the company or individual out there who has figured out which wires to tap into. (Some good keywords to search for are RGB, NAV, screen, and rearview camera, as well as the make of your car.)

 Needless to say, this may be a good way to void a factory warranty. When hacking something as tightly integrated as a factory screen, use the same quick-release connectors that the screen harness uses and avoid cutting wires. You want to be able to restore the wiring to stock (original) condition for troubleshooting, or if you're taking it to the dealer for warranty work. This method is also effective for leased vehicles, depending on how strict the lease agreement is.

While you will probably be able to find an adapter to get video on your NAV screen, the ability to send the touchscreen or button presses to your in-car computer is highly unlikely unless you tap into and reprogram the factory navigation system itself. At this level of difficulty, you're better off replacing the screen.

Custom Screens

Many of the commercially available screens use the same electronics and simply change the enclosure. They may also add some buttons or video source switching capabilities. In fact, you can purchase the screens from electronics catalogs without enclosures in a very plain-vanilla configuration.

Sub-$100 video screens are easy to find in large retail chains, though, and they can be disassembled and custom-installed wherever you need them. For instance, some people have installed screens in the center of their side-view mirrors, so they can see both behind and another view, by way of mini-cameras located at the rear of the vehicle. Others have installed whole banks of screens in the rear seat, making a video wall of inexpensive screens, just like you see in stores and clubs.

Mounting Your Screen on the Dashboard

If you are going to be setting up a temporary in-car screen installation, you can use the mounting equipment that comes with most small screens.

There are several standards relating to mounting screens. Almost all screens come with an integrated nut (Figure 3-2) that is the same as the one you find on cameras. This allows the screen to be mounted from below on a tripod or other bracket. Another standard mounting system is a slot in the back of the screen, also shown in Figure 3-2. A slotted nut can be slid into this bracket and tightened. Many pivoting arm supports for screens use this mounting system.

When you purchase a screen, you should check what mounting hardware it comes with to ensure that you get what you need for your configuration.

If your vehicle doesn't have room in the console or radio area to install the screen, you can use the mounting hardware that comes with the screen, shown in Figure 3-3, to mount it on top of the dashboard. The VGA touch-screens from Xenarc, Lilliput, and Pixellon all come with mounting posts. These posts have flexible metal bases with double-stick tape. Although not the prettiest installation, this tape will stick firmly to most dashboards and will hold the screen in place. While some of these mounting posts have screw holes as well, if you ever decide to remove the monitor you'll find it a lot easier to remove some sticky tape from the dashboard than to fill in and patch any holes you've drilled.

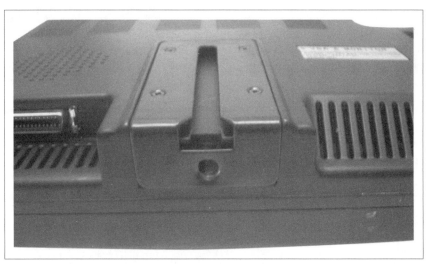

Figure 3-2. A standard mounting nut and mounting slot

Figure 3-3. A touchscreen mounting bracket

If the screen you've set your heart on doesn't come with the mount you need, that doesn't mean you shouldn't buy it. When deciding to tear into your vehicle, it's a good idea to find out how good you are at fabricating brackets and the like. It's not nearly as difficult as you think. Most brackets are simply bent sheet metal with holes. With a vise, a few different hammers, a drill or drill press, a hacksaw, and a grinding wheel, you'll be all set to make the majority of brackets and fittings you'll need. A good way to see what kind of bracket you need is to make a mock-up using malleable materials. Strapping tape, which is not actually tape but comes in a similar rolled-up narrow strip, is a good way to make a test fitment. It can be found at any hardware store and is simply a thin-gauge metal strip with holes every half-inch. Use it to make the basic shape of the needed bracket, fit it up with the screen to be mounted, and once it fits right, use it as a model for a sturdier version. If you know of any metal fabricators in your area, make friends with them. Little brackets can mean the difference between your screen fitting or falling out.

—Damien Stolarz and Lionel Felix

HACK #25 Install a Headrest Screen

Headrest screens are safe, inexpensive, and very easy to install without ripping your car apart.

Headrest screens are probably the most popular aftermarket installation. Giving your vehicle an "in-flight entertainment" look, they can be cleanly installed into a vehicle without expensive or difficult modifications.

There are several ways to get screens installed or attached to headrests so that passengers in the rear seats can enjoy video.

Replacing Your Headrests

Figure 3-4 shows one way, which is simply to buy a headrest with a screen preinstalled. Companies such as Visualogic and Audiovox make these units for a range of vehicles, including many popular SUVs with gray or beige leather headrests. These headrests are slightly wider than OEM headrests, so that they can accommodate 7" wide-screen monitors. They also have the benefit of being tested to comply with Department of Motor Vehicles standards for head protection in a crash (the primary purpose of a headrest). Another company, Starvision, makes a model that can adapt to any size of headrest. And as always, you can just Google "headrest screen kit" and see what you find.

Clamping onto Your Headrests

Another option for installing screens is to use a bracket that connects to the headrest posts. These brackets come in various shapes and provide a standard mounting screw that can support a headrest monitor.

Although these screens are easy to mount, the cables will be somewhat visible even in the neatest of routings. A good way to hide the cable harness is to use mesh sheathing and shrink tube on the ends. You can pick the color, and the mesh looks better than three wires running down the headrest.

Figure 3-4. Headrest with preinstalled screen

Digging into Your Headrests

If there are no pre-manufactured headrest solutions for your vehicle, or you don't mind modifying your headrests, you can install screens yourself (or have them professionally installed). If you're going to do it yourself, you can often get inexpensive used headrests for your car from a local dismantler or junkyard—you can then keep a set of unmodified headrests in reserve, so you can restore the car to its original state if you decide to sell it or move the screens to another car.

 Most LCD screens for cars come with a plastic frame that encloses the screen, and some even have an up/down swivel to adjust the screen angle. Make sure you check your screen to see how good it looks at different viewing angles—you don't want to mount the screen in such a way that it looks dim, or that the backseat passenger can't see it if the driver tilts her seat back.

To install a headrest screen, the first step is to remove the headrest from the car. Many cars have a button you can press at the bottom of one of the metal posts that frees the headrest and lets the posts slide all the way out. Other cars require you to insert a paper clip in a small hole to release the lock.

Once you have the headrest out, center the screen's frame in the headrest and verify that the headrest is deep enough to embed the frame and screen. If it is, draw an outline of the frame on the headrest in the exact location where you plan to install the screen. Make sure that the rectangle is the *inside* dimension of the frame, so that the frame lip of the installed screen will cover your ink mark (Figure 3-5).

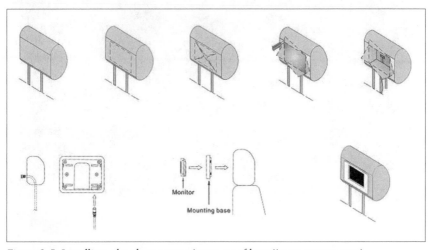

Figure 3-5. Installing a headrest screen (courtesy of http://www.xenarc.com)

You won't be cutting a rectangle to install the frame. Instead, draw an X from corner to corner in the square you've drawn. Once you're sure the square is in the right place, take a razor blade or knife and cut along this X, so that you have four triangular flaps to fold out.

To make room for the screen, you will need to remove some of the guts of the headrest (such as foam or stuffing). You can use whatever cutting tools you have on hand; razor blades or scissors will work, but an adjustable-length utility blade is best. Dig out the stuffing until you have enough depth (usually about an inch) to push in the screen frame. If you run into harder stuff than foam, you may have to cut it away with another tool, such as a rotary cutting drill (i.e., a Dremel). You should not cut to the very edge of the lines, but rather cut inward so that there is enough material to tightly hold the frame once it is inserted.

After you have removed an inch or so of material and made a nice indentation for your frame, you need to secure it. Most likely, your headrest has hard material in the middle, such as plastic, that you can screw the frame into. (Use short screws, because you don't want these screws impaling your head should you subsequently whiplash into your headrest while driving.)

Velcroing onto Your Headrests

I wanted to simply purchase new headrests with screens installed for my vehicle, but none of the models I could find matched the gray fabric interior of my 2005 Dodge Grand Caravan. So I went to get a pair of screens that I could install in the headrests—again, no luck. My headrests are unusually thin, only a couple of inches deep. I was frustrated, because I wanted a clean look. I initially zip-tied the metal stand that came with the screen to the metal posts of the driver's-side headrest, but that didn't look very good, and I kept having to tighten the nut on the stand or the screen would sag and point at the floor.

Finally, I got a bright idea. I have a reel of strong industrial Velcro that I bought at Fry's Electronics. I had been using it for a temporary installation of a touchscreen on my front console, and it was holding well. I decided to sew two strips onto the back of the headrest. You can see the result in Figure 3-6.

Figure 3-6. Mounting a headrest screen with Velcro

Voilà! I'm not much of a tailor and this Velcro does not match my fabric color, but one day I may try to dye a patch of gray Velcro. The handy thing is, I can now quickly take off the screens and stash them if I need to, and if I ever decide to upgrade the screens (e.g., to wide VGA touchscreens for head-to-head computer gaming), I can replace them easily.

If you use sufficient Velcro (I use a 2" by 5" strip) the screen should be quite securely fastened; however, a permanent installation is safer in an accident because there is no chance of it flying off the headrest. Sun visor screens [Hack #27] are only half as deep as screens designed for headrests (less than 1"), and could be adapted to fit in a particularly shallow headrest or behind a racing-style seat.

Installing the Wiring

Once you have a screen mounted, you need to get the video to the screen somehow. Most good screens have a single wire (or two, in the case of USB touchscreens) that carries the video and the 12V power to the screen. The screen comes with only a couple of inches of wire, which mates with a longer cord that breaks out into the video and power inputs.

Facing the screen, you can see whether the thick wire (or bundle of wires) comes out of the right or left side. You will need to pull the longer wire up to that side through the seat itself, in the space between the seat covering (fabric or leather) and the padding of the seat. Starting on the appropriate side, insert the wire into the side or back of the seat and start fishing it upward. If you pull the end of the video cable with your fingers through the fabric while pushing on the wire from below, you can inch the wire up a bit at a time. Eventually you'll get to the top of the seat. Another approach is to straighten a coat hanger, create a hook on the end, lower it down between the seat fabric and foam, hook the wire, and pull it up. If you wrap the hook end in tape it won't tear the fabric as you pull it back up.

If you look at the plastic receptacles that the headrest poles insert into, you should find that the fabric or leather underneath them has a little bit of play. If not, you will need to carefully choose where you want to cut a hole, or extend the hole under one of those receptacles. You will need to feed the wire that goes to the screen through this hole.

Once you connect the short pigtail wire that comes from your screen to the long wire you've fed through the seat, you should have a working screen. Most screens are designed so that they're powered off when you start the car, and the passenger can turn them on by pressing the power button. If you've supplied multiple video sources to the screen, your passenger will be able to select them with the screen's input button.

Some higher-end screens come with their own audio jacks or even infrared audio receivers, allowing each passenger to have wired or wireless headphones connected to their audio/video sources. To get the most out of this setup, you'll want to get a multiple-in, multiple-out video switcher so that each passenger can fully customize his or her video [Hack #35].

HACK #26 Install a VGA Touchscreen in Your Dashboard

Although it's a more challenging project, a cleanly integrated center console screen can provide you with a high-resolution touchscreen that's ideal for controlling your in-car PC.

Many of the newest cars come with a factory-installed navigation option. However, you are invariably stuck with the software that came with the car, and these navigation units usually can't play DVDs and certainly can't play video games. Also, after 5 years you'll find yourself with an old, clunky navigation unit, even though computers will have increased in speed by 10 times.

If you instead had a simple touchscreen that controlled whatever state-of-the-art computer you felt like installing in the trunk, you'd be ahead of the game. You'd be able to read sharper text and view clearer maps, because VGA screens run at higher resolutions than the RGB screens that come in cars. And you'd be able to continually add new programs and new features, while maintaining the clean look of a factory install.

There are several early manufacturers in this market, all of whom use similar screens with different enclosures and features. Xenarc (*http://www.xenarc.com*) and Lilliput (*http://www.newision.com*) are two such vendors, and Figure 3-7 shows some of their screens.

Whether you are replacing your existing screen or installing a new one, there are a number of planning steps to take before you make a purchase.

Maximizing the Screen Size

VGA touchscreens come in sizes ranging from 7" wide-screen monitors to 10" traditional 4:3 monitors, and all the way up to full-size LCDs. If you're replacing a factory screen, you want to get a screen as close to the original size and shape as possible, in order to both minimize the amount of customization you need to do and leave open the option of reinstalling the original screen if you ever need to (e.g., when selling the car, returning it after the lease is up, or returning it to the friend you borrowed it from).

If you are doing a new installation in a vehicle that did not come with a touchscreen, you have a couple of options. First, if your vehicle was not

Figure 3-7. Two Newision Lilliput touchscreens

originally designed to have a screen at all, you may have to fabricate a completely new dashboard panel. A good custom audio shop can create any shape you need, using fiberglass.

If you are going to have to build the screen-mounting frame from scratch, you do have the option to "go big" or "supersize" your screen. You may be able to squeeze a 10" or even 12" screen into your center dash panel—just be sure the laws in your state won't keep you off the road with your oversized video unit.

If your car has a factory navigation option but you didn't choose it, you have more options. You may be able to buy the navigation-ready dashboard framing from the dealer or, even better, from a car parts distributor (not a chain—look in the phone book for replacement parts for your particular car) or a salvage yard. If you can find a totaled version of your car with the navigation option installed, you may be able to get all the dashboard pieces you need, and if you say you don't want the screen the price may not be that bad.

Determining the Placement

Installing the screen involves more than simply finding an empty space in your dash and sticking the screen in it. Before you even purchase a screen, you should make a cardboard mock-up and place it where you anticipate installing it. Make sure that the driver and the passenger can reach it (if it is a touchscreen) and that any other controls it may be displacing can be reached in their new homes as well.

Many of the controls in a car are oversized by design, to take up more space on the dashboard. For instance, the temperature controls on many cars are simply three dials and two sliders, which could fit in a 1" by 4" panel if the knobs were smaller. Instead, they are put in a modular 2-DIN panel that dominates the dashboard and takes up more room than the radio. Often these can be moved to another part of the dashboard, or even into the glove compartment if there is not enough room on the dash.

The more planning and purchasing you do yourself before you go to the fiberglass masters, the cheaper your project will be and the faster it will be completed.

Adjusting the Angle

Most in-dash screens are not adjustable. Thus, it is imperative that you get the viewing angle right. While preinstalled screens in modern dashboards are presented at a nice viewing angle, older dashboards are straight up and down, and a naïve flush installation will result in a screen that you have to slouch down to look at.

Even if you get the angle perfect for yourself, you should try to ensure that taller and shorter people, both passengers and drivers, can also see the screen. You may have to evaluate several screens, because different screens have different viewing angles, and the touchscreen layer on the screen decreases the brightness and affects this angle.

Some screens do have a few degrees of pivot in their mounting, so they can point more toward either the left or the right. However, some cars with center consoles that point toward the driver may make a center-mounted monitor useless for anyone but the driver. In short, "screen test" your setup (pun intended) before you commit to its final position.

Ensuring Brightness

If the screen is going to be used in an SUV with tinted windows all around, the amount of ambient light competing with the touchscreen should be minimal. If you are installing the screen in a convertible car, however, it's important to make sure that the display on the screen isn't completely washed out by sunlight.

Before installing *any* screen into the dash, you should verify its brightness qualities and behavior under different lighting conditions. Many of the screens preinstalled in cars, while low resolution, have been designed to deal with diverse lighting conditions, or use buttons on the side for user input and thus do not have the brightness reductions caused by touchscreen capabilities.

Fortunately, there is a high-bright option available for VGA touchscreens. Some vendors (such as *http://www.karpc.com*) will sell you a Xenarc touchscreen that they have modified with a reflective back panel. While this washes out the colors a bit, it reflects incoming light and makes the screen usable even in bright sunlight.

Unfortunately, no current LCD screen is readable in direct sunlight. The most practical solution today is to shield the LCD from sun with good (deep) placement within the dashboard. If you look at many factory NAV units, you will see that they have a large frame around the screen and that the screen is inset several inches. This helps to keep the screen "in the shade" and viewable.

> Gamma Control is a program that adjusts your gamma, brightness, and contrast levels based on the time of day and sunrise/sunset times in your geographic location. This makes it unnecessary for you to adjust your screen's brightness as the day changes into night. This program is also fully integrated into the voice-recognition program NaviVoice [**Hack #60**] by the same author. You can find both of these programs at *http://www.whipflash.com/vamr/*.

Exposing Infrared Controls

Because these screens are VGA, they can autosync to standard PC resolutions, and even switch between VGA and several composite video inputs. They also have built-in brightness, contrast, and other settings. However, if the screens are cleanly installed, the buttons to adjust these settings may be hidden away in the dashboard.

Luckily, many of the in-car computer screens (such as the Xenarc and Lilliput models) come with an external remote control that has brightness and source controls on it. If you expose the infrared receiver during your installation (just leave a small hole over the IR receiver eye on the screen), you can keep a remote in the center console and use it when you need to adjust these settings.

Integrating Existing Navigation and Video Features

One difficulty in replacing the factory screen is that the factory features, such as navigation, are designed to work only with that screen. Furthermore, factory systems never give you something nice like a standard VGA or composite port to plug into. Most of them use a multi-wire video connection called RGB (red-green-blue), which sits between composite video (low quality) and VGA (high quality). This allows their navigation screens to be fairly crisp, but it will make it difficult to connect your navigation system to your new screen.

One option you have is to convert the NAV unit's RGB output *down* to composite and connect that to your replacement screen. This is a straight-forward solution, but it gives you an unacceptably lower-quality image than the factory RGB. The other option is to convert the RGB *up* to VGA, but this requires relatively expensive hardware and the addition of yet another item: a VGA switcher to switch between the PC and the factory navigation. So, if you replace your factory screen, you pretty much have to give up the factory navigation system—which you may or may not want to do, depending on how much of an improvement the computer-based navigation system you're installing is. (An alternative to replacing the screen is to make your computer talk to the built-in factory RGB screen [Hack #32].)

If you have a DVD player in your car, factory or aftermarket, you probably want to be able to display its output on your front screen as well. Most VGA touchscreens for cars have two additional video inputs for items such as rearview cameras [Hack #33] and DVD players. Optionally, you can play DVDs on your car PC, which gives a higher resolution on the VGA screen.

Finishing the Installation

While the passengers can manually turn on their headrest screens, you expect a dashboard screen to automatically power on when the car is started. Some of the models automatically turn on whenever there is power, but others need to be turned on by pressing the power switch. If your screen doesn't turn on with the car, read "Power Your Car PC" [Hack #42] to learn how to fix it.

Once you have your screen installed, if your PC is in the trunk, you may need to get 3-meter VGA and USB extension cables for the touchscreen interface. You should also configure your car PC to match the native resolution (e.g., 800×480 or 800×600) of your VGA touchscreen. Although it will display other resolutions, such as 1024×768, the native resolution of an LCD display is usually the sharpest and clearest image. If your car computer cannot output the right resolution, there is aftermarket software for Windows that may help. Linux users running X11 can simply set the right resolution and refresh numbers in their X configuration files—if their video cards support it, it will work.

As always, check the functioning of the system at various points during the install to make sure that you're on the right track. Having to take everything apart at the end to fix one forgotten connector is a waste of your precious car PC hacking time.

Install a Sun Visor Screen

#27 With headrest and fold-down screens, the front-seat passenger often gets left out of the picture.

Sun visor screens are a stealthy way to give a customized video experience to the front-seat passenger. The back seats of many compact and sports cars are used only for pet and grocery transport or general storage, and people only sit in the front seats. If the laws in your state do not allow screens visible to the driver, a sun visor tilted away from the driver may be the perfect solution for your front-seat passenger.

As with headrests, there are two basic models available: replacement visors, and screens that you dig into the visor to install. Replacement visors have the screens built right in and come in a few styles that hopefully match your interior. They also come with vanity mirrors and lights, just like normal visors.

Figure 3-8 shows one of the many kits that install into your existing visor. These come in sizes ranging from just a few inches to 7" wide-screens. They have especially shallow (about 0.5") frames that can be mounted in today's puffier SUV visors.

Figure 3-8. A visor screen kit

To install one of these visor screens, you need to dig into your visor. Naturally, the first thing to do is to remove the visor from the car. There are usually several screws that hold the adjustable pole of the visor to the ceiling near the front pillars of the windshield. Also, visors with lighted screens or other electronics are connected by a wire, which can hopefully be unplugged—there should be a mating connector somewhere that can be un-mated to release the visor. If you need to remove the pillar cover to get to the wiring, go ahead, because you will need to take it off later anyway.

Once you have taken out the visor, the installation is similar to installing a screen in a headrest [Hack #25], but with a smaller hole. Position the frame of the visor monitor on the correct side of the visor, and trace it lightly. Then draw an X connecting the corners of the rectangle, and cut along the lines of the X.

Once the hole is cut, you must remove the fluff or other padding from the center outward, to make a firm-holding fit around the frame when it is installed. Because you don't have the clearance for screws, the frame must be affixed with different materials, such as strong double-stick tape or adhesive glue.

With the screen mounted, you now need to run the video and power cables through the corner of the visor and down through the pillar of the vehicle.

 If your pillar has side-impact airbags, do not dismantle it. Instead, find another route from the ceiling to the floor, or at least go to a professional install shop and ask what they would do first.

If the screen's wires are black and the original wires were beige, gray, or another color, you may want to spray paint the short bit of wire that will be exposed to better match the car's interior. Also, the thicker wire for the screen may not fit in the existing visor, roof, or pillar holes, especially if the existing power wire travels through the metal visor pole itself. If this is the case, you need to make a small hole in the corner of the visor, and then put the wire down the top of the pillar. Don't cut into the headliner.

If you haven't yet removed the pillar cover, do so now. Find the screws and clamps and carefully loosen it. You may not need to completely remove it in order to thread the visor video cables down into the dashboard area.

Once you have the cables in place and have taken out most of the slack in the wiring, temporarily mount the visor without closing up the pillar. Check the full range of motion of the visor—some visors extend on their mounting rails and thus require some slack in the wire.

Before you fasten everything back into place, do a final screen functionality check by giving it 12V and a video signal. If it works correctly, you can close up the pillar, finish fastening the visor, and run the power and video cables to their final destinations.

Install a Motorized Fold-out Screen

HACK
#28

Motorized fold-out screens are relatively easy and noninvasive to install.

If you don't have room in your dashboard to mount a screen, already have a factory screen that only does navigation, or don't want your screen visible when you're not using it, a head unit with a motorized video screen (as shown in Figure 3-9) may be your solution. Due to the continual miniaturization of electronics, it's possible to fit a 7" touchscreen, a DVD player, and a standard radio receiver head unit into a single-DIN (the size of a normal car radio) enclosure.

Figure 3-9. A compact fold-out screen

Installing a head unit with a motorized video screen is as straightforward as installing a new head unit. The only difference is that there are a couple of extra wires you need to connect.

Some of these screens have a built-in DVD player; others are "DVD-ready" and connect to an external DVD component. In the U.S., however, none of these players are supposed to play DVDs when the car is in motion. In order to prevent this playback, all of the units have a wire that tells the DVD player when the car is in motion.

Professional installers are supposed to connect this wire to something that supplies 12V only when the car is safely stopped—i.e., when the transmission is in park or the emergency brake is on. The emergency brake is commonly used for this purpose, because it is easy to find and connect to.

 If you are going to use your in-car computer to display track and title information, just like your existing head unit does, then you may not need to disable the video input when the car is moving to remain in compliance with traffic laws. However, even if I were a lawyer, I wouldn't give legal advice in a book on hacking your car—it's up to you to stay legal and, more importantly, safe to yourself and others.

Other wires that need to be routed correctly are the audio and video inputs. Since you are probably installing the head unit as a display for an in-car computer, you need to run shielded video and stereo audio cables from the computer to the head unit.

Depending on the features of your fancy new head unit, it may have four audio outputs, or even six-channel surround sound with an optical digital audio output. When you upgrade to a DVD player head unit (or any higher-end head unit, for that matter), you often need to add an amplifier. This is because while most factory and less-expensive ($250–300) aftermarket head units usually have an integrated amplifier that can connect directly to your car speakers, higher-end units expect to connect to an external two-, four-, or six-channel amplifier. For more on surround sound and upgrading your amplifier, read "Put Multi-Channel DVD Surround Sound in Your Car" [Hack #39].

While some of the high-end head units with fold-out screens have touch-screen features, don't expect to be able to use these to control your computer. The touchscreens in the head units from manufacturers such as Pioneer, Kenwood, and others work only with their own built-in user interface and other components by the same manufacturer.

Several manufacturers have been working on PC-compatible, VGA-resolution motorized fold-out touchscreen head units. However, these have been plagued by quality issues—pressing against a screen gradually weakens the motorized parts and hinge—and thus have not yet made it to market. Even the name-brand touchscreens are prone to weakening.

Make sure that your head unit screen has audio and video auxiliary inputs before you buy it. Some of the units "have" AUX-in but require another external component to bring it to the head unit, which costs extra. Look at your equipment, and make sure it isn't "AUX-ready" but actually has RCA or S-Video inputs for audio and video. If it doesn't, either choose a different screen or buy the correct adapters.

HACK #29 Install a Fold-Down Ceiling-Mounted Screen

While individual headrest screens give each passenger the potential for individual entertainment, to entertain everyone at once go with a big fold-down screen.

If you buy a new vehicle with a factory DVD player, it comes with a fold-down screen for the rear passengers, and often wired or wireless headphones as well. However, these screens are usually a bit undersized and are not the highest resolution available.

Aftermarket fold-down screens are often bigger, have higher resolution, and even have touchscreen features—but installing things on the roof of your car can be difficult. While factory installation is usually a safer option, it's not crazy to try to install your own ceiling-mounted screen, as long as you do it in a sensible way.

Selecting Your Screen

The first thing to do when considering installing a ceiling-mounted screen is to make sure that you have enough room, that there's enough ceiling clearance, and that the screen won't hit someone in the head when it folds down. Before you buy a huge screen, make sure that it will be comfortably visible for all the passengers. If you have multiple rows of rear passengers, such as in larger SUVs or vans, you should take a piece of cardboard the size of the screen, pin it up to the ceiling, and sit in the rearmost row of seats, with two people in the middle seats. Make sure you can see. Also sit in the middle seats, and make sure the screen isn't six inches from your face, making you feel like you're in the front row of a movie theater.

If any screen you're mounting is going to block your rearview mirror, make sure that you install a rearview camera [Hack #33] to restore rearview mirror functionality. Seeing traffic behind you may not be just a convenience issue, but a legal one. Some states will fine you if you obstruct your rearview mirror. Check the local laws, and ask around at custom shops if people in the area are getting hassled for having 17" ceiling flippers. You don't want to be driving blind.

Once you have established that a screen will work in your car, you want to make sure the screen has the features you're looking for, such as the right aspect ratio. If you plan to watch primarily DVD movies, you can get a wide screen, but if you plan to use the screen mainly for satellite or TV reception, you might not want the stretched look for everything and should instead get a traditional 4:3 (TV-shaped) monitor, or something a bit in the middle. You also should consider getting a VGA fold-down screen if you can. Since you are powering this screen with a computer, you might as well make use of all your available resolution. Your DVD movies can then be shown in their native resolutions or higher HDTV resolutions, depending on how good a fold-down VGA screen you buy.

Another consideration is whether you want to get a brand-name stereo manufacturer's DVD system. These systems often have higher-resolution connections between the DVD player and the screen, providing a more satisfying DVD experience. They also usually provide an auxiliary A/V input for other devices, such as video game consoles or in-car computers. The main drawback is that Alpine, Pioneer, and other vendors create complete solutions with proprietary interconnects, so buying one item locks you into buying other accessories from that manufacturer. This makes it harder to, say, play the DVD on multiple screens with an A/V switcher [Hack #35].

If you can't find the screen you're looking for in a fold-down format, or you already have a nice monitor or old laptop you want to use, then check out "Install a VGA Touchscreen in Your Dashboard" [Hack #26] and "Turn Your Laptop into a Fold-Down or Dashboard Screen" [Hack #31].

Scouting for Locations

The main challenge of installing a fold-down screen is to not screw up your headliner. To mount your screen, you are going to need to screw it stably into the ceiling of your vehicle. Since you don't want screws sticking out through the roof, you will need to mount the screen to the roof's *crossmembers*, which are the metal beams or ribs that travel across the roof at regular intervals from front to back, giving the roof support.

To find these crossmembers, you need to peek under your headliner. The headliner is usually just a thin layer of fabric with spongy backing glued to a firm cardboard frame. Depending on your vehicle, getting underneath this headliner is usually a fairly involved process, requiring a couple hours spent unscrewing plastic panels. It's not that hard to do; it's just a bit boring. Before you start, it's a good idea to read up on either the factory manuals (which are available on CD or at the dealer) or the Chilton's manual for your car—these are available at any auto parts chain or online (*http://www.chiltondiy.com*), and they usually give you full instructions on how to replace the headliner for your car. Make sure you keep track of all the screws you remove in the process and of where each plastic brace, frame, or panel goes.

Taking digital pictures of something before you remove it is a quick and easy way to record how it was assembled, so you can put it back correctly later.

You do not have to completely remove the headliner to install a screen. You should be able to loosen the mounting for the front half or front quarter (passenger's side or driver's side) of the headliner and drop it down, looking under it to find the crossmembers and noting their locations. You'll have to remove all the plastic hardware—ceiling lights, top pillar panels, plastic and rubber door frames, clothing hooks, passenger handholds, and any other hardware that helps to hold up the ceiling. You'll also have to remove the pillar seatbelt holders, and possibly the seatbelt itself, in order to create a clear path for the wiring that needs to go from the ceiling to the floor.

The main risks in removing a headliner are denting or folding the flimsy cardboard that makes it up, or breaking the tabs off the plastic panels that mount to the body and hold up the headliner. Don't let a corner of the headliner hang down unsupported, and be careful to remove the interior plastic panels without breaking their clips (although you can get new ones from the dealer if you need to).

If you have to mark any positions on the headliner itself, since you don't want to mark it permanently, you can use painter's masking tape. You can find this non-tacky tape at a hardware store—like a Post-it note, it should pull right off when you're done. Once you have dropped enough of the headliner (see Figure 3-10), you can use a flashlight to scout around and see where any wires should be run along the ceiling.

Figure 3-10. A dropped headliner

Building the Set

Most ceiling-mounted screens come with a special mounting frame. This metal bracket mounts to the crossmembers (metal ribs) on the ceiling, and the flip-down monitor screws into the frame.

Sometimes, if the crossmembers aren't in the right place, an installer will create a custom mounting bracket out of plywood (or metal). In this approach, a piece of plywood is cut to fit into the space between crossmembers and glued to the roof of the car using metal-to-wood construction adhesive. Pictures of this type of bracket can be found at *http://www.audioinmotion.com/generic48.html*.

If you have a welder, or know someone who does, it may make sense to tack weld a small bit of angle iron to fit up to the rest of the mounting holes. Weld *only* to the crossmember, and make small tack welds using the coolest setting. A hot weld may damage paint on the other side of the roof, so never weld directly to the roof skin. If done right, it will be a very solid mount. Don't forget the welder for trunk and floor work as well. Those places are less sensitive to paint issues.

Once you have established a surface for accepting screw holes (either plywood or existing metal crossmembers), you need to drill mounting holes. This is the penetrating moment; you are impaling your headliner, so be conservative and be accurate where you drill. The fortunate thing is that these are small holes, and if you favor the center of where your screen will be installed, you can cover any mistakes with the screen. You need to support the headliner during this drilling, but don't put everything together yet, because you still need to run all the wires from the screen.

Costumes

If you're a stickler for matching (or if you aren't but your spouse, with whom you must share the vehicle, is), then you want to make sure that your screen matches your interior. Many of the screens you can purchase come in black plastic, but the interiors of many cars are a standard beige, gray, or other color. Luckily, it's all pretty much the same plastic, and even more fortunately, you can paint the plastic of your screen to match your interior. Painting techniques for plastic or other items are beyond the scope of this book, but here is a useful tip: go to any used car lot and ask them who does their interior vinyl and leather dyes. They will refer you to a vendor who can mix a paint to match your interior.

While this is particularly applicable to the highly visible fold-down screens, any of the plastic frames and screen enclosures can be painted to match your interior.

Action!

Once you have your screen dressed up how you want it, the same rules apply to installing any screen. Your goal is to find a way to get the video and power wires from your screen, across the roof, down one of the pillars between the front and rear seats (the B pillars), and to the floor, where they can be stealthily routed to their destination.

All this pillar-talk can get a little confusing. Fortunately, there is a way to indicate what pillar you're talking about. The forward-most pillar that holds the windshield is called the "A" pillar. The pillar where the front door strikes the body is the "B" pillar. In a two- or four-door coupe or sedan, the pillar that holds the sides of the rear window is—you guessed it—the "C" pillar. For wagons and SUVs, we continue on down the alphabet.

To route these pillar wires, you must carefully remove most of the plastic or other covering on the B pillars, being careful not to break any clips (once again, the take-apart manual for your car is a cheap, essential tool for this stage).

Most of the wiring will be going down the pillar, but if you're installing the screen where there was once a dome light, you should be able to tap into that light's 12V and ground wires to power your screen. Once you have the wires routed, you can reattach the headliner and start putting a few framing pieces back in place. Then you can position the monitor frame and insert the screws.

It's good to have a body panel tool for this type of work, but don't fret if you break clips—most of them are not intended to be pulled out and put back in over and over. Know what clips to ask for when going to the dealership and ask for new ones.

Make sure that the screen is fully working by connecting it to your DVD player or computer before you replace all the interior pieces. Make sure it turns on appropriately, by temporarily wiring it to something that supplies 12V. You don't want to be driving around in a semi-disassembled car for the next week, and if you start this project on a Sunday and then find that you didn't connect the wires to the screen correctly...well, you get the picture.

—*Damien Stolarz and Lionel Felix*

Supersize Your Fold-Down LCD Screen

A lower-cost, higher-quality fold-down screen awaits you with standard ceiling- and wall-mounting approaches.

If you want a big screen in your car, you can go to your local car stereo shop and spend $1,000 on a 14" fold-down monitor. While flashy and large, the quality of this monitor will leave much to be desired because of its composite-only video inputs and its low TV resolution.

Alternatively, you can go to your local computer shop and spend $199 on a 15" LCD flat-screen monitor. The lowest-end flat-screen computer monitor, with a VGA input and at least 1024×768 resolution, has far better quality than a high-end car screen.

The difference, of course, is that the car screen has a custom molded fold-down enclosure, whereas the desktop LCD has a stand. But fortunately the Video Electronics Standards Organization (VESA) has standardized a mounting system for flat-screen monitors. As a result, most LCD monitors use either a 100-mm or 75-mm square bolt pattern on the back, and companies such as OmniMount (*http://www.omnimount.com*) and AVF Vector (*http://usen.avfgroup.com*) offer a large array of inexpensive mounting solutions that can be adapted for in-car use.

If your car ceiling's crossmembers happen to line up where you want your screen, you can securely screw the VESA mounting bracket into the metal crossmembers. Otherwise, you can secure a metal or plywood bridge between two adjacent crossmembers, and attach to that [Hack #29]. (Installation will vary from vehicle to vehicle.)

> If your seats are big enough, you could mount a 15" flat screen for each passenger! Instead of headrest screens, you can use OmniMount's QM-100F (a $50 flat-screen wall mount) to give each passenger an in-car theatre experience—for under $250 per seat!

In my own installation, I tried using the OmniMount first. It installed fairly easily and looked great, but each time I folded down the screen it torqued the wood block I had glued to my ceiling, which eventually broke loose. I kept shopping, and finally at Home Depot I found the AVF Vector LCD005 (Figure 3-11). This unit, also designed for mounting an LCD screen under a cabinet, worked great, because it folds down with no tension and stays up by sliding and locking into place—a lower-tech solution than the Omni-Mount, but better suited for the vehicle. In my 2005 Dodge Caravan, the crossmember over the front seats had a fortuitously located metal bracket with a small hole in it. I simply widened the hole with a drill bit, put a nut above it, and bolted the unit into the ceiling. (You can see other pictures from this installation in "Install a Mac Mini in Your Car" [Hack #54]).

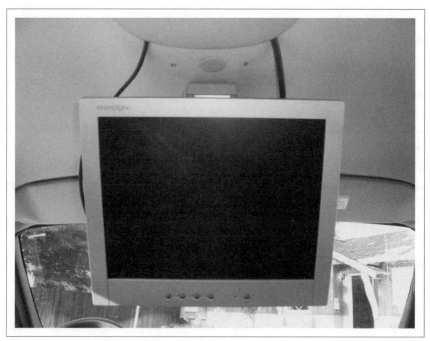

Figure 3-11. A 15" fold-down LCD screen

These VESA screen mounts are generally attractive, but they won't be mistaken for a factory install. Still, mounting a high-resolution 15" LCD screen in your vehicle for the street price of an 8" car screen is a much better upgrade, in my opinion.

H A C K   Turn Your Laptop into a Fold-Down
#31   or Dashboard Screen

You may already have a nice LCD screen for your car, in the form of an old laptop.

We haven't yet exhausted all the ways to get a flat screen into your car. A laptop, old or new, can be an excellent solution for an in-car installation.

Laptops have beautiful, large LCD screens, but they do have a few drawbacks. For one thing, they almost always have thin, fragile, proprietary connectors for which you can't easily make extension wires. Second, except for a few specialized models, laptop screens usually have a big keyboard and computer sticking out of them. Finally, if a laptop screen is mounted on a ceiling, it will be upside-down. But don't worry, there are solutions to all of these problems.

In-Dash or In-Seat Monitor

In the late 1990s, when computers weren't even powerful enough to play DVDs, Sony made a thin laptop called the Clié that had a strange screen resolution: 1024×480. It was about the size of a VHS cassette tape. My friend used one as a portable MP3 player in his Mazda RX7 years before there were any MP3 players on the market. At the time, I was upgrading the stereo system for my 1950 Nash Ambassador, which has a radio that hides behind a roll-down cover. The size of the radio slot is huge—as you'd guess, about the size of a Sony Clié screen.

The big problem was that the Sony Clié would not bend 270 degrees backwards, as I wanted it to, without threatening to break. So I did what any hacker would do—I took it apart to see if I could encourage it to rotate. And indeed I could (see Figure 3-12).

In practice, while you will find that it's difficult to extend the length of the cord between a laptop and its monitor, reversing the position of the monitor 180 degrees will work. To do this, you have to do a lot of disassembly. (Although manufacturers usually don't publish the take-apart manuals for their laptops except for authorized service, you may be able to find this information by searching the Web for your make of laptop, or by contacting the manufacturer.)

First, take off the outer plastic of the LCD *bezel* (the thin plastic frame that surrounds the screen). Then, remove the casing from the top of the laptop around the LCD hinges. Depending on your model, you may have to remove the entire laptop case. You will now have several ribbon cables and the power cord exposed. There should be two to four screws mounting the hinges to the body of the laptop, and once you remove these the LCD screen should be free from the body of the laptop. You can turn the LCD screen 180 degrees at this point, and in many cases, you will see how you can screw the hinges on in this reversed orientation.

You can usually carefully flip over the thin plastic ribbon cable that goes to the LCD so that it still fits neatly into the thin path through the plastic or metal hinge covers. You may find that there is some asymmetry in the design, and while the hinges will fit, the cover will remain about 15 degrees open instead of closing completely. This may affect your ability to mount it flat (for instance, in a dashboard or flush in a seat back). However, if you don't reattach the hinges, but simply securely Velcro your screen to the

Figure 3-12. A reversed laptop screen

bottom of the laptop, it will pack flat, providing you with a compact screen and computer combination, ready for flush mounting in your dashboard or the back of the front driver's or passenger's seat.

Fold-Down Laptop

Perhaps you have a working laptop that you want to suspend from your car's ceiling, rather than embedding it in the dash or a seat back. A laptop already has a tidy closed position, and if it's a newer laptop it will have an optical drive for you to play DVDs.

The first step is to make sure that your laptop screen can be inverted. Portrait Displays, Inc. (*http://www.portrait.com*) makes software called Pivot Pro that can invert your screen. The software is inexpensive, and you can download a free trial to make sure it works before embarking on a large upside-down laptop installation.

If you can invert the screen, the next step is to figure out where to mount the laptop on your ceiling. To mount a laptop, you want to create a very secure mounting bracket. Since you probably want the lid to close flush, you can't have anything too thick going around the laptop to hold it up. Also, since you want to be able to remove the laptop without taking it apart, you need a two-piece mounting solution: something that connects to the laptop, and another bit that connects to the ceiling.

The basic approach is:

1. Create something that clamps securely to the laptop.
2. Mount a bracket to the ceiling.
3. Connect the ceiling mounts to the laptop.

How you do this depends on how heavy your laptop is, how clean a fit you want, and how good you are at fabrication. Since a laptop does not come with a convenient mounting bracket and is generally heavier than a fold-down screen (it also includes a computer!), you have to make sure you mount it securely enough to support its weight.

In my installation, I used OmniMount's QM-100F, a two-piece flat wall-mounting bracket for LCD screens. Figure 3-13 shows how I mounted one of the brackets to the bottom of my laptop, using zip ties, metal L-brackets, and some screws. This step varies from laptop to laptop, and is left as an exercise for the reader.

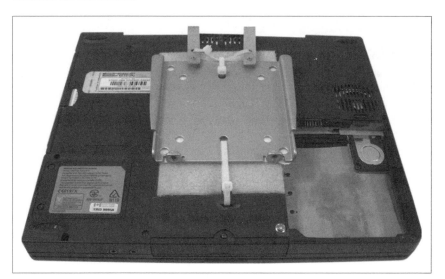

Figure 3-13. A ceiling-mount laptop bracket

Once you have chosen your laptop mounting solution, you need to drill the holes to attach the ceiling bracket, and then mount it. You'll also need to figure out what wires you need to route, and run them above the headliner [Hack #29]. Once you get all the wires to the edge of the vehicle, run them down one of the door pillars. Depending on how many wires you want to run to elsewhere in the vehicle, you may need to get extender cables for USB, VGA, and even the power cord. (If you use a wireless mouse and keyboard, you can run fewer wires.) Note that running the VGA cable is useful—you can use it to drive another screen elsewhere in your vehicle, such as a dash-mounted VGA touchscreen [Hack #26]. You need to get a 12V car power adapter for your laptop, and you need a wire that runs from your laptop through the ceiling and down to the floor, where it then meets the power. You don't have to buy a power cord extender; you can extend the power cord with any wire of similar thickness by splicing it, soldering it, and heat shrinking it [Hack #4], as long as you preserve the polarity by making sure the center wire and outer wire stay connected correctly.

For a clean look, you may want to cover the exposed portions of the laptop frame with plastic, vinyl, leather, or a similar covering that matches your interior. You should be able to get plastic covers for the screws you use as well. For a completely clean installation, you can have a fabricator make a fiberglass shell that covers the front and back of the laptop, and even paint your laptop case cover to match your car's interior. But most laptops close up pretty flat and tidy, and you only need to cover the bundle of wires that comes out of the back of the laptop.

HACK #32 Connect a Car PC to Your Factory Screen

Almost any factory screen can be connected to your in-car computer with the right adapter.

Usually, in the U.S. market at least, auto manufacturers are too cautious to enable DVD features on a dash-mounted monitor, even if the car is not in motion. Thus, one of the most popular aftermarket hacks is to connect DVD players and video games to these screens with a video AUX-input adapter. Some of the vendors listed in "Get Computer Audio into Your Head Unit" [Hack #14] also make adapters for factory screens, but as new vehicles and screen configurations are coming out all the time, it's difficult for the manufacturers of these adapters to keep up.

The factory rear-seat entertainment screens in most vehicles are easier to hook up to play DVDs. There are fewer product-liability concerns with these screens, and because they don't have to integrate with a navigation friends at the dealerships loan them cars, they reverse-engineer them and make new adapters.

But what if you have a brand new car that no one has yet made the hardware for? Or what if you have a vehicle that the vendors won't make an adapter for, because they're worried they'll disable the OnStar, or because it would take too much modification and they can't make a plug-and-play kit? And what if you want to move your adapter from your other car into your new car? Well, you can do the same thing the adapter makers do: open up the dash and take a look.

The best starting source of information on your car is the manufacturer's manual, which is an invaluable reference if you are taking apart your navigation system. Also, if your car is popular, you can find a lot of additional information with Google. If you can find someone who has done a take-apart of your car, analyzed the pieces, and made a web page describing the process, you're golden.

But even without a manual, you can do the investigation yourself—and if you don't totally understand what you see, you'll at least have gathered more clues for further searching online. In fact, even if all you find out is that you'd rather just throw in the towel and install a replacement screen, you'll still have moved the project along. So get your screwdriver and start carefully taking apart that dash.

If you can get into your car and identify the manufacturer part numbers of the screen and navigation unit, you may find that the same model is also used in a different car. Try Googling for that NAV unit (instead of your make/model of vehicle), and if it's used in any other vehicle, you can see if there's an adapter for *that* vehicle that will work for you. Even if it's a one-of-a-kind NAV unit not used in any other cars, once you've identified the actual manufacturer of your screen and accessories, you can contact them and ask for the wiring and video format information. It may be publicly available, or just an email away.

Alternatively, if you truly crave adventure, you can get a pair of wire snips, some electrical tape, and a multimeter and just jump in. Like disabling a bomb in a spy movie, you want to find good candidates for the R, G, B, and sync wires, and then carefully turn off the vehicle, snip one of them, turn on the vehicle, and see if you've disabled one of the colors. If you snip the sync wire, you should have a wavy picture. The ground wire is usually black. If you snip a wire that doesn't seem to be one of the ones you're after, you'll need to connect the wires back together [Hack #4] and verify that things still work.

This procedure of snipping wires is for the courageous—as with any device, if you power it up with some of the wrong wires disconnected, you could damage something. Unless you possess the right skills and equipment (i.e., an oscilloscope), or the same reckless overconfidence that I possess, you should stick to what others can discover for you.

VGA to RGB Conversion

The adapters listed earlier work for most applications, such as DVDs and video games, and if you're using your computer to play MP3s or movies they should work acceptably. However, you will notice that with any of these adapters, your image is not as sharp and clean as the factory video. The reason is that converting from composite or S-Video *up* to RGB is much cheaper (for the manufacturer) than converting from VGA *down* to RGB.

If you need the same sharp, readable text that your NAV system produces from your computer, and the S-Video input is still too fuzzy, you're going to have to get your computer to output the right RGB signal. Although a full explanation is outside the scope of this hack, there are two paths you can pursue: find a video card that outputs RGB (like the video output of the NAV unit itself), or find a *scan converter*, a small device that can translate the VGA signals down to the RGB the screen expects.

Composite Video Screens

Now, if your screen *does* have a factory DVD option that connects to a rear-seat entertainment fold-down screen, or even the front screen in European setups, you should be able to connect your computer to it as well.

DVD players almost always use composite video outputs, so finding where to plug in your computer is as easy as removing the DVD player itself and finding where the wires lead. If you're very fortunate it will even use conventional RCA cables, but in any event you should be able to figure out which cables are power, which are audio, and which are video.

The basic approach is the same with all this investigative work—trace the source of your video, follow it to the screen or to the video source, and find out where you can splice into it. Then, insert a switcher so that you can pipe multiple sources into it, including the original.

As a parting reminder, use high-quality (thick, well-shielded) video cables for this work—when video is run long distances through a car in unshielded cables, its signal weakens and the quality suffers.

Install a Rearview Mirror Screen and Camera

Rearview monitor and camera combinations can double as a convenient display for your car PC.

With the progressive miniaturization of LCD display technology comes the option of putting screens everywhere. Rearview mirrors can now be purchased with embedded 3–5" screens, and coupled with tiny video surveillance cameras, they've become a great option for improving rear visibility in large vehicles.

Trucks and buses without rearview mirrors were the first to really benefit from rearview monitors and cameras. But now, tall SUVs with tinted windows are just as likely to crush small obstacles when backing up, unless they are enhanced with video surveillance technology.

However, hindsight is not the only use for these rearview mirror screens. For in-car computer applications, the rearview mirror is ideally located to provide information to the driver while minimizing eye movement away from the road. Rearview screens are necessarily small, perhaps only 4–5" diagonally, but that's enough space to show a few lines of large-point text, such as the title of the currently playing MP3 or album, just as you would get on a modern digital radio receiver (see Figure 3-15).

Figure 3-15. A rearview mirror screen in action

One of the nice things about the way screens are integrated into rearview mirrors is that the screens are reflective, so the entire length of the mirror still serves as a rear view, and by simply changing the focus of your eyes you can read the text on the screen.

Installing the Screen

Rearview screens install in a similar way to sun visor screens [Hack #27], except that the video cables need to travel under the headliner [Hack #29] before they make their trip down a pillar.

Another difference is that rearview screens have another wire that detects when the car is in reverse and automatically switches the video to the rear camera. The installation of this backing-up activation feature is discussed in the section "Installing an RGB Screen Adapter" in "Connect a Car PC to Your Factory Screen" [Hack #32].

Installing the Camera

There are several options for installing a rearview camera.

The easiest to install are the units that are integrated into the license plate holder. Since there are usually already wires running power to a rear plate light, you can pass the camera wires through the hole that they use. Another popular unit is a cylindrical camera that replaces the trunk or rear door lock fixture. Since most cars can unlock the trunk using a keyless entry remote, and lifting the trunk gate or back hatch does not require the key, this is a good place to install a camera. These units have a longer lens and thus a better picture, and they install very seamlessly.

The more conventional rear cameras require a hole to be drilled, either on the back hatch or in the roof of the vehicle. These come in a variety of configurations, and it is probably best to have them professionally installed unless you feel comfortable drilling a hole in the exterior of your vehicle. Figure 3-16 shows a rearview camera.

All of these cameras terminate with a video cable somewhere in the back of the car, in either the trunk or the back hatch area. In the case of a trunk install, the wire can be snaked around the edge of the trunk and clips can be used to mount the wire until it enters the body of the car, where it can be fed under the carpet to the rearview screen. Find a place to pass through the wire that won't encourage water to come in and spoil the party. Any gap in the door or hatch seals will leak to some degree. Finding a spot between the seal and the outer skin and drilling a small hold to gain access to the interior is one way to keep the seals sealed. If possible, remove the connector head, or the hole will have to be bigger than the wire diameter to let it pass through. Then, once it's all in place, use silicone sealant (available in any hardware store) to plug up the hole.

In a back-hatch install (i.e., in SUVs or vans) you have to remove the paneling on the hatch, and in the process figure out how to get the wire up around the hatch window and through the watertight wire pipe that connects the hatch and the body of the vehicle (as in Figure 3-17). Depending on how close this wiring is to the inside framing, you should be able to run the video cable either above the rear headliner, or to one of the rear pillars and down to the floor of the vehicle.

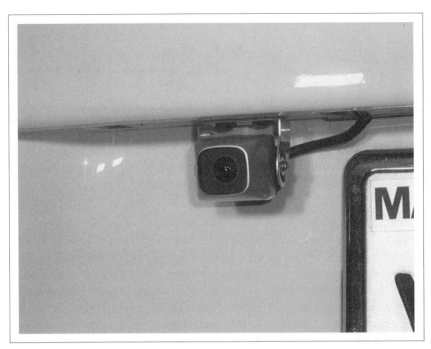

Figure 3-16. A rearview camera

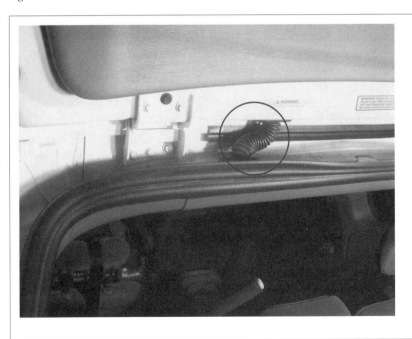

Figure 3-17. The watertight wire pipe, an important part of the wiring of your camera

Hacking the Hack

There are some interesting hacking possibilities with the rearview screen and camera combination.

In terms of the user interface, some of the very popular in-car computer motherboards have dual-video-output capabilities. You can connect one screen to your PC as your primary, and connect the rearview mirror screen as a second monitor. You can then display a skinned media player such as Winamp on the small screen (in a big font) to get track and album information while you're playing tunes. Better yet, you can run any application that gives you useful information—the time, compass directions, a GPS map, WiFi signal strength while wardriving—and have that information available at a glance.

Another interesting hack is to *record* the rearview video. Since you have a full-fledged PC in the car, you can use a capture card, or a USB 2.0 video-capture device, to pipe the rearview video into your car PC. If you install a program that automatically starts recording the video to disk when the computer is turned on (webcam software with an archiving feature is good for this), you will have a built-in surveillance camera for behind your vehicle. Then if you need the license plate of that hit-and-run or the guy who was tailgating you, you're in luck, because your vehicle is recording it all.

HACK

#34   Boost Your Video Signal for Multiple Screens

You don't have to put up with poor-quality video when displaying your car computer's output on multiple screens.

If passenger video entertainment in your vehicle is handled by one large fold-down screen, you don't need this hack. If you have multiple screens, though, this hack can help you improve the quality of the picture they display.

If you're simply driving a pair of rear-headrest screens, using a simple RCA splitter is one approach. This will work, but because the voltage coming out of the video card has to supply two screens, each screen will get a correspondingly washed out and weaker signal. Start splitting the voltage to three or four screens, and you will get an unacceptable picture on all the screens. Retail stores, which have dozens of TV sets all showing the same signal, solve this problem by using a *video booster* to amplify the signal.

Video boosters are inexpensive—a 1×4 (1 input, 4 outputs) booster can be purchased for around $25–30. Figure 3-18 shows a unit by Fahrenheit Technologies (*http://www.farenheitusa.com*), a popular manufacturer of in-car boosters.

Figure 3-18. Fahrenheit's video booster

To install it, simply connect the composite output (or S-Video output with an S-Video-to-composite adapter) of your computer to the amplifier input, and then run the wires from each video screen to one of the outputs. Many units have adjustable gain (amplification) for each output, so you can tune it for each monitor until the picture looks right—the color should not be either washed out or bleeding and oversaturated, and the picture should be crisp and solid.

Video boosters are designed to send the *same* video to all your monitors. If you would like to have different video at each screen according to the preference of that passenger, "Customize Each Passenger's Video" [Hack #35] is a must-read.

Customize Each Passenger's Video

Imagine a peaceful cross-country road trip in which you never need to endure someone else's choice of music or movies, because everyone has a personalized entertainment center.

If you carry around many passengers on a regular basis, or if you just want to make sure that *everyone* is amused on a long road trip, provide your passengers with adequate facilities to enjoy themselves.

The number of video devices you can have in a vehicle is limited only by your budget and cargo space. I personally would not find it unreasonable to have one of each current video gaming console, a DVD player, and one or two computers in a vehicle. I even have a 12V VCR for showing old movies, and the very bored can always check out the action from the rearview camera [Hack #33]

Enabling all of these devices doesn't require you to have a switchboard operator climbing around in the trunk and trying to route video hookups between devices and screens. Instead, you need a video switcher.

There are several kinds of switchers to choose from.

Built-in Switchers

Many of the better headrest screens can switch between two or three video sources via a button on the front of the monitor, and/or a handheld remote control. These units do not switch the audio, but if your goal is to tune into a head-to-head video game or a DVD movie, where the audio is already being piped into wireless headphones, then this solution does work.

For the scenario shown in Figure 3-19, you need one video booster per video source [Hack #34], and you must run those outputs to each switchable screen. Each screen can then choose between multiple sources, such as a video game, a DVD player, or the computer.

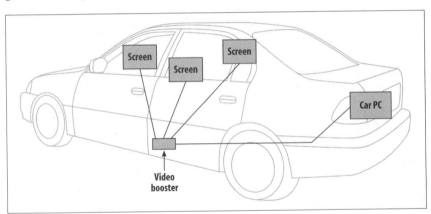

Figure 3-19. Use video boosters to provide a clean signal to all screens

Automatic Switchers

Simple automatic switchers allow a screen to auto-select between two sources depending on a voltage line. This is good for situations where you don't want to have to select, but you simply want one device to override another. An example would be to have the overhead screen usually show the output from the DVD player, but for the 12V output of the computer to trigger the auto-selector when it gets turned on and make the computer the image that is shown. Precision Interface Electronics (*http://www.pie.net*)

makes this sort of adapter, and when you don't want to have to hit switches to get the right video, it's a good solution.

Matrix Switchers

The third approach to switching video is to connect all the screens and video sources to a single video switcher, which incorporates routing and amplification features. These switchers can switch a number of inputs to a number of outputs (3×3 and 4×4 being common numbers), allowing each viewer to select any of the available video sources. (See Figure 3-14 in "Connect a Car PC to Your Factory Screen" [Hack #32].)

Some of these units come with a wired remote for each screen, which is intended to be installed near the screen. Viewers then use the remote to select the input signal for that screen. These units are relatively inexpensive, but you have to run additional wires and install unsightly switch boxes near each screen. Other units come with multiple wireless remotes, so that each viewer can wirelessly select his or her desired programming—but be sure you don't misplace the remotes!

Many video switching units incorporate audio switching as well, so you can use a single set of headphones for all audio sources. The best units broadcast the audio wirelessly and come bundled with wireless headphones. This provides for a customized A/V experience for any passenger, with a minimum of wiring. The audio lines of each video source need to be connected through the switcher, so that the passengers can select from the DVD player, game console, or computer, for instance, and their headphones will switch to the appropriate sound. One of these outputs should be routed to the car's head unit or amplifier, so that the DVD or computer sound can be put through the car speakers as well.

2.4 GHz is a great frequency for wireless audio—unless you're also trying to use WiFi and Bluetooth, which use the same frequency. My own experience with dueling 2.4 GHz audio/video repeaters, which mangled my home WiFi signal, revealed that these devices don't play well together.

Proprietary Switchers

"Proprietary" is used here not in a critical sense, but merely to describe video selectors that work only with a specific hardware vendor. Blaupunkt, for example, has its own high-resolution RGB head unit screen that can be connected to a Blaupunkt navigation system. Instead of having to degrade the navigation signal down to composite video when you add AUX video inputs, their switch box has an RGB input as well as four additional video inputs for games, a DVD player, a computer, and so on. If you have a high-end after-market head unit, go to your vendor's web site to see what viewer customizations are available to you.

Tune in TV in the Car

#36 With the right antenna, the TV tuner card in your PC can expand your viewing choices and entertain your passengers.

While many in-car TV systems are available, in-car computers expand the options even further. A computer-based TV system can combine the functions of playing, recording, and archiving TV programs. With digital video recorder (DVR) software, passengers can have all the latest TV features that they've come to expect, such as being able to pause and rewind live TV.

There are many systems for tuning TV broadcasts in a computer, ranging from external USB 2.0 TV capture systems to built-in TV/FM tuner PCI cards. The USB units are sometimes better, because they don't have to deal with signal interference inside the PC case. However, the features and video speeds are better on the PCI cards. PCI cards (such as those from *http:// www.hauppauge.com*) are also good because they integrate FM and TV tuning and have built-in MPEG encoding capabilities—essential for soft personal video recorder (PVR) programs, so that you can have TiVo-like features on the road. The Hauppauge units also have some of the best Linux driver support of any card on the market for their PVR series.

The trick to picking up good TV signals in the car is a good car antenna. If you have ever seen the small wings on the trunk of a limousine, you've seen one type of TV antenna for vehicles. However, you don't have to install an external antenna to pick up TV—there are many antennas that can be mounted on the inside of your car.

You can pay from around $10 to $100 for an in-car TV antenna, depending on the quality of the model. The easiest to install are like in-home rabbit ears—they have two antennas that stretch out to the left and right, and these can be mounted high in the rear window.

During your antenna search, you will see the term *diversity*. With a diversity antenna, you mount two antennas in different places in your car. Receivers can then choose which antenna has a better signal at any given time, providing better reception than with just one antenna.

There are two main connectors for antennas. Conventional antennas for homes use what is called an *F* connector. In the U.S., this connector is commonly referred to as a *coaxial* connector. This is the same connector type

that screws onto the back of TVs, cable boxes, and VCRs. However, many car TV systems use a 3.5-mm connector (like a headphone jack) instead. Your car TV tuner most likely uses an F connector, so make sure that your car antenna has an F jack. If it doesn't, you can buy a 3.5-to-F connector, or build one with parts available at Radio Shack.

If you can, get an antenna that comes with an amplifier, either integrated within the antenna housing or as a separate 12V device. It's an inexpensive addition, and given that the TV tuner on a car or in a computer is probably less sophisticated than a TV set, you need all the signal strength you can get.

With a starting cost of less than $10 for some antennas, it's cheap and easy to test out the reception of your in-car computer television. If you find you need a better signal, you can go to a more expensive internal or even external-mount solution.

Now that you have TV in the car, you need a PVR so that your shows are waiting for you when you get in the car. For more information on setting up these PVR features on your PC, see "Put a Video Jukebox in Your Car Theater" [Hack #70].

HACK #37 Receive Satellite TV While Driving

While RVs have been tuning in satellite TV while parked for years, recent technologies allow you to tune in while your vehicle is in motion.

Years ago, millions of rural dwellers envied their urban cable-ready friends who were able to get dozens of cable TV channels at a low cost. However, with the advent of digital satellite television, people who lived in remote places were able to get comparable service to cable—provided they could see the southern sky. It didn't take long for RV owners to jump on this opportunity and equip their vehicles with satellite dishes.

At first, these dishes needed to be manually aimed whenever the RV parked up for a while. Then, signal-finding kits were developed that provided audio feedback to speed up the process of aiming the antenna. Finally, motorized automatic signal finders hit the market.

However, each of these solutions still required a large, 18" dish to be pointed at the sky, which had to be folded down when the vehicle was in motion. Fast forward to now to see a new solution that works not only for RVs, but for everyday vehicles with big, flat roofs, such as Hummers and SUVs. A roof-mounted digital satellite receiver integrates a spinning array of tiny, half-dollar-sized antennas into a package that is only 5" inches tall.

Made by KVH Industries (*http://www.kvh.com*), this device is expensive at a little over $2,000—but not overpriced considering what it does. Combine the ability to receive digital satellite at any time, while driving or not, with the PVR software available to modern computers, and you can have the novelty of watching your favorite shows *in your car* whenever you want to view them—and the real hack here is that KVH has built an antenna to pick up signals that were never designed for mobile reception. (For more information on setting up PVR features on your PC, see "Put a Video Jukebox in Your Car Theater" [Hack #70].)

DirecTV has dozens of audio-only channels similar in format to XM and Sirius, so in addition to rear-seat entertainment, you can use this as another option for satellite radio. Furthermore, if you already have DirecTV, adding the mobile package is very cheap—essentially just the $10 cost of adding another receiver.

It's worth noting that the DirecTV channel package for in-car use is a bit restricted—you can't watch HBO, for instance. However, if you get the RV or trucker package, the full coast-to-coast mobile package with all the channels is available. You have to designate what type of vehicle you're installing the system in when you subscribe, but with the size of SUVs these days, I think you could make a case for getting the RV or trucker package if you really feel you need all the channels.

HACK #38 Play DVDs with Your in-Car Computer

The most obvious reason to install video in the car is so your passengers can watch movies, and with a computer, the in-car DVD experience can be even better.

DVD entertainment is the major driver of in-car screen sales. In-car video entertainment was once rare, but now you can purchase a DVD player and two headrest screens for the rear passengers for under $300.

But this cheap solution doesn't give you the best DVD experience possible. In-car portable DVD players are limited. Most of them include only stereo sound, not surround sound (Pyle, at *http://www.pyleaudio.com*, and Phoenix Gold, at *http://www.phoenixgold.com*, are notable exceptions), and most of them are limited to composite video output, which is the lowest acceptable video quality.

A modern personal computer is a much more powerful DVD player. For about $50 you can get a full-featured software DVD player that does *progressive scan conversion* (a method of enhancing the visual quality of DVD video for flat screens and computer monitors), offers surround sound, and can be set to play DVDs from any region (U.S., Europe, etc.). Computer-based DVD players can drive high-resolution screens at the full DVD resolution of 720 × 480, and even higher on larger flat screens.

Locating Your DVD Drive

There are several approaches to getting DVD drives into a car. Many in-car computer enclosures have an integrated CD/DVD drive, either tray- or slot-loading. However, most computers are too large to fit in the dashboard, or even under the seat.

If you have a large vehicle with a center console between the driver and passenger seats, you may be able to hide your computer in that unit, mounting the DVD drive so that it can be accessed by the front or rear passengers.

However, the standard location for an optical drive in cars is in the middle of the dashboard. Thus, for the driver's convenience, you want a small drive that you can install seamlessly in the dashboard alongside any existing CD drive. Figure 3-20 shows one of the many slim-line CD/DVD enclosures that are excellent for this purpose. Several models exist that provide both USB and FireWire connectors, are less than 1" tall, and can accommodate any laptop-sized DVD drive. Although a conventional 5.25" CD drive enclosure (also pictured in Figure 3-20) could fit in a single-DIN slot, your dashboard would look like the front of a PC case—not a very attractive install. Instead, you should mount a slot-loading, laptop-sized optical drive (or a Mac Mini [Hack #54]) using an existing or fabricated horizontal slot in the dashboard for a very stealth install.

Figure 3-20. An internal DVD drive, a laptop DVD drive, and a Mac Mini

Connecting Your DVD Drive

The easiest approach is to mount your DVD drive externally from the computer, so that your computer can be located wherever you want. If you have a full-sized computer installed in the trunk, you can use three-meter cables to connect it to your DVD drive in the front area. But what interface should you use?

Since it's likely you'll want USB connectors near the dashboard [Hack #51] anyway, you may simply want to connect a USB hub for your in-dash DVD player. This install looks best if you cleanly flush-mount the USB adapter, but it looks bad to have the USB cable from the DVD drive looping out of the dash to plug into the front of the hub. So, for a clean install, you need to either use *two* USB hubs, with one facing inwards for a connection to the DVD drive, or run a pair of USB cables from the computer up to the front of the car.

Another consideration with USB is power. Optical drives take around 600–800 mA of power at 5V. This is above the 500-mA limit provided by USB 2.0 hubs. I've personally tried half a dozen USB hubs to no avail—they purposely limit the power. Thus, the DVD drive has to be separately powered, requiring another 12V-to-5V adapter. These are cheap and easy to find—at Radio Shack and any auto shop, you can find cigarette lighter adapters that adapt 12V down to 9V, 6V, 3V, or 1.5V with a switch. And a company called ZIP-LINQ (*http://www.ziplinq.com*) even makes a unit that is basically a 12V-to-USB adapter.

It's important to note that these units may not provide the clean, regulated 5V power your DVD drive needs and may be designed for more robust equipment. If you want a safer power environment for your DVD drive, use a regulated adapter (Google "12V to 5V DC-to-DC power supply").

With smaller motherboards, such as the popular VIA EPIA models, the USB power output isn't enough to power an external DVD drive by the wire itself. However, if you have a larger computer and a hearty power supply, you may be able to get away with a single USB cable that can power the device.

The motivation for having only a single wire is more than just to reduce clutter. A *bus-powered* device (which gets its power from the cable, not a separate power supply) ensures that the DVD drive is on only when the computer is on, and avoids synchronization problems when the DVD drive is suddenly powered off (e.g., when you pull the key out of the ignition) when the computer is still on or, even worse, reading from the disk (which won't hurt the player but will probably crash your operating system). Another benefit of bus power is that you don't have to install yet another power adapter in your dash.

The most successful bus power approach is to use FireWire cables (the larger, 6-pin version). FireWire has very solid power characteristics and was designed to drive fairly thirsty external devices. The maximum rated length of a FireWire cable is about three meters, and in practice they work at longer distances than that. FireWire cables are nicely shielded, and I've purchased a 15-foot cable at Fry's Electronics for around $12.

FireWire is also nicely compatible with the 12V in cars. Similar to the 12V-to-5V cigarette lighter adapter mentioned earlier, the older FireWire iPod rechargers can be used to power FireWire devices. FireWire devices have

additional circuitry to deal with a range of input voltages, and they aren't likely to suddenly give up on life if the voltage fluctuates.

There's one more reason to use bus power. Many of the power adapters for external devices are *barrel plugs*. These cylindrical plugs can pull or fall out easily, requiring you to take your dashboard apart to get the DVD player working again. USB and FireWire connectors plug in more firmly and are less likely to pop out after installation.

Running the Right Software

It wasn't until computer processors reached 400 MHz that PCs had enough power to decode DVD MPEG-2 video using software. Modern processors with speeds greater than 1 GHz have no problems decoding DVD video, but the multitasking features of computers can still cause jitters and quality problems when the PC has other work to do, such as driving multiple monitors or accessing networks.

There are a number of DVD programs and hardware solutions available for PCs. WinDVD (*http://www.windvd.com*) and PowerDVD (*http://www.gocyberlink.com*) are two mainstream Windows applications, both of which play DVDs with high quality on any GHz-class machine. They each come as $15 add-ins to Windows Media Player, or you can buy the full-fledged versions of the programs for $50–70, depending on which additional features you choose (such as 5.1 surround sound).

The very popular, compact VIA EPIA motherboards are used extensively for in-car computing. They are low power, low heat, and run an Intel-compatible processor at speeds around 1 GHz. However, these CPUs have lower floating-point performance than real Pentiums, and thus DVD playback taxes their processors. While they advertise built-in MPEG-2 decoding hardware assistance, the only DVD player that implements this is a closed-source version of Linux DVD software (a bad mix, if you ask me). PowerDVD and WinDVD seem to run fine on these machines (not the 600-MHz versions, but the 1-GHz and above models), but it's a shame that they don't use the built-in hardware support.

I'd have to say my favorite DVD player is MPlayer (*http://www.mplayerhq.hu*), which runs on Linux, Windows, and Mac OS X. One of the features I like most about it is that it runs from a command line from which you can configure all sorts of features, such as which screen to start playback on and which track or scene in the movie to start with. This allows you to start playing the movie on a DVD instantly, without going through all the trailers and the menu system. This also makes it safer for the driver—if you can hit one button on your touchscreen and play the movie, that's better than having to hit Play, wait for a menu, and then hit Play again.

Putting It Together

My own car-computer setup is designed so that I can put in a DVD and start it playing in the front seat without having to watch the video. I remain in control of the media, but those in the back seat get to watch. I can also choose whether to pump the DVD sound through the car's speakers or let the back-seat passengers listen on their own headphones.

To accomplish this, I use the dual monitor setup available on the VIA EPIA boards. They have a VGA output (which I've connected to my dash-mounted VGA touchscreen) and both a composite and an S-Video output.

I run one of these outputs to the rear monitor (I only have one headrest monitor, but the output could be split and amplified to any number of other screens) and the other to the composite input of my VGA touchscreen.

While I'm driving, I leave my software running on the primary (VGA touch-screen) monitor. If I insert a DVD, I have my software configured to play the DVD on the second monitor (the composite output).

If I want to watch too (i.e., while stopped or to quickly check what's playing), I press the SOURCE button on the VGA touchscreen and switch from VGA to the first AUX video input. Then I switch back to my VGA signal when I want to run the primary desktop on my PC.

Once you get DVD working well in the car, you may realize that you have four or more speakers, yet you're only playing back a stereo soundtrack. "Put Multi-Channel DVD Surround Sound in Your Car" [Hack #39] tells you how to correct this shortcoming.

Put Multi-Channel DVD Surround Sound in Your Car
#39

If you already have four or more speakers in your car, it's a straightforward upgrade to go from stereo to multi-channel sound.

Surround sound is a term used to describe a number of different approaches to "surrounding" the listener with sound in a movie theater, home theater, or, in our case, automotive theater.

The basic concept of surround sound is to place multiple speakers strategically around the audience, giving them sound from all directions. By sending different types of sounds to each speaker, a 3D effect is created, where things can be heard coming from behind, passing by, and going off into the distance. Even dialog can be positioned in space around the listener.

The unique sound sent to each individual speaker is called a *channel*, and the number of channels in the sound determines how many speakers you

need to reproduce it. Each channel of sound in these systems has a specific function and helps to produce the overall 3D sound experience.

Surround sound systems usually have an array of speakers in front of and behind the listener, as well as a low-frequency channel for special effects such as explosions and rumbling. The designation *5.1* describes a system with five normal audio channels and one low-frequency effects channel. If you add a rear center speaker, you get six audio channels plus a bass track, and this is called *6.1*. If you go to *four* rear speakers—left surround, right surround, left rear, and right rear—you have *7.1* sound. Figure 3-21 shows the normal elements of a surround sound system.

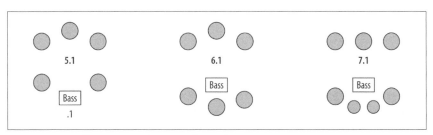

Figure 3-21. Different types of surround sound

Although your car might have eight speakers, it really has only two basic channels (stereo). The bass amplifier usually uses a *crossover* to extract the low frequency from these two channels and sends that to the bass speaker. In cheaper subwoofers, the crossover, amplifier, and bass speaker are in a single self-contained unit. The other four to eight speakers (front and rear, midrange and tweeter) play back either the left or the right stereo signal. Your car probably has balance and fade controls, but these simply adjust the relative volume between left and right or between front and back. You're still listening to the same two channels of sound; they're just being sent to you from all directions.

In the specification for surround sound systems, each speaker is supposed to work at a certain frequency range (like the tweeters, midrange, and bass speakers in a car) and be positioned at a precise distance from the listener. In the car, though, you generally won't want to move the speakers you already have. Instead, you simply want to change their purpose, and add a couple of additional speakers to fill out the missing roles.

Figure 3-22 demonstrates that for each distinct channel in a car, you may actually have two speakers—a midrange and a tweeter. The different channels in surround sound really describe *where* the sound is supposed to come from (rear right, behind, center front, etc.). Most cars have stereos that output four signals, which are then split into eight speakers. To install true surround sound, you'll use these eight speakers (four pairs) as the front channel and rear surround speakers, and then add a center channel and a subwoofer.

Figure 3-22. Surround sound in a car

DTS Versus Dolby 5.1

There are several competing surround sound systems. DVDs usually come with tracks in both the DTS and Dolby 5.1 formats, as well as in stereo. Surround sound processors are designed to take the sound from a DVD player and split it into the six or more surround sound channels.

In a home theater setup, you usually have a separate amplifier unit that performs this function, connected to the DVD player via a single digital link. For an in-car computer, you can use DVD player software such as Power-DVD (*http://www.gocyberlink.com*) or WinDVD (*http://www.windvd.com*) to decode all the surround sound formats without requiring any additional hardware.

Audio Connectors

Naturally, if you're decoding six channels of sound, you need six physical audio outputs, and thus you need a sound card that supports this. There are two basic approaches to implementing six-channel sound.

Analog approach. The analog approach is to get a sound card with six outputs (three stereo pairs). Then, you can use two or three car audio amplifiers [Hack #15] (depending on whether they are two- or four-channel) to amplify these six audio signals.

The VIA EPIA boards, for instance, have a mode where the three audio connectors—normally line-in, line-out, and microphone—become six-channel sound. By connecting a 3.5 mm to RCA out pair to each of these, you get the six audio outputs you need for the surround sound.

You can also get USB 5.1 sound output devices that have the necessary six outputs.

Digital approach. The digital approach to surround sound decoding allows the signal to travel digitally from the computer to the amplifier or sound decoder. In this arrangement, the digital to analog conversion occurs nearer to the amplifier, reducing analog losses.

S/PDIF (which stands for Sony/Phillips digital interface) is a protocol and physical standard for sending multiple channels of sound digitally over a wire. Actual implementations of S/PDIF can travel over coaxial wires or optical cables.

Many sound cards have both S/PDIF inputs and outputs for compatibility with any audio equipment you might have. The coaxial S/PDIF interface uses the common RCA connector. Optical S/PDIF comes in two physical connector formats.

Toslink (Toshiba link) is an optical connector format (shown in Figure 3-23) that can carry S/PDIF and other optical audio transmission protocols. A Toslink cable consists of a single, flexible, insulated optical cable, with squarish connectors on both ends that click into the female receptacles of Toslink devices. There is also a smaller version of this connector format, called mini-Toslink (found on devices such as MiniDisks), that can be converted to Toslink with a simple adapter.

Figure 3-23. Toslink connectors

By using digital cabling as much as possible, you increase audio quality and reduce the number of wires, because one digital cable can carry all of the audio channels.

Surround sound is becoming popular in cars, and the aftermarket has started to realize this. You can already get an all-in-one 5.1 sound card and amplifier combo for your computer from Creative Labs, and companies are starting to manufacture the same type of product for the car. For instance, the company Phoenix Gold (*http://www.phoenixgold.com*) makes a six-channel (5.1 sound) amplifier, called the OCTANE-R 5.1MT, that has optical Toslink inputs and coaxial inputs, and powers five car speakers at 100W and a subwoofer at 200W. It even has onscreen computer controls, which are a really nice feature. If space is at a premium, or if you don't want to fill your trunk with amplifiers because you want to leave room for computers, this is a great solution.

Auto Upgrades

Part of the beauty of using a computer in your car is that you get to upgrade to the latest technologies without getting a new car, and sometimes without even getting new hardware. If DVD software evolves to support an enhanced DVD feature, you can simply install the new program in your car, and you're up to date.

If you want to upgrade to some new audio or video technology in your car, even HD DVD, you can bet that your computer will allow you to shortcut the delays of consumer electronics and get the feature before most people know that it even exists.

HACK #40 Install a Video Game Console Computer in Your Car

Video games are an extremely effective way of burning time on the road, and they're an essential tool for enduring long-distance drives.

Unsurprisingly, many of the people who like to enhance their cars also enjoy playing video games. And even "soccer moms" and other unexpected car hobbyists enjoy the ability to placate their children with the backseat entertainment provided by a game console.

Installing a Game Console

PlayStation 2 units, Xboxes, and Nintendo GameCubes are all candidates
for in-car installation. There are several considerations when installing these
in the car:

Power

> The car voltage needs to be converted and regulated to safely power
> these devices, and you need to make sure that they won't stay on when
> the car is off and kill the battery, so they should be connected to auxil-
> iary switched outlets. A simple way to power one of these devices is to
> use an inverter [Hack #11] and plug in the wall adapter that came with the
> unit. A better way is to find a 12V adapter designed for your specific
> video game unit, which should be available at any store that sells video
> game console accessories.

Integration

> The easiest units to install in a car dashboard are ones where the optical
> drive tray slides out. You want the units to be installed in a stable way,
> so that the optical drives don't get shaken around. GameCubes, origi-
> nal PlayStations, and new PlayStation 2s have top-load drives and are
> more difficult to mount.

Video delivery

> If you are going to have head-to-head gaming, you need multiple pas-
> sengers to be able to tap into the video signal. Thus, it's probably best to
> either run the game to all screens or, even better, install a video switcher
> [Hack #35] so that each passenger can select their screen's video source.

> If you would like to install two game consoles for head-to-head gaming
> (for instance, so that four rear passengers can play head-to-head, each
> with their own screens) you can use a 4×4 video splitter [Hack #35]. Put
> the two game consoles as two of the inputs, and each of the passengers
> can select the appropriate game console as their screen's video source.

Control

> The best solution for game control is to get wireless (preferably radio
> frequency, not infrared, which require line of sight to work) controllers
> so that they can be passed to whoever needs them without creating a
> tangled mess of wires. If you have infrared receivers, mount them high
> and central on the ceiling so anyone in the car can use the controllers.
> You can also run controller extensions to each seat and plug in a con-
> troller only when needed—this involves more labor but uses fewer
> expensive parts, and you won't run into any interference problems (as
> you may with the IR and RF solutions).

Hacking the Hack

One of the benefits of Xbox and PlayStation 2 installation, and one of the reasons why they are so popular, is that they double as DVD players. When cleanly integrated in the dashboard, you get DVD, CD, and gaming capabilities all in one unit.

But you needn't stop there. Most of the consoles on the market are powerful enough to run Linux. Some of the consoles require a *mod chip*, a chip with a hacked version of their internal software, in order to run Linux or other software, but once you get the modification your console becomes a powerful, versatile computing platform. Sony actually supplies a Linux distribution for their console (*http://playstation2-linux.com*). You can find Xbox Linux at *http://www.xbox-linux.org* and GameCube Linux at *http://www.gc-linux.org*. A full-featured car PC frontend package for Linux can be found at *http://www.dashwerks.com*.

CHAPTER FOUR

In-Car Computers
Hacks 41–54

In the first three chapters, I covered the basics of automotive computer integration: car power, car audio, and car video. Now you finally get to hook up your computer. There are many considerations that go into what kind of computer to put in a car. A large, modern, multi-gigahertz computer provides the smoothest in-car gaming experience, but it takes a lot of power and space. A laptop seems an obvious choice for in-car use, but laptops are awkward to mount and difficult to smoothly integrate in a vehicle's interior. Industry standards exist for rugged, low-power-consumption computers, but these are usually too expensive for consumer use. Fortunately, there has been a lot of recent investment and development in the area of set-top boxes and home theater PCs (HTPCs), which has resulted in the creation of small, quiet, low-power, gigahertz-class Intel-compatible motherboards and processors with excellent multimedia capabilities—perfect for in-car computing.

When you go to install a PC in your car, one way to approach it is from an engineering perspective. Draw up a detailed list of requirements, along with notes on the physical and power constraints of your car. Search for industry-standard solutions for rugged, shock-mounted hardware. Locate memory, motherboards, and hard drives that deal well with the temperature extremes of an uninsulated vehicle trunk. Create a budget for your expenditures, and while you're at it, solicit quotes from at least three vendors for each component.

Well, that's one way to do it. The more conventional way to hack a computer into a car is to say, "I'm going to build a computer for my car this weekend—I think I have enough spare parts." This is the approach addressed in this chapter. Each of the following hacks covers one important aspect of getting a computer to work in a car. Once you've worked through the hacks in this chapter, you should have a car PC well integrated into your car and ready to use.

Choose an in-Car PC Hardware Platform

HACK #41

Speed, size, noise, power efficiency, and price are some of the trade-offs to consider when building a car PC.

There are many ways to build an in-car PC. The "right" way depends on what you want to use the PC for, and whether you are building from scratch or using parts you have on hand.

If you are an IT guy with too many spare computers to count, you probably want to see if you can put your existing parts together to make a PC for your car. Or perhaps you just upgraded your laptop and you figure that the older one, which can play DVDs and still has 10 minutes of battery life, could be adapted to power your in-car entertainment system. Maybe you're a gamer with a top-of-the-line Alienware (*http://www.alienware.com*) machine, and you expect to get in some extra time on your massive multiplayer online role-playing game over your new broadband wireless cell phone connection while someone else drives. Or maybe you're a hacker who wants the computer to run all the time, so you can remotely control your car windows and an in-car camera through your computer's wireless Internet connection.

Let's look over the major considerations that go into selecting a car PC hardware platform.

Fast Computers

If you have a top-of-the-line PC on your desk, your first impulse may be to build the same sort of system for your car. Certainly, if you are doing seriously demanding work, such as playing 3D, 2D, or online games, or running platform game emulation (i.e., emulating a PlayStation, Xbox, Nintendo 64, or older console), you need the fastest computer money can buy.

If you plan to run your high-end PC only when the car is on, you should have enough power if you use a high-wattage inverter **[Hack #42]** and upgrade your car's alternator **[Hack #9]**.

Extremely fast computers have the drawbacks of being expensive, noisy, power-hungry, and bulky. If you mount the computer in your trunk and don't mind the space it takes up, that solves the size and noise issues. But if you have an SUV, you may not have a sonic barrier between your rear area and the cabin of the car. In this case, you will want to reduce the noise your PC makes.

Another consideration is temperature. Keeping your PC cool enough requires there to be adequate airflow, and the trunk of a vehicle tends to be fairly leaky, allowing some of this hot air to get out. For in-trunk high-end

PCs, though, you'd do well to make sure you have fans that are heat-controlled, so that their speed increases (and the computer is possibly even shut down) in response to high-temperature conditions.

If you have an SUV, minivan, or luxury car that has air-conditioning vents in the rear of the vehicle, you can run a ventilating pipe from an A/C vent to the intake fan of your PC. With SUVs, using the A/C can help reduce the effort required by PC fans to keep the computer cool, and tinting the rear windows keeps the sun off the PC and helps it to stay cool.

Cheap Computers

If your main consideration is cost, you can build a car PC out of whatever you have lying around. Depending on what you want to use it for, you can get away with an old or low-powered computer. Older computers tend to run cooler and make less noise than anything you purchase today.

If you only want to play MP3s and run Winamp visualizations on a screen, anything over a 90-MHz Pentium is sufficient. Computers below 200 MHz might even have an old AT power supply (with an on/off toggle switch on the front of the case), which are much easier to get working in a car. (For more on startup and shutdown, see "Start Up and Shut Down Your Car PC" [Hack #43].)

If you need to play DVDs, you can supplement a slow processor with a circa-1999 DVD decoder board from your junk pile. Software DVD decoding requires a 450-MHz Pentium III at a minimum, but with a DVD decoder board or a video card with onboard DVD decoding capabilities (such as some ATI Rage 128s), any PC can do it.

Even if you can't play current PC video games on a low-end system, many older video games from the 1980s and 1990s can be run with emulation software. And because these types of games have simple keypad controls (most don't require a full PC keyboard), they are well suited for in-car passenger entertainment.

If you plan to use the PC just for web surfing, you have even more options—any computer with a processor speed of over 200 MHz should be able to run a web browser without too much trouble.

Small, Power-Efficient Computers

If you want to operate the computer when the car is off, its power usage is a primary consideration. You might only want to use the PC for brief moments while the car is stopped, or you might try to design a system where the computer is always powered so that it can "phone home" for *telemetry* functionality (remote measurement and control, such as downloading music, video, and emails; tracking your car's location; or even viewing a live security webcam installed in your car).

When both space and power are considerations, the best solution is to use small motherboards that are designed for compact, low-power environments. Over the last few years, computers have been shrinking—and not in the traditional sense. Instead of packing more functionality into the same ATX form factor, there has been a trend to make smaller, cube- or pizza-box-shaped PCs that can fit in the space of a VCR or a DVD player.

One manufacturer of cube-sized PCs is Shuttle (*http://www.shuttle.com*). While quiet and high-performance, Shuttle PCs are almost as power-hungry as traditional desktop computers.

VIA Technologies (*http://www.via.com.tw*), a major motherboard manufacturer, has developed and standardized entirely new PC form factors that they have dubbed Mini-ITX (pictured in Figure 4-1) and Nano-ITX. On their embedded web site (*http://www.viaembedded.com*), you can find links to their wide selection of feature-packed EPIA series motherboards.

Figure 4-1. The Mini-ITX M2 motherboard

VIA's EPIA boards use their own low-power, Intel-compatible processor, running at speeds of around 1 GHz. The boards are only 17 cm square, have every connector and port you could want, and consume only 20–30W of power. Their newest board, the Nano-ITX, is only 12 cm square—about the size of a CD case. The community surrounding these boards is quite extensive, as people have begun using them to hack computers into any conceivable device or object. Mini-ITX.com (*http://www.mini-itx.com*) has a long list of creative projects for which these boards have been used, as well as links to the many small cases in which you can install these boards.

If you are building a car PC from scratch, your best starting point is an EPIA board such as the EPIA M2, which has a PCMCIA slot (essential for the many wireless Internet connectivity options) and a CompactFlash slot (great for shock-resistant nonmechanical flash file storage), and can run at speeds as fast as 1.3 GHz.

If you're looking for a computer that's already all put together, you should also take a look at the Mac Mini as a hardware solution [Hack #54]. Capable of running both OS X and Linux, the Mac Mini is almost exactly the size of a single-DIN car radio and has a slot-loading CD drive. Buying one of these can be even cheaper than building an EPIA-based PC (Mac Minis start at about $500); what's more, they're more powerful, more compact, and already assembled.

The Mac Mini

The best reason to switch to Mac for your in-car computer is the new Mac Mini. At 6.5" square and 2" tall (see Figure 4-35 in "Install a Mac Mini in Your Car" [Hack #54]), it seems like it was designed for a single-DIN automotive slot (7"×2"). Though the Mac Mini had only just been released when this book was being written, there are already vendors specializing in Mac Mini-to-car installations, such as Classic Restorations in New York (*http://www.classicresto.com/macmini.html*).

The Mac Mini costs only a little more than the iPod, yet it can turn your car into the "digital hub," instead of just an accessory to it. It is a powerful multimedia machine with a cool-running 1.42-GHz PowerPC processor; it comes with VGA and DVI video interfaces, USB and FireWire peripheral interfaces, and also has options for integrated WiFi, Bluetooth, and even a DVD burner in the same tiny package—just about every conceivable technology and interface necessary for in-car computing.

Laptop Computers

Using a laptop with an automobile power adapter is a quick, easy way to get a computer into your car. You can even leave the laptop plugged into the cigarette lighter adapter when the car is off for several hours without any harm, but if you leave your laptop charging overnight it *could* discharge your car battery. If you want to permanently install a laptop in your car, you still need to use a startup/shutdown controller [Hack #43], as you would with a regular PC.

Laptops are great if you simply want to play MP3s and surf the Web in the car on an occasional basis, but it's difficult for the driver to safely operate a laptop that's just sitting on the passenger seat, and it can go flying in an accident. The excellent thing about laptops is that they are compact and power efficient; also, many used laptops available on eBay include DVD players, making any laptop over around 600 MHz suitable for in-car audio/video entertainment.

The drawback of laptops is that you can't disconnect the screen on them and put the laptop in the trunk and the screen in the ceiling, so the screen becomes a wasted resource. Out-of-warranty laptops with cracked screens or many dead pixels are great candidates for in-car computers ("Hey boss, can I take your broken Dell off your hands?"). But if your laptop is slim and stylish enough, you may find you can get the screen *and* the computer in your car if you mount it on the ceiling [Hack #31].

Non-Obvious in-Car Computers

Your in-car computer does not have to be a "computer" at all. All the most recent game consoles, such as the Xbox, PlayStation 2, and GameCube, have interfaces for hard drives, networking, and keyboards. Each of these platforms can even run Linux, with easily available modification chips.

The benefits of using a game console as an in-car computer are obvious. For one, consoles are far cheaper than PCs, as well as smaller and quieter. You can install one console for each passenger if you really need to. Although the consoles can't play ordinary console games when booted to Linux, they can run thousands of other applications, including MP3 players and Linux-based games and game emulators.

The latest Palm (*http://www.palmone.com*) and PocketPC (*http://www.microsoft.com/pocketpc/*) devices are multimedia-capable, with processor speeds exceeding 600 MHz. Their portability ensures that their power consumption will be low, making them viable in-car computers. In fact, there are a variety of PocketPC and PalmOS GPS/navigation solutions, where the GPS unit plugs into the top of the handheld device and the handheld is mounted on the dashboard, facing the driver. The only problem is that there aren't any good docking stations (yet) that enable you to plug this type of portable multimedia device into the dash without having wires everywhere.

Another diminutive option is the recently released OQO (*http://www.oqo.com*) computer, which uses a low-power Intel-compatible chip to squeeze a 1-GHz processor into a handheld computer. With a simple docking adapter, this device connects to a VGA monitor and a standard keyboard. It has an integrated 800×480 touchscreen and a 20-GB hard drive, and it can power itself for a long time when connected to a car battery. You could simply Velcro the OQO to your dashboard and drill a small hole to pass through the USB and power cables.

As more powerful, pint-sized devices like this come on the market, the task of getting computing into the car becomes easier and easier.

Cases and Enclosures

Though a variety of companies make cases for Mini-ITX form factor boards, only a few companies have created motherboard enclosures designed for in-car use. You can see a sampling of car PC cases in Figure 4-2.

Figure 4-2. Car PC cases: two Morex, a Solar PC, and a CarBot

Morex (*http://www.morex.com.tw*) cases are some of the cheapest. They adapt easily to in-car use but don't have any car-specific power connectors, so power wires will have to pass through some hole into the case.

Opus Solutions (*http://www.opussolutions.com*), makers of some of the best power supplies **[Hack #42]**, also make several in-car computer enclosures that are solid, expandable (they add an additional PCI slot for the VIA motherboards), and have optional shock-absorbing rubber spacers for industrial vehicle (or sports car) installations.

In-Dash PC (*http://www.indashpc.org*) makes an inexpensive single-DIN enclosure for car PCs. Their approach is unique in that they've managed to squeeze a VIA motherboard, a slot-loading optical drive, and bootable flash memory into a box that can fit in your dashboard. This is excellent if you really don't have room in the trunk, and it saves you the trouble and expense of running wires to a computer in the trunk.

CarBot (*http://www.carbotpc.com*), my own company, has been selling a very pretty (but expensive) brushed aluminum enclosure for Mini-ITX boards. One of the features of the CarBot case is that it has all the PC-related ports on one side and all the car-related ports (such as 12V, ground, ignition, and RCA audio input and output) on the other side. This makes it possible to take a CarBot case into an install shop and say "hook it up" without getting blank stares from the installers, as you do with many other car PC enclosures.

There are dozens of other cases on the market. The following links will help you find some other options that may fit your needs.

See Also

- *http://www.mp3car.com*—Premier forum on car PCs
- *http://www.karpc.com*—Car PC reseller
- *http://www.logicsupply.com*—Car PC parts distributor/reseller
- *http://www.carhacks.org*—Car PC blog site

HACK #42 Power Your Car PC

While you could just use an inverter to power a normal PC AT or ATX power supply, there are several power supplies on the market designed specifically for in-car computer use.

An in-car computer must be able to run on 12V, instead of the 120–240V found in a house. More accurately, an in-car computer has to put up with a voltage that fluctuates around 12–14V when the engine is on, and that can drop well below 12V when the engine is off or while it is starting. Computers are fairly sensitive to voltage fluctuations and can easily get "fried" by voltage spikes.

A *regulated* power supply is a power supply that ensures that its output voltages do not fluctuate significantly. All internal computer power supplies and many external AC adapters are regulated, meaning that minor fluctuations of input voltage do not show up on the output to the motherboard.

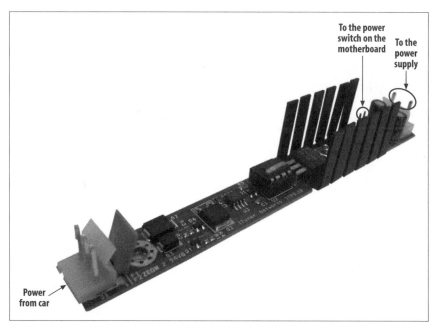

Figure 4-6. The ITPS

If the car turns on, the ITPS will "press" the power switch to turn on the PC and let it start booting. When the car turns off, the power switch is hit again—but instead of immediately cutting power to the PC, the ITPS gives the PC another 45 seconds to shut down smoothly. If the computer hangs somewhere in the shutting-down process (as many user-oriented operating systems commonly do, for example by leaving up a dialog box that says "Do you want to save this document before quitting?"), the ITPS will cut the power after 45 seconds to ensure that the PC doesn't keep running and kill the car battery.

The ITPS doesn't include a power supply, but it does supply 12V to another power supply or a voltage inverter. ITPS units are relatively inexpensive (less than $40) and work extremely reliably. They draw very little power when the PC is off (around 10 mA).

The drawbacks of the ITPS are that it requires an input of over 13V (not always available with weak batteries when the car is turned off), and it can only pass about 60W (5A), so it can't be used with larger 120W or 200W power supplies. To solve these problems, Mini-box also just released their M1-ATX **[Hack #42]**, which integrates ITPS startup controller functionality with a solid, compact 90W power supply. Improving on the ITPS, the M1-ATX has several jumpers that allow you to configure how long you want the computer to stay on after you shut down the car—key for sending and receiving data wirelessly **[Hack #64]**.

Mpegbox (*http://www.mpegbox.net*) also makes a startup/shutdown controller: the microShutdown (uSDC20D), pictured in Figure 4-7. Not only does it do the standard job of turning on the car PC when the power is activated, but it has the additional benefits of measuring the automobile battery voltage and the ambient temperature inside your car PC case, and shutting down the PC if either the voltage is too low or the computer is too hot.

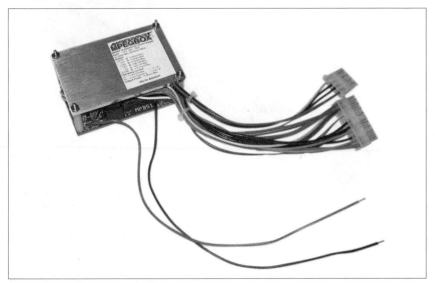

Figure 4-7. Mpegbox's microShutdown board

Dashwerks (*http://www.dashwerks.com*), makers of the Linux in-car software DashPC, also make a feature-rich startup controller board (Figure 4-8). It uses the Advanced Configuration Power Interface, or *ACPI* (*http://www.acpi.info*), to control starting up and shutting down the computer via the Wake-on-LAN connection. In addition, the unit interfaces with the serial port of the computer and communicates with software (such as DashPC or the open source Perl scripts provided at *http://www.dashwerks.com/dw_dssc.php*) to let the OS know when the car is on or off. The unit even allows the computer to control five other 12V devices, such as amplifiers or screens, through software.

As mentioned in "Power Your Car PC" [Hack #42], Opus Solutions makes 90W and 150W power supplies that combine power regulation and startup/shutdown control.

Carnetix (*http://www.carnetix.com*) makes an external power regulator and startup controller that also provides power regulation and survives engine cranking, like the Opus, but can work with any other power supply. It also

Figure 4-8. Dashwerks's startup controller board

has the unique feature of a delayed 12V output—this line doesn't turn on
the amplifier until after the computer is started, avoiding the loud "pop"
that PCs sometimes output to the speakers when they first turn on.

If you're using an inverter to power your car PC, you need to tie it to a
switched 12V voltage source, so that it doesn't kill your battery when you're
away from the car. However, if the inverter is simply connected to the *ACC*
(on or accessory) 12V, you'll end up cutting power to your PC when the car
turns off. To prevent this from happening, use a startup/shutdown controller with an inverter by wiring the 12V output of the controller to the input of
the inverter. When the car power is activated, the inverter will power on; the
ITPS, microShutdown, or similar unit will then activate the computer's
power button.

Alternative Solutions

Most people building car PCs simply buy a startup controller, or a power
supply with integrated startup control. Nonetheless, there are some circum-
stances where the startup controller doesn't do what you want. Here is some
additional theory on computer startup and shutdown that you can use in
creating a custom startup control system.

There are several things that can make a computer wake up:

- Pressing the power switch
- Wake-on-LAN (WOL)—many PCI Ethernet cards or network cards built into motherboards can turn on a PC
- Activity on the serial port
- Pressing the "on" button on recent-model keyboards
- Return of power after unexpected power loss
- Timed wakeup based on a setting in the BIOS

To monitor all these conditions and power up successfully, the computer must have a small trickle of current, called *standby power*. All modern ATX power supplies provide this small 5V signal even when the computer is "off." (For more on standby power, see "Boot Your Car Computer on a Schedule" [Hack #47].)

Switches and long wires. The simplest way to rig up your car computer is to run a switch to the dashboard and manually hit this power switch to power up the PC. You could even run the power switch, the reset switch, and the power LED and hard disk LED wires to the dashboard, drill small holes for them, and mount them in the dash. This technique requires long wires but the least amount of inventiveness, and it's a straightforward way to get things going.

If you are running wires to a laptop located under the seat or in the trunk, you need to find a way to remotely power the laptop. If you don't mind voiding your laptop's warranty (since you're reading this book, you probably don't), you can solder a pair of wires to its power button.

Take-apart instructions vary for any laptop, but once you have exposed the power switch, you can solder a pair of wires to the existing switch. You can then either run the wires through an existing hole or slot in your laptop, or poke a new small hole in the plastic casing. Since this is a small switch with probably only 1V going through it, you can use fairly thin wires (such as phone cord), run them to the dash, and hook them up with another switch installed in your dash, as shown in Figure 4-9.

Relay circuits. Ideally, a car computer should act just like a car radio—it should automatically turn on and off with the car, and be ready to use shortly after you start the vehicle without you having to press a power switch.

The first hack I ever came up with for automatic startup and shutdown was a relay circuit. *Relays* are simple voltage-activated switches used to isolate one power system from another. They don't take much circuit-building skill to

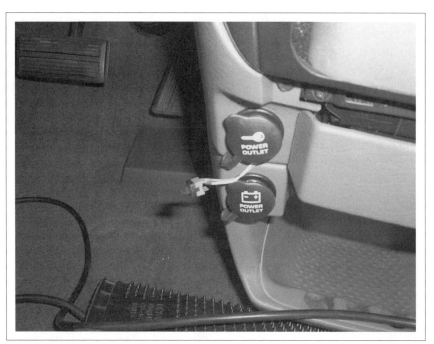

Figure 4-9. A small dashboard switch

use. If you look up the specifications of a Wake-on-LAN (WOL) *header* (the pins sticking up from the motherboard) in your motherboard manual, you will see that it is made up of pins for 5V, ground, and WOL. To get your computer to wake up, you simply have to connect the 5V and WOL pins for a moment (for this to work, WOL must also be enabled in the computer BIOS).

For my hack, I used two relays. One relay was connected to the accessory 12V of the vehicle; it closed one switch and opened another whenever the *car* was on. The other relay was connected to the 12V of the computer power supply; it closed one switch and opened another whenever the *computer* was on.

I rigged up the two relays in sequence, so that the 5V pin connected to the WOL pin only when the car's accessory 12V was on *and* the computer was off. In other words, WOL is off when the car's 12V is off and when the computer is already on, but if the computer is off and the car is on, WOL will be triggered until the computer switches on (which activates the second relay, turning WOL off again).

One of the attributes of this solution is that it always keeps the computer on when the car is on. If you manually shut down the computer (i.e., choose "shut down" from an OS menu), it will dutifully shut down, and then the relay circuit will dutifully turn it back on.

This relay circuit is crude, but it works, and it only costs around $10 to build with Radio Shack parts. After I discovered the next solution, however, I stopped using this reliable but complex relay circuit.

Capacitors. After six months of using the above relay solution, my friend pointed out an elegant solution that made me smack my forehead.

Capacitors are small, cylinder-shaped electronic devices that hold a voltage for a short time. Large capacitors can be used to keep your voltage levels stable [Hack #8], but this hack uses a tiny capacitor to create the effect of a momentary button press.

Capacitors work by filling up with electricity (up to their capacity, measured in *farads*) until they match the voltage that's being fed to them. They don't let any voltage pass through; they only fill up. Normally, when you press the power switch that connects to a motherboard, you are shorting (connecting) the power switch pins on the motherboard, which causes a voltage on one pin to travel to the other pin.

If you put a capacitor across these pins, as in Figure 4-10, when the motherboard first gets standby power (the trickle of 5V power from the power supply when the computer is off but plugged into a wall socket), the power switch will also have power. The capacitor will start to fill up, and during this filling period the other power pin will feel a surge in voltage, turning on the computer. Once the capacitor is filled (within a second or less) it doesn't change the voltage, so the computer will remain on until it is manually shut down or the power to the unit is cut.

In my experience, a 10uF capacitor works well with the EPIA M2 motherboards. Increasing that number increases the length of time for which the button is "pushed"; you may need to experiment with a couple of different capacitors for your particular motherboard. The capacitor has a little + and – diagram on its label, and these should correspond to the + and – pins on the power header on the motherboard.

This capacitor trick can be used for other soft power devices, too. For instance, some video displays have power switches and don't automatically turn on when power is supplied. To solve this problem, you simply solder a capacitor across the power switch. Now, instead of having to hit the switch, the unit will always turn on when it receives power.

Shutting down. Although both the relay and capacitor solutions get the computer turned on, you also need some way to turn it off.

Manually powering down in software is one approach. If you choose "shut down" in your OS, the computer will turn off. If you used a capacitor to

Figure 4-10. A 10uF capacitor acting as a power switch

power up, it won't power on again until you turn the car off and on again. If you used a relay circuit and the car is still running, the computer will shut down and the WOL relays will cause it to power right back up, as mentioned earlier.

However, depending on the driver to manually shut down the computer every time is a recipe for a dead battery. A more automatic solution is to use your OS's energy-saving features. Most OSs have a control panel where you can tell the computer to shut down after a set period of inactivity. If you set it for 30 minutes, the computer should usually shut down (or hibernate) about 30 minutes after you leave the car.

Yet another option is the simple hack I did for some versions of my company's (*http://www.carbotpc.com*) in-car computers. I wanted the ability to let our software determine when to shut down the computer, based on whether it was done downloading email or software from the house when the driver parked at the house at the end of the day.

I used a "car is on" relay—simply the ACC 12V and ground across a relay—to tell the computer whether or not the car was on. Many small motherboards have one serial port on the back and another as a header on the board itself. In my hack, I ran pin 1 (the carrier detect, or CD, pin, usually used to notify the computer if a modem is online) through the relay switch to pin 4 (the data terminal ready, or DTR, pin, usually used to tell the modem the computer is ready). Since my motherboard has COM2 (the second serial port) on the inside, my software can simply open COM2 and monitor the CD line. If it's up, then the car's ACC 12V must be on, and our software doesn't shut down. If it goes down, our software knows the car is off; if it's off for long enough, and if all software updates and email downloads are finished, the software shuts down the computer.

HACK #44 Reduce the Boot Time of Your in-Car Computer

There are dozens of tricks you can use to reduce the boot time of your in-car PC.

In 1980, if you turned on a car stereo, it turned on. Instantly. If you left the volume up from the last time you'd used it, the sound would come blaring out as quickly as the tape could start spinning and the analog amplifier circuits could charge their capacitors.

Nowadays, when you turn on your car radio, it boots up just like a computer. Since it only loads a tiny bit of microcode out of nonvolatile memory, though, it boots too quickly for most people to really notice. And by saving a bit of state information, it usually returns to the last radio station or CD track you were listening to.

NAV systems also have to boot up. When you turn on your modern navigation screen in a luxury car, you may have to wait a few seconds for everything to settle down, but the splash screen comes up almost instantly, and it feels more like starting an appliance than like booting a computer.

User-interface designers have often been critical of the modern PC boot process. Every modern operating system usually takes several minutes to boot up and load its graphical user interface. But why? You'd think that an operating system would be able to figure out what hardware is in the machine and, barring any changes, simply snap right back to where it was the last time the machine was shut down.

The general solution to the lengthy boot process has been to create energy-saving modes. Instead of shutting the machines off when not in use and then making them boot faster, the simpler approach is to allow the computers to *sleep*, by turning off some of the most power-hungry devices during down time (i.e., the monitor and the CPU) and supplying power only to keep the OS and programs paused in memory.

Another energy-saving mode is *hibernation*, where the contents of memory are quickly saved to the hard disk, and the computer is shut down completely. Then, when it boots up again, it restores the memory from the hard disk and picks up where it left off.

Hibernation is one of the most common tricks used for getting a car PC to boot a bit quicker. Most PCs can be configured to hibernate when the power button is pressed, instead of shutting down. This can cut boot times down to 30 seconds or so, but awakening from hibernation still takes a long time because hundreds of megabytes of memory have to be refilled—and the more memory you have, the more Windows will fill, and thus the longer it will take to restore. A trick for quicker hibernation wake-ups is to reduce the amount of RAM to the minimum you really need.

Breaking It Down

It isn't just the operating system that contributes to boot time. The BIOS power-on self-test (POST) and device detection, the hard drive spin up, and the boot loader delays are all factors, not to mention the multi-second delays added by startup/shutdown controllers [Hack #43] in an attempt to stabilize the car power.

Figure 4-11 breaks down the boot process into all the steps, from turning the key to hearing the audio resume where it left off when the computer last shut down.

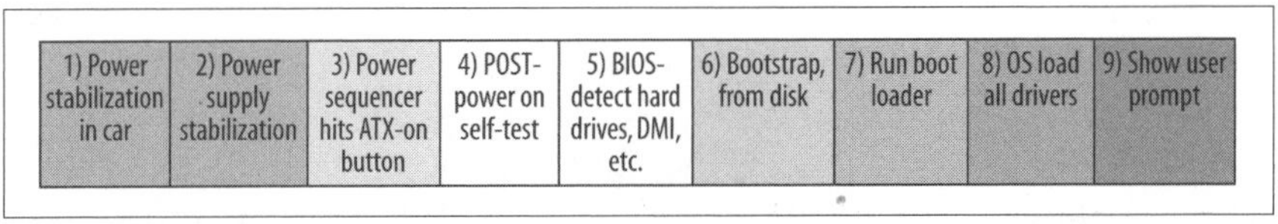

1) Power stabilization in car	2) Power supply stabilization	3) Power sequencer hits ATX-on button	4) POST-power on self-test	5) BIOS-detect hard drives, DMI, etc.	6) Bootstrap, from disk	7) Run boot loader	8) OS load all drivers	9) Show user prompt

Figure 4-11. The steps of an in-car computer boot process

Stabilizing power. The power stabilization step is just how long it takes for the voltage to level out in the car. When you start to crank the engine, the 12–14V suddenly drops to 8V or lower. Your computer's startup process will be reset unless its power supply can deal with this much of a voltage drop. "Keep Your Computer on During Engine Cranking" [Hack #45] discusses how to alleviate this problem. You're pretty much stuck with the delays built into your chosen hardware and power supplies, but having a good alternator and a good strong battery can save a little time.

Once the power has stabilized in both the car and the power supply, whatever on/off circuit you are using will "press" the power switch to turn on the computer. The computer's POST takes a few seconds at a minimum, just to test the memory. If you're adventurous you can actually replace the computer's BIOS (*http://sourceforge.net/projects/freebios*) to reduce the boot time, but normally you'll only be able to optimize the BIOS by changing settings, as outlined next.

Optimizing the BIOS settings. There are several simple setting changes that can greatly reduce boot time. For one, setting the desired boot device as the only boot option simplifies the process of looking for CD-ROMs and floppy disks to boot from. Eliminate legacy devices and settings such as floppy disks, floppy seek at boot, the floppy controller, and any other setting having to do with floppy disks to prevent hardware detection delays. Definitely disable any LAN boot, as this is useful only when booting from a server (i.e., quite useless for a car PC). Set the BIOS error setting on the main page to not stop on any errors—you want the car PC to boot even if no keyboard is attached.

Whether you are using Linux or Windows, you can gain time by disabling onboard devices. If you aren't using the onboard Ethernet for anything, disable it. If you aren't using serial ports or parallel ports, disable those as well. Every device that must be auto-detected and configured takes a few milliseconds to a few seconds. If you aren't using the second IDE channel for hard disks, disable that—and definitely disable any unused onboard SCSI cards, as this setting consumes a lot of time during boot.

You can sometimes also disable the summary screens and graphical splash screens of the BIOS—although these don't add much time (if any), they add visuals you probably don't need to see in a car PC.

Optimizing boot loading. Once you have trimmed down the BIOS, you should have a computer that hits the boot loader screen within a few seconds. Many boot loaders for either Linux or Windows sit there for several seconds to give you the option of pressing keys to change the booting process. Since your car computer system is supposed to boot the same way each time, you can disable these options—you want the OS to start booting immediately. Depending on the boot loader, this change can save another two or more seconds in the boot process.

Trimming the operating system. If you are going to rely on hibernation to decrease your boot times, you need to actually reduce your total system memory. Counterintuitive as it is, less memory makes for faster resumption from hibernation. The more memory there is, the more the operating system uses, and thus the more "stuff" there is in memory that must be saved to disk and later restored. Since the multitasking demands of a car PC can be less than those of a desktop, you should be able to get by with less memory than you might think—even 128 MB might be sufficient.

If you are going to do a full OS boot instead of restoring from hibernation, however, you should trim down services and disable anything not needed that tries to find and dynamically configure devices. While this is fairly easy to do on Linux, Windows has less granular control over the boot process.

An excellent reference for optimizing boot times on Windows XP, titled "Beginners Guides: 99 Performance Tips for Windows XP," is located at *http://www.pcstats.com/articleview.cfm?articleid=1590*.

Optimizing Linux can vary by distribution, but the complete configurability of the sequence of boot processes offers many more options than Windows for tuning the system. An article I wrote, "Reducing Boot Times in Linux" (available at *http://www.linuxjournal.com/article.php?sid=7594*), summarizes several of these options.

Giving the user something to see and hear. One of the ways to make a user interface appear to be "working" is to make sure that video is on the screen and sound is coming out of the speakers. The Windows boot loader normally briefly shows the Windows 98 or Windows XP screen. If you're working with Linux, with either the GRUB or LILO boot loaders, you can get a splash screen up almost instantly, and it can show animation throughout the boot process. You can find GRUB and LILO boot resources at *http://ruslug.rutgers.edu/~mcgrof/grub-images/* and *http://www.gamers.org/~quinet/lilo/help.html*, respectively.

In Linux, if you load the sound drivers early on in the boot process, you can activate a "splash sound" to let the user know that the car PC is booting. You can even put your MP3 player as an extremely early-running service, so that MP3 playback from the last-known position in the playlist resumes before the rest of the software (for instance, an X Windows environment) boots. (However, if you run a new GUI MP3 player, once the GUI boots it will interrupt that command-line MP3 player.)

More Hardware Approaches

After doing everything possible to the software, you'll still be stuck at 20–30 seconds for booting up. How do you get it down from there? If you are willing to try a brute-force solution, there's some more hardware you can throw at the problem.

Using faster hard drives. The 2.5" IDE drives that come in many in-car computers and laptops are usually 4,200- or 5,400-RPM drives. You can upgrade to a 7,200-RPM drive in the laptop form factor, such as the Hitachi Travelstar 7K60. You can also use 3.5" drives, and get a 10,000-RPM drive such as a Western Digital Raptor WD740GD. But these faster hard drives are power hungry, so why not go for a solid-state solution? You can get a multi-gigabyte drive such as M-Systems's (*http://www.m-systems.com*) Fast Flash Disk (FFD) 2.5" Ultra ATA or BitMicro's (*http://www.bitmicro.com*) E-Disk. Designed for use in fighter planes, these drives essentially eliminate seek times, reducing them to microseconds. Of course, be prepared for sticker shock—solid-state hard drives can be hundreds of times costlier per megabyte than mechanical hard drives.

Starting the computer earlier. Another way to "reduce" the boot time is to have the computer already on when you get to your car.

Why should the computer start booting only when you turn the key? One user read an article I wrote and suggested that the car PC should start booting as soon as you open the car door. Another approach is to start the computer with your remote keyless entry system [Hack #46].

But why wait until you're near your car? If you drive on a schedule, there's no reason not to boot your car PC minutes *before* you get to your car, with your email and traffic information already downloaded and your music queued up. You can set up this solution using "Boot Your Car Computer on a Schedule" [Hack #47].

Note that these "early-bird" booting approaches only work if your computer can stay on during engine cranking [Hack #45].

HACK #45 Keep Your Computer on During Engine Cranking

An already booted car PC will reboot whenever you start the car, unless you install the right hardware.

The primary reason cars have large batteries is to turn the starter engine and start the car. When you crank the engine to start the car, the voltage drops—from the normal 12–14V, it can drop all the way to 7V or lower. As soon as the car is started, the voltage goes back up, but in the meantime, your unprotected car PC will hang or reboot.

In many cars, the turning of the ignition switch temporarily cuts power to the radio, the headlights, and the A/C—turn your car on to see if it does this. If so, the other problem that occurs is that the 12V line going to your computer is *completely* cut off during engine cranking, and your computer shuts down immediately.

After you've made sure that the 12V line to your car PC **[Hack #11]** doesn't get switched off when cranking the engine, you then have to figure out how to stabilize it.

Stabilizing the Voltage

There are a couple of ways to solve this problem, but they all boil down to keeping the voltage to the computer level while the car's voltage fluctuates. Normal voltage regulators are designed to level out small fluctuations in the input voltage, not massive brownouts like those caused by engine cranking. To survive it, you need devices that can maintain 12V for as long as it takes to start the engine.

Adding a second battery. "Add a Second Car Battery" **[Hack #10]** provides the technical instructions you need on how to set up a car with two different batteries. Figure 4-12 shows how you can run your car PC off the second battery, turning it on either with its own power switch or with a power sequencer connected to the car's ignition. Doing this ensures that your car PC is unmolested by the power fluctuations in the primary battery.

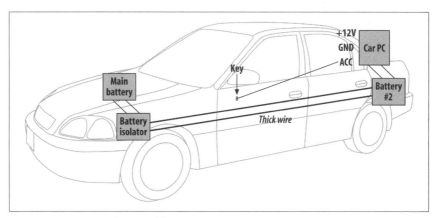

Figure 4-12. Wiring of a second battery

Adding a small 12V battery. Another, less drastic approach is to get a small 12V battery, rated at around 1–2 Ah, and use it as a voltage stabilizer, as shown in Figure 4-13. You can find these batteries at an electronic surplus store or any larger electronic hobbyist store. Make sure the battery you purchase is *deep cycle*, so that you can completely discharge it without killing it. You need to put a *diode* (a device that only lets current go one way) in between the car's 12V line and the 12V line of the battery, so that if your car is off, the little battery doesn't try to power your accessories. The trickle current passing through it on the way to the device will charge the battery, and this may slowly drain the main battery over time. So, if you're not driving the car frequently (which recharges the main battery), you'll want to make sure the 12V line to this battery and to your computer is switched off when the car is off.

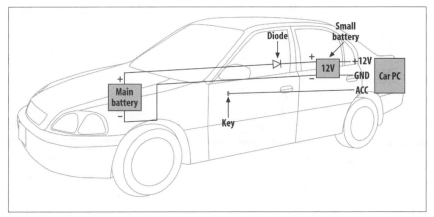

Figure 4-13. Using a smaller 12V battery

Using a crank-proof power supply. Opus Solutions, Mpegbox, and Mini-box all make power supplies that can survive engine cranking. Each of these power supplies has its own power range, and they are getting better all the time.

Opus Solutions's (*http://www.opussolutions.com*) 150W power supply, which leads the bunch, can deal with input voltages ranging from 7.5V to 18V. Mpegbox (*http://www.mpegbox.net*) makes a 70W power supply that can regulate to 12V voltages from 8V to 15V. Mini-box (*http://www.mini-box.com*) has recently released the M1-ATX, a 90W ATX power supply that is the smallest and, at $80, the cheapest fully crank-proof power supply.

Carnetix (*http://www.carnetix.com*) don't make a power supply, but they make an external power regulator and startup controller [Hack #43] to supply crank-proof 12V to any non-crank-proof power supply. It takes a battery input of +7.5VDC to +18VDC and provides a regulated +12VDC output at up to 5A. It's designed to be used with the common ITX cases (such as the Casetronic C-134 case) with their own internal power supplies (which require regulated 12V input) and to replace the external conventional AC/DC power brick with one that's DC/DC.

Although Morex (*http://www.morexintl.com*) manufactures 60W and 80W power supplies rated to survive voltages from 9–16V, they are *not* crank-proof. Their "Car Power Kit" power supplies are intended for automotive applications, but they have not worked in my extensive testing, and I do not recommend them.

For a full rundown on the power supplies, check out "Power Your Car PC" [Hack #42].

Using a big capacitor. "Use a Huge Capacitor to Sustain Power" [Hack #8] describes how a large capacitor can help deliver consistent high-amperage output to bass speakers. Capacitors are designed to keep the car lights from dimming when your amplifiers are pumping out sound. If you're already installing a large farad capacitor for your audio system, check if it lets your computer stay on when you start the car. You have to ensure, however, that the input to the capacitor doesn't turn off when the car is cranking (i.e., that the car's battery connects directly to the capacitor).

HACK #46 Turn On Your Car Computer Before You Start Your Car

Most cars today come with keyless entry systems that can be used to turn on your car PC remotely.

"Reduce the Boot Time of Your in-Car Computer" [Hack #44] suggested that one way to reduce the perceived boot time of your car PC is to have it boot when you open the car door. This way, by the time you get the engine started, the computer is fully booted and waiting for your commands.

When you open your car door, the dome light usually comes on. This behavior is controlled by a small plunger between the car door hinges in the frame of the car itself. It turns off when the car door is closed and on when it is open.

Opening the door causes 12V to activate somewhere in the system. This 12V may not be directly connected to the dome light—for instance, it may trigger some computer that turns on the dome light for a while. Regardless, you can simply use the door opening or dome light 12V signal as a "start" command for the startup controller you selected in "Start Up and Shut Down Your Car PC" [Hack #43], by running a wire from the door button or dome light to the ACC/KEY input on your startup controller. Figure 4-14 shows how this works.

The door opening or dome light turning on will cause the computer to start booting. Depending on your startup controller, you will then have a short

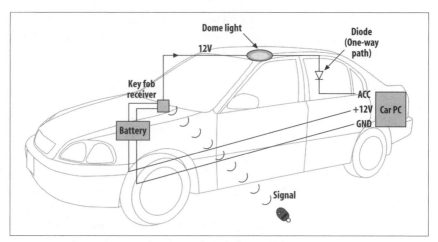

Figure 4-14. Booting up your computer using the dome light switch

while (from 45 seconds to a couple of minutes) to bring the ACC/KEY line *high* (up to 12V) again after the door is closed or the dome light goes back off. As long as you start your car, or at least turn the key to the accessory position, in this time window, the startup controller will remain on and the computer will continue to receive power, and thus the computer will finish booting without interruption.

If you start blending different 12V trigger inputs to the car PC, such as dome light and ACC, you *must* use a diode between each input and the startup controller to ensure the voltages don't "backwash." Otherwise, the dome light may come on whenever the car is on, or the car radio may try to power up whenever the door opens. Figure 4-15 shows how you can do this.

Once you've completed these steps, your car PC will start to boot the instant a door is opened, because the dome light will go on, which will also make the startup controller think that the car has turned on.

For many cars, using a remote keyless entry device ("key fob") to unlock the doors also activates the dome light, so using such a device may have the side effect of giving you remote activation. As long as you get to the car before your dome light goes out again, you won't lose power to your computer. (The light is usually on a timer, and it will go out a little while after you activate the lock or press the remote's unlock switch.)

You might want your car computer to go on only if you *unlock* your car. This is almost as straightforward; you need to find a wire that goes to 12V when the car is unlocked. A Chilton's or other shop manual for your car will provide you with wiring diagrams. Although cars vary, the harness of wires going to the driver's door will contain the wire you need. The wire

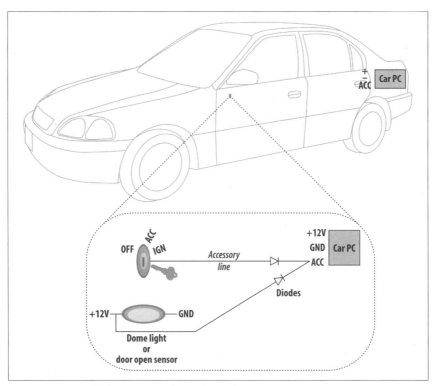

Figure 4-15. Use diodes to ensure that voltages don't mix

that actually triggers the unlock will most likely be 12V, and you will find it running to a small unlocking motor if you pull the panel off your door.

But, if you are using a momentary 12V pulse such as the unlock signal to activate your PC, you need to ensure that the pulse is long enough to turn on the power supply, and that your startup controller doesn't immediately shut the computer back down when the pulse is over. The Opus power supply (described in both "Power Your Car PC" [Hack #42] and "Start Up and Shut Down Your Car PC" [Hack #43]) has the ability to wait up to one hour *after* the ACC/KEY line goes down before it tries to shut down the PC, so it is good for this application. Even better, the P1260 and P1280 startup regulators from Carnetix (*http://www.carnetix.com*), also described in "Start Up and Shut Down Your Car PC" [Hack #43], have this "Pulse Start" feature built in, and they are designed to allow you to power up your car PC with momentary door lock, car alarm, or wireless device triggers.

Another option for remote booting is to purchase a remote car starter that has buttons to turn on the car, roll down the windows, open the trunk, and so on. (For more information, Google "remote start.") If you want a dedicated "turn on my computer" button, you can use one of the remote car starter's unused switches for this task. If you configure your startup/shutdown controller to boot up the computer and leave it on for a while after it is triggered, you can tie it to any one of the 12V pulses from a remote starter.

Some aftermarket remotes have extended ranges, allowing you to turn on the car PC from very far away (e.g., 1,000 feet).

See Also

- "Transfer Data to and from Your Car PC" [Hack #64]

HACK #47 Boot Your Car Computer on a Schedule

To get your in-car computer to do work when the car isn't on, you'll need to get it booting on a schedule.

OnStar, a service that comes preinstalled with certain U.S. vehicles, allows you to call a live person over a hands-free cellular connection to obtain a variety of concierge services, such as reservations, directions, and roadside assistance. One of the features of the OnStar computer is that, if you get locked out of your car, you can call them, and within 10 minutes they can unlock your car by sending a code to your OnStar system. You have to wait 10 minutes because this is how often the OnStar computer turns on to "phone home," making itself available to the OnStar mother ship through a cellular network.

"Phone home" is only one of the important features that can be enabled by periodic wakeups. You could configure your in-car computer to take time-lapse photographs of the parking lot with an attached camera, or to pull down traffic information from an online traffic web site (using your web browser's timed web site retrieval) so that it's there when you get in the car before and after work. Or you might want it to sync up every night with a directory on your home computer (using file synchronization software) over a wireless connection, in order to download music, videos, or other data.

Computer BIOS Wakeup

Most computer BIOS settings include the ability to wake up on a schedule. The feature is designed for client/server machines that must perform periodic tasks but may not be powered on when the tasks are due. This is great if you want a computer to turn on at 2 A.M., dial your other office, and perform one or more tasks, or if you want to push software updates to hundreds of machines in the middle of the night.

There are even utilities to set the wakeup time. On Linux, using tools such as NVRAM wakeup (*http://sourceforge.net/projects/nvram-wakeup*) or Wakeup

Clock (*http://www.malloc.de/tools/wakeup_clock.html*), you can program your computer to wake up every hour (or whenever you need) by using a cron job or scheduled task that shuts down the PC but sets the wakeup time before it goes down.

On Windows, utilities such as PowrClik (*http://genntt.webs.com.ua*) allow you to set scheduled wakeups and run Visual Basic scripts and command-line programs.

Problems with timed wakeup. The problems with using timed wakeups in a car are twofold. First, each of these wakeups uses a lot of power, even if the computer only wakes up and shuts down within a span of two minutes. While not as taxing as starting your car, these startup/shutdown sequences take their toll on the battery, especially if the vehicle is only driven every few days or on weekends. Second, the car computer requires something called "standby power"—that is, the computer must still be plugged into a live source of power for periodic wakeups to function, and this means it is constantly drawing small amounts of power.

The OnStar computer is a small, low-power, embedded computer that takes only as much power as a car alarm. A desktop computer, even when powered off, can draw 10 times that power. In a wall-power setting, this tiny trickle of current is no problem. In a car, however, supplying this 300 mA of current is the equivalent of leaving your dome light on—after a couple of days or a week it can kill the car battery.

Using a second battery. The simplest approach to letting your computer wake up on a schedule is to allocate the power for it. If you install a second deep-cycle battery **[Hack #10]**, there is no risk of killing your main battery. Since a deep-cycle battery doesn't mind being completely discharged, there's no problem if you don't drive for a week and your computer drains it. And because the standby power for a PC (around 300 mA) is much, much lower than the rated output of the battery, you should be able to get weeks of standby power without discharging the battery too much—perfect for scheduling your car PC to record a radio program for you while you're on vacation.

Using a startup controller. Most of the startup/shutdown controllers described in "Start Up and Shut Down Your Car PC" **[Hack #43]** cut power completely from the car computer when the car is turned off. While this is good for the battery, it essentially precludes the PC from waking up on its own because it has no standby power.

However, the startup controller I like the best, the ITPS (*http://www.mini-box.com/itps.htm*), can be reprogrammed. Why would you want to do this?

Well, when you turn off your car and go into your house or office, you may want your computer to stay on for another 30 minutes so you can copy files to its WiFi connection [Hack #64], for instance. iTuner Networks even provides the source code to the microcontroller they use, a 12-series PIC chip. You can download the source code at *http://www.mini-box.com/ITPS/itps3.zip* and reprogram it to suit your needs. You'll need a PIC chip writer, but these can be purchased for under $50 (Google "PIC programmer").

Using the ITPS, my own company, CarBot (*http://www.carbotpc.com*), has tried to solve the problem of starting car computers on a schedule. At CarBot, we wanted a way to have a car computer start up every couple of hours so we could periodically check email and download of new versions of the software.

We also wanted the computer, not the ITPS, to be in charge of when to shut down. Ordinarily, the ITPS has two wires, both of which connect to the power switch on the computer. Since we use a 10uF capacitor across the power switch to automatically start up the computer when power is applied. [Hack #43], we decided to repurpose the two pins on the ITPS (both of which go directly to pins on the 12-series PIC chip). You can get the source code for our PIC modification at *http://www.oreilly.com/catalog/carpchks*.

We use one of the pins for output, and one for input. The output pin is wired directly to the carrier detect pin (pin 1) of the onboard COM2, and the status of the ACC line (whether the car's ignition is on) is sent to the computer. That way, when the car is turned off, the computer knows about it—but then it's up to the *computer* to determine how long to stay on. The input pin is wired to a 5V line on the motherboard audio header. This allows the ITPS to monitor when the computer is on. When the computer finally turns off, the ITPS then cuts the power to the motherboard. This drops the power consumption from the 1.5–2A that a normal EPIA-M board takes when running with a laptop hard drive, or 300 mA when turned off, down to the 10–30 mA trickle of current that the ITPS consumes. The ITPS then continues to wait until the car turns on again, and when the power comes back, the motherboard starts up again.

HACK #48   Choose an in-Car PC Software Platform

You can use any major operating system for your in-car PC. Here are a few pointers to help you decide.

The major choices for an in-car operating system are the same as for a desktop: Windows, Linux, and, if you "think different," Mac OS X. The primary deciding factors are what software you want to run, what hardware you want to run it on, and of course what system is easiest for *you* to work with.

Windows

Windows XP is your most flexible choice in terms of hardware and software support. Though you can run older versions of Windows, such as Windows 2000 or Windows 98, most of the car computer application development occurs on XP.

Windows tends to have support for the latest multimedia features. I know that sounds very buzzwordy, but it isn't intended to be; it merely means that you get the best driver support, both hardware and software, when using the latest version of the Windows OS. If you're trying to run the latest DVD software with surround sound, a handful of video game emulators, and some 3D games, as well as supporting a number of USB networking, storage, and input devices, you'll have the smoothest experience if you run XP.

One of the drawbacks of Windows XP is the way it handles new hardware. If you so much as change the USB port of a network device, GPS unit, or other similar device, Windows acts as if it has never seen that hardware before. It pops up dialogs asking you to find the driver (even though it knows full well where the driver is), and then it creates a completely unconfigured "new" entry for the device in its hardware list. This has the frustrating result of changing the COM port of your GPS unit, or resetting the "connect to non-preferred networks" setting of a USB network card, making your GPS and networking stop working until you reconfigure them in the Windows control panel.

Another Windows choice is Microsoft's *embedded* operating system, Windows CE. Embedded operating systems are designed to run on appliances and other special-purpose computers. The BMW 7 Series uses this OS in its navigation computer, and the Windows automotive group (*http://www. microsoft.com/automotive/windowsautomotive*) is trying to get this OS into new vehicles from other manufacturers. Windows CE also powers the Pocket PC computing platform, which has gained market share over the Palm Pilot after half a decade of fierce fighting. But while you can install applications on a Pocket PC, Windows CE alone isn't sold directly to end consumers. Embedded operating systems expect to be configured with only the necessary drivers and software, burned onto a flash disk, and run for years without any changes. While this ultra-reliability is important for an OS that might be communicating with the engine computer, it's very uninteresting for those of us who want to hack new functionality into our cars on a regular basis.

Windows runs only on *x86* instruction set processors, which include Intel, AMD, and VIA Eden processors. Intel's own market-leading Pentium 4 processors get notoriously hot—not an ideal condition for an in-car computer.

But recently, VIA and Intel itself (with the Pentium M) have begun to make hardware that consumes tens of watts, not hundreds. While the "real" in-car computers that auto manufacturers preinstall in their cars are unlikely to ever be x86 processors (or to run Windows XP or its successors), Windows is still one of the strongest options for in-car entertainment computing.

There are actually several different editions of Windows XP suitable for in-car computing: Home, Professional, Media Center Edition 2005, and Embedded. Windows XP Home edition is the cheapest, at less than $100 for the OEM (Original Equipment Manufacturer) version. You can buy an OEM version of Windows when you purchase computer hardware such as a motherboard or processor, as opposed to the *retail* version, which upgrades your existing operating system. Windows XP Home has almost everything you need for car PC computing (despite the irony of its name), but it lacks one must-have feature found in Windows XP Pro: Remote Desktop. When that feature is enabled, you can log into your computer remotely (say, when you go into the house after parking your car) and see the full screen, enabling you to control and configure things, run programs remotely, and so on. While there are many other remote desktop services that you can install (including VNC, at *http://www.realvnc.com*), the one built into XP Pro is probably the most bandwidth-efficient version you can get.

Windows XP Media Center Edition 2005 is essentially Windows XP Pro with a special media player application, and for an additional $30 you can get an infrared remote control designed for it. Like the OEM version of XP Home, you can purchase this in conjunction with just a minimum amount of computer hardware from a licensed vendor. Media Center can play MP3/WMA (Windows Media Audio) collections and WMV (Windows Media Video), but not DVDs—for that, you need a separate DVD player plug-in or application. It also can control a radio or TV tuner if you have the correct hardware (check out *http://www.microsoft.com/windowsxp/mediacenter* for more info). Since it is designed to be used with a remote and not a keyboard, it is a decent option for rear-seat entertainment, although you will find that most dedicated in-car computer frontend software has far more features.

The final version of Windows XP that I recommend for in-car computing is XP Embedded. This version of the OS is designed to work on embedded (dedicated-purpose) computers, not as a general-purpose computing OS. It is purchasable only from Microsoft's embedded licensing companies, such as Bsquare (*http://www.bsquare.com*), and you have to sign several license agreements to get hold of it. The license takes great pains to make sure that you don't ship XP Embedded with general office-productivity applications as a desktop OS replacement, and it has a lot of other language intended to ensure that you use it only for appliance-type computers.

Once you get through these rings of fire, in small volumes XP Embedded costs about the same as XP Home, and you get a lot of features you'll wish XP Home had. For instance, XP Embedded has a read-only filesystem driver that allows you to use a hard drive so that unexpected shutdowns won't corrupt the drive [Hack #49]. Another cool feature of XP Embedded is that you can throw away all the features you don't want—*really*. It's as if you were given a bag of all the thousands of drivers in XP Home/Pro and told, "Have it your way." The learning curve on XP Embedded is high; it's designed for system integrators, not car PC nuts. But the results of customization can be vastly reduced boot times; exact control over startup activities and their sequence; and the ability to make bootable, very small footprint XP drives. A reasonably capable XP Embedded *image* (all the files that boot XP) can be squeezed onto a small flash drive. "Install Windows on a CompactFlash Card" [Hack #49] goes into more detail on using XP Embedded.

Information on a nice selection of in-car frontend software for Windows can be found in the MP3Car.com forums under Mp3Car Technical, Software & Software Development, as well as in Chapter 7 of this book.

Linux

Linux runs a strong second to Windows in terms of versatile in-car multimedia support. Linux has strong hardware support for all the popular hardware peripherals useful in a car, such as wireless remotes, video capture cards, and networking peripherals. Plus, Linux is much more easily customizable than Windows XP. Taking out unneeded drivers and resources is as simple as editing a few text files, and advice abounds on the Net on how to make a good Linux box do all sorts of things.

The drawback with Linux is that it requires familiarity. If you aren't a command-line edit-config-files type of person, and aren't willing to learn, Linux can be a rough road for you. However, Linux will ultimately get you the most bang for your buck—your computer will boot faster, react more responsively, and act more predictably between boots than it will with Windows XP. Linux's graphical user interfaces, to date, lack most of the "helpful" wizards that pop up demanding explanation of new networks, devices, updates, and how much disk space you have left. Although these bells and whistles are arguably useful for a desktop user, they are a hassle to deal with when you don't have a keyboard or mouse, and they disturb the experience of an in-car computer user.

The major strength of Linux is its command-line and scripting capabilities. Just about every scripting language runs on Linux, and almost everything you would want to do can be done from a command line. This comes in quite handy when you don't want to write a full-blown program, but you want to, for example, quickly make a nice button on the screen that the driver can press to instantly play a DVD on the car's second screen (for instance, with MPlayer, available at *http://www.mplayerhq.hu*).

It's perhaps somewhat unfair to describe Linux only in terms of how it differs from or is better than Windows, but the common wisdom of the desktop world applies here as well: Linux is more open, more configurable, and arguably better for programmers, but it has fewer available applications. While there are dozens of navigation and car PC frontends for Windows, only a small selection is available for Linux. SourceForge is a good place to look for projects.

An excellent, full-featured, open source in-car PC project for Linux can be found at Dashwerks (*http://www.dashwerks.com*); the SourceForge project for Dashwerks can be found at *http://sourceforge.net/project/showfiles.php?group_id=43989*.

Another Linux-based car PC frontend project is Headunit, found at *http://sourceforge.net/projects/headunit*. You can find more information about it at the MP3Car web site (*http://www.mp3car.com*).

Mac OS X

Mac OS X is a strong solution for in-car applications. It's no secret that the iPod pretty much owns the portable MP3 market, and one obvious (if overkill) way to get your iPod integrated into your car is to use a Macintosh computer running iTunes as the go-between.

OS X has fantastic multimedia support with its QuickTime architecture, and iTunes alone can be used as a dashboard jukebox with a remote control. OS X also has an integrated DVD player application that will play DVD video right off the hard drive or DVD drive, without you having to buy additional software. Almost every application on the system is accessible by the native scripting language AppleScript, and the OS has built-in speech recognition for launching commands. Thus, with a few lines of relatively painless programming, everything in the OS can be made "speakable" (i.e., respond to voice commands).

Besides the built-in apps, there are some really promising individual projects out there [Hack #53], such as Dash Mac (*http://sourceforge.net/projects/dashmac*) and iDash (*http://sourceforge.net/projects/idash*).

A good resource for Mac car PC software is *http://carmac.acmelab.org*. Along with iTunes frontends, they have a number of more advanced projects and general discussions. But the biggest reason to switch to a Mac for in-car computing is the new Mac Mini, which is described in "Choose an in-Car PC Hardware Platform" [Hack #41] and installed in "Install a Mac Mini in Your Car" [Hack #54]

DOS and Other Operating Systems

Depending on the hardware you're using, DOS may be a viable OS choice for you. DOS, including the simple DOS that comes with Windows 95, 98, or ME, is by far the fastest-booting OS on Intel hardware. Using an MP3 player such as DAMP (*http://www.damp-mp3.co.uk*), you can get your music playing mere seconds after you start your computer, instead of a minute later, as with modern bloated GUI OSs.

DOS also runs on very old hardware. If you have an old Pentium or AMD processor, for instance, you can *underclock* it (say, run a 500-MHz chip at 300 MHz or a 200-MHz chip at 133 MHz). Underclocking will reduce the processing power and thus the amount of heat generated. Since you only really need a 90-MHz (or faster) Pentium to play back MP3s, underclocking can let you build a simple media computer that draws small amounts of power and generates little heat.

Any other orphaned OS that still has an online community can be adapted for in-car use, as long as you can get it to talk to whatever touchscreen, remote control, or other user-interface device you want to use. If you just want to have a fixed menu of options (say, music, videos, and some games) and you can develop a simple menu for your computer, there's no good reason not to, and you may get some brief Internet notoriety when you post screenshots of the only BeOS or OS2/Warp in-car computer system out there.

HACK #49 Install Windows on a CompactFlash Card

Microsoft's XP Embedded OS can help you do what XP normally can't—boot off a CompactFlash card.

The car PC community is constantly searching for hardware and software solutions to improve the system's boot speed and reliability and reduce the physical size of the computer. One of these solutions is to build a system that boots off a *CompactFlash* (CF) drive. Flash storage is used in many commercial devices because it's small, has no moving parts, uses less power than a hard drive, and holds up much better than a hard drive when exposed to vibration and extreme temperatures.

Using only a CF-to-IDE adapter (Google "CF to IDE") and any off-the-shelf CF card (Figure 4-16), flash-based systems can be built relatively easily and affordably. One of the disadvantages of using flash, however, is that due to its construction it can withstand only a limited number of writes. This is fine for digital cameras, but since operating systems like to constantly thrash around on the hard drive with temporary files and virtual memory, flash requires special support by the operating system to filter out or completely disable these writes. Many users have turned to custom versions of Linux, while Windows users have had no viable option other than Windows CE or XP Embedded.

Figure 4-16. A CompactFlash-to-IDE adapter

For those willing to try, Microsoft provides a free trial of XP Embedded (XPe) from its web site that allows developers to build a fully functional boot image that will work for 90–120 days. It takes a few tries to get it working right, but it's a very powerful tool. After spending a good amount of time playing with it and reading as much as I could about it on Microsoft's MSDN site, I decided to investigate how XPe was able to work on flash disks. Since XPe is just a componentized version of XP, I figured there was no reason why a regular XP install couldn't be made to use some of the XPe components in order to boot from a CF disk.

Microsoft provides a component called the *Enhanced Write Filter* (EWF) for developers planning to deploy their systems to a CF disk. EWF is simply a storage filter driver that can be configured to protect one or more volumes from any unwanted writes. All changes to a protected volume are filtered by EWF, which then stores them in RAM rather than writing them to the disk. Upon system shutdown or reboot, changes can be either committed to the volume or discarded. Since the volume is not written to during normal operation, the system is also more resistant to data corruption in case of a sudden power loss.

MinLogon is a component Microsoft added to XPe for devices that need quick boot times and as little overhead as possible. Normally, when an XP system is booted, an executable called WinLogon is started that performs the user login, sets the security policy settings, and runs the logon scripts. This can be a lengthy process and seriously hurt boot times. Car PC developers don't typically need this level of functionality in our systems—we just want the system to boot up as quickly as possible and start playing music like a normal radio would. MinLogon was created for just these types of devices, and coupled with EWF, you can use it to turn a regular XP install into an OS capable of quickly booting off a CF disk.

The first step in preparing a CF install is downloading the XPe trial from *http://msdn.microsoft.com/embedded/windowsxpembedded/default.aspx*. The install will create a network share on your system called *Repositories*. This is where all the XPe components are stored, and all the files I use in this hack come from this directory. The best way to experiment with this hack without corrupting your desktop system is to use machine virtualization software, such as VirtualPC (*http://www.microsoft.com/windows/virtualpc/default.mspx*) or VM-Ware (*http://www.vmware.com*). Set up your XP install and make sure you've got a way to transfer files between the virtual machine (VM) and the desktop. After I set up my system in VirtualPC, I created a second VM using a differencing drive of the first VM. This was so that if I screwed up I wouldn't have to go through the lengthy reinstall process all over again. (See the VirtualPC documentation for directions on how to set up a differencing drive.)

If you have any disk-cloning software, such as Symantec's Ghost (*http://www.symantec.com/sabu/ghost/*), you can use that too. Clone the drive you want to experiment with onto some old 1-GB drive you have lying around, and try changing that version so that you can re-clone it if you mess it up.

Setting Up MinLogon

First we'll set up MinLogon. This is an optional component—it is not necessary for running XP from a CF card, but it does improve boot time. Search the *Repositories* directory on your main hard disk for the latest version of *minlogon.exe* and transfer it to the test virtual machine or hard drive:

1. First go to the *Windows\System32* directory of your virtual machine and rename the file *winlogon.exe* to *winlogon.exe.bak*.

2. Copy the *minlogon.exe* file to the *Windows\System32* directory and rename it *winlogon.exe*.

3. If a Windows File Protection warning comes up warning you about changing the filename, just cancel the dialog to ensure that the new MinLogon file isn't replaced by Windows File Protection.

4. Next, create a text file called *minlogon.reg*. Edit the file and enter the following text:

   ```
   Windows Registry Editor Version 5.00

   [HKEY_LOCAL_MACHINE\SOFTWARE\Microsoft\Windows NT\CurrentVersion\Winlogon]
   "Config"=dword:00000017
   ```

5. Save the file and then merge it into the Registry by double-clicking on it. Double-check the Registry to make sure the entries were entered properly.

6. Reboot the system.

As long as you entered everything properly, the VM will boot into XP using the System account. The first time you boot up it will prepare the user settings for the System account, so it'll take a bit longer than usual. Once that is done, go ahead and reboot again to make sure everything is working properly. MinLogon may cause problems for some applications, so if you find that it doesn't fit your needs, just restore the original *winlogon.exe*.

Setting Up Enhanced Write Filter (EWF)

Now that MinLogon is working properly, you can go ahead and set up EWF. Before you do so, make sure you disable the paging file by right-clicking on My Computer, clicking the Advanced tab, clicking the Performance button, clicking the Change button in the Virtual Memory section, and selecting "No paging file." You'll also want to disable system restores, by right-clicking on My Computer, selecting the System Restore tab, and checking "Turn off System Restore." (These features interfere with EWF.) One bug I've found is that when booting with EWF, XP always brings up the recovery options at bootup. You can disable this by deleting the file named *bootstat.dat* in the *Windows* directory. You'll need to search the *Repositories* directory again for three files: *ewf.sys*, *ewfntldr*, and *ewfmgr.exe*. Since the directories may change with each release, make sure you search for the latest versions and place them on the VM system.

1. Rename the *ntldr* file on your root drive to *ntldr.bak*.
2. Move the *ewfntldr* file to your root drive, and rename it *ntldr*.
3. Move *ewfmgr.exe* to your *Windows\System32* folder.
4. Move *ewf.sys* to your *Windows\System32\drivers* folder.
5. Create a text file called *ewf.reg* and enter the text from Example 4-1. (You can download these files at *http://www.oreilly.com/catalog/carpchks*.)

Example 4-1. Registry entries to set up Enhanced Write Filter

```
Windows Registry Editor Version 5.00
[HKEY_LOCAL_MACHINE\SOFTWARE\Microsoft\Dfrg\BootOptimizeFunction]
"Enable"="N"
[HKEY_LOCAL_MACHINE\SOFTWARE\Microsoft\Windows\CurrentVersion\OptimalLayout]
"EnableAutoLayout"=dword:00000000
[HKEY_LOCAL_MACHINE\SYSTEM\CurrentControlSet\Control\FileSystem]
"NtfsDisableLastAccessUpdate"=dword:00000001
[HKEY_LOCAL_MACHINE\SYSTEM\CurrentControlSet\Control\Session Manager\Memory
Management\PrefetchParameters]
"EnablePrefetcher"=dword:00000000
[HKEY_LOCAL_MACHINE\SYSTEM\CurrentControlSet\Control\Session Manager]
BootExecute=""
[HKEY_LOCAL_MACHINE\SYSTEM\CurrentControlSet\Enum\Root\LEGACY_EWF]
"NextInstance"=dword:00000001
[HKEY_LOCAL_MACHINE\SYSTEM\CurrentControlSet\Enum\Root\LEGACY_EWF\0000]
"Service"="EWF"
"Legacy"=dword:00000001
"ConfigFlags"=dword:00000020
"Class"="LegacyDriver"
"ClassGUID"="{8ECC055D-047F-11D1-A537-0000F8753ED1}"
"DeviceDesc"="EWF"
"Capabilities"=dword:00000000
[HKEY_LOCAL_MACHINE\SYSTEM\CurrentControlSet\Enum\Root\LEGACY_EWF\0000\Control]
"ActiveService"="EWF"
[HKEY_LOCAL_MACHINE\SYSTEM\CurrentControlSet\Services\ewf]
"ErrorControl"=dword:00000001
"Group"="System Bus Extender"
"Start"=dword:00000000
"Type"=dword:00000001
[HKEY_LOCAL_MACHINE\SYSTEM\CurrentControlSet\Control\Class\{71A27CDD-812A-11D0-
BEC7-08002BE2092F}]
"UpperFilters"="Ewf"
[HKEY_LOCAL_MACHINE\SYSTEM\CurrentControlSet\Services\ewf\Parameters\Protected\
Volume0]
"Type"=dword:00000001
"ArcName"="multi(0)disk(0)rdisk(0)partition(1)"
```

6. Save the file. Before you merge it, you need to alter the permissions on one Registry key. In *regedit*, navigate to HKEY_LOCAL_MACHINE\SYSTEM\CurrentControlSet\Enum\Root. Right-click on Root and click Permissions. Set "Everyone" to have Full Control, and then merge the file by

double-clicking on it. As you did for MinLogon, ensure that all the values were entered properly, and then reset the Root key permissions to the way they were before.

7. Reboot the system.

Pay special attention to the last entry, ArcName. That points to the volume you want protected. This script will default to the first partition of the master drive on the primary IDE controller, so as long as you have your CF card set as the master drive on the primary IDE controller you'll be fine.

The first few entries are optimizations for EWF-enabled systems. To minimize disk writes, we've disabled automatic defragmentation and prefetch. I also included a tweak to disable the NTFS last-access file timestamp. If you use NTFS on your system, you don't want the OS constantly updating timestamps for files you access and creating unnecessary disk writes.

Once the system boots, pull up a command line and run **ewfmgr** *n*:, where *n* is the letter of the protected drive (typically "c"). The output should be similar to this:

```
Protected Volume Configuration
   Type            RAM (REG)
   State           ENABLED
   Boot Command    NO_CMD
     Param1        0
     Param2        0
   Volume ID       87 0B 88 0B 00 7E 00 00 00 00 00 00 00 00 00 00
   Device Name     "\Device\HarddiskVolume1" [C:]
   Max Levels      1
   Clump Size      512
   Current Level   1
     Memory used for data 1294336 bytes
   Memory used for mapping 4096 bytes
```

If instead you get an error stating that no EWF volume could be found, pull up the Registry Editor and recheck your settings, make sure that *ewf.sys* is in the *System32\drivers* directory, unplug any other hard drives, and restart.

ewfmgr gives you some important information about your protected volume and tells you how much RAM your overlay is taking up. That's an important factor to keep in mind: the more changes you make to your protected volume, the more RAM it'll take up, until you finally run out of memory. So be careful what you do to your system with EWF running.

Here are two important commands to remember:

```
C:\ ewfmgr c: -commitanddisable –live
```

This will immediately disable EWF and commit all changes to the volume.

And this command will enable EWF on the next bootup:

```
C:\ ewfmgr c: -enable
```

The typical process for making persistent changes to your volume is to run the `commitanddisable` command, make your changes, run the `enable` command, and restart.

Another useful feature for car PC systems is what Microsoft calls "Hibernate Once, Resume Many" (HORM). If you have hibernation support enabled in your system, this basically allows you to hibernate your system once, and then always resume from that same hibernation state every time you boot up. This minimizes writes to the CF card and improves boot and shutdown times. All it takes is a simple file called *resmany.dat* on the root of your drive. Just create an empty text file and name it *resmany.dat*. When this file is present on the root drive, the EWF NTLDR knows not to reset the hibernation file as it normally would; thus, you never have to re-hibernate, unless you specifically request it. If you decide you don't want to resume from hibernation, just hit F8 while the system is booting to delete the restoration data and boot up normally.

The hibernation process bypasses EWF, so there's no need to disable EWF before you hibernate. However, make sure to disable EWF when you create the *resmany.dat* file, or it won't be written to the flash drive. (You'll then need to re-enable EWF and reboot before hibernating.) Most likely, you'll have an external drive containing your MP3s. Microsoft recommends setting the hibernation point without any other hard drives plugged into the system, because if the write cache still has data in it when you hibernate, every time you resume that data will be in the write cache and could potentially corrupt the partition. XP will automatically detect any new drives that are attached to the system, so once you set the hibernation point you can leave your drives plugged in.

Setting Up Your XP Installation

Now that you have successfully created an EWF system in a VM, you can start planning your final system. My recommendation is to first make a customized XP install, using a program such as nLite (*http://nuhi.msfn.org/nlite.html*) to remove any excess features you don't need. You want to get your XP installation as small as possible so that it can fit onto a CF card. You'll probably have to choose between a 512-MB or 1-GB card. Do some research, and try to find the fastest CF card you can afford. Keep in mind that if you plan on using hibernation, your space requirements will increase by the amount of RAM you install in the system. In other words, if your XP installation takes up 320 MB and you have a 256-MB stick of RAM, you'll use up about 576 MB of space and will need to get a 1-GB card. However, if you don't need hibernation, you can make do with a 512-MB card and save yourself some money. You'll also need to buy a CF-to-IDE adapter. Do a search on Google, and you'll find quite a few different adapters out there. Some can even plug directly into the IDE port rather than using cables, which saves space.

The best way to go about putting your XP installation on a CF card is to first set up your system on a regular hard drive. Load up all your drivers and third-party tools, make the necessary configuration changes, and of course install EWF and MinLogon. Once you're happy with the system, you need to initialize your CF card. Microsoft recommends using a FAT filesystem to improve the performance of EWF and minimize writes to the drive. Also, many retail CF cards come configured as removable drives, and as Windows XP will not allow you to partition and format a removable drive with NTFS, you must use FAT for these cards (although you can sometimes get a utility from the manufacturer to configure the CF card to appear as a *fixed*, or non-removable, drive).

XPe includes a special tool called *Bootprep.exe* that is used to enable FAT-formatted disks to boot into Windows XP. To configure a FAT-formatted CF disk to boot XP, you'll need a DOS boot disk with *fdisk.exe*, *format.com*, and *bootprep.exe*. Here's what to do:

1. Start by installing your CF card as the master drive on the primary controller and your hard drive on the secondary controller.

2. Boot into DOS and partition your disk, and then run the command **format c: /s**. This command formats the disk, and the /s switch copies over the DOS system files to make the CF disk bootable. Reboot, and if all goes well the system will boot into DOS from the CF disk. If not, you need to check your BIOS settings.

3. Once you've confirmed that your CF card boots successfully, boot with your DOS boot disk (not the CF card) and reformat the card by using the command **format c:** (without the /s switch). Then use the **bootprep /dc** command (the /d switch specifies which drive to use) to run Bootprep.

If you are using NTFS, simply use Windows Disk Management to partition the drive and format it.

Now you are ready to copy over your XP install. Since Windows won't allow copying of files from the currently running OS instance, you need to boot into another OS, or attach both the hard drive and the CF card to another machine. Use whatever method you prefer, whether it's booting into Knoppix, DOS, or another XP installation. Just make sure that whichever method you use, it copies all hidden and system files and keeps the file attributes (hidden, read-only, archived, and so on) intact.

Once the transfer is done, connect your CF card to your system, remove all other hard drives, and boot up. As long as all the files were copied over properly, the system will start booting into your XP install, just as it did from the hard drive. Once the system boots up, take a look around and make sure everything is working right. Bring up a console by running **cmd** from the Start menu, and check that EWF is running.

With your system now running on a CF card, you have a small, fast, and reliable installation of XP to use for your car PC or any other small, embedded device you plan to use. I suggest you experiment a little by using the standby power function, as well as taking a look through Microsoft's MSDN site for embedded technologies (*http://msdn.microsoft.com/embedded/*) to see what tips they may have.

If you're going to be making significant changes to the system, you may want to consider doing it on the hard drive first and then redeploying to the CF disk. That way, you can clean out log files, temp directories, and any other leftover junk that'll take up precious space on your CF disk.

—Silvio Fiorito

Power Your Portable Devices in the Car

Almost any small consumer device can be run on car power, and if you can't find the right adapter you can usually make one.

There are many portable devices that can bring music to your car, but unless your device is very popular there may not be a specific car adapter for it. Nonetheless, by figuring out a few vital statistics about your device, you can adapt it to work in the car.

The main data you need to get a device working is:

Voltage
> You need to know the voltage of the device, and whether it runs on AC or DC. The ideal candidates for running on car voltage are DC and between 1.5V and 12V.

Amperage
> You need to know how much current your device wants. More amps, in general, require thicker wires and a bigger adapter. The easiest devices to power are under 1 or 2 amps.

Plug size

The common barrel plug is a cylindrical plug with an inner and an outer metal contact separated by insulating plastic. There are many sizes of these, and you need your power adapter to fit correctly in this plug.

Polarity

Polarity is simply which of the contacts in your barrel plug is positive (+) and which is negative (−). These are usually indicated by a small diagram.

Most consumer electronics devices, especially those that run on batteries, are designed to run on DC voltage in the 1.5V to 9V range. This is fortunate, because it is very easy to "step down" a car's 12V to one of these voltages. Figure 4-17 shows one such adapter from Radio Shack with a switch to select 9V, 6V, 4.5V, or 3V, depending on your device.

Figure 4-17. A 12V car multi-adapter

The second thing to determine is whether your device wants too much current. Any power adapter you purchase should specify a maximum amperage at which it will run, such as 1000 mA (1A). Any device you wish to power should have a corresponding amperage on its label, such as 800 mA. As long as the device's amperage is less than the maximum for the adapter, you can safely power the device.

Getting plug sizes right is straightforward enough. The 12V, 1A cigarette lighter adapter shown in Figure 4-17 comes with four common plugs on the end. If none of these is the one you need, however, all is not lost. You may need to buy a different plug end, or snip the plug end off the wall adapter that came with the unit and splice it onto the 12V adapter to make it work in your car (you can always splice the original wall adapter back together [Hack #4] if you keep it). If you don't want to cut your wall adapter, you should be able to find the right adapter; Radio Shack has a full collection of common adapters and wires to hook them up.

As long as you have a proper barrel plug that fits your device, the only thing you have left to worry about is respecting the *polarity* of the wires (positive to positive and negative to negative).

> You don't want to reverse the polarity (+ and – connection) of wires to your devices, even for a moment, as it can damage the devices.

There are a few rules of thumb that can help you figure out the polarity of your power supply wires, to make sure that plus goes to plus and minus goes to minus. On AC-to-DC wall adapters, the negative wire is usually black, and the positive wire is often black with a white stripe. Sometimes there is a little diagram on the device and/or the power supply, with a letter C around a dot. The outer C circle indicates the polarity (+ or –) of the outside of the barrel plug, and the inside dot signifies the polarity of the inside of the plug. The key is to make sure that the + and – going into the device are what the device expects.

The most effective way to make sure that you get the polarity right is to purchase and use a *multimeter*. Set the multimeter to the 20V range, and put one lead on the middle plug and one on the outside of the plug to the wall adapter that came with your device. It should indicate the voltage coming out of the adapter, with a plus or minus sign. Then, when you get your new power adapter wired up, do the exact same test on your new in-car power adapter. The voltage should be around the same (e.g., 5V), and the + or – polarity should be the same as it was for the wall adapter. If you do this, you'll know you've wired it up right.

Powering Hard Drives and Optical Drives

USB is notoriously bad for powering devices such as portable hard drives and DVD drives. The 500-mA limit on many USB ports and hubs is less than the 600–1000 mA needed to power a device with a spinning disk. FireWire is much more reliable with regard to bus power, and since most of the car PC motherboards of choice come with FireWire ports built in, it is a good choice for powering both CD drives [Hack #38] and portable hard drives, assuming you can use a short enough cable (less than 15'). FireWire may fail to power your devices if you use a longer (15–25') cable.

If you have a dual FireWire/USB device and you don't want to rewire a power supply for it, there is a simpler approach: connect the device to the computer via USB, then power it with 12V on the FireWire port. You can use a device such as the Griffin Powerpod (*http://www.griffintechnology.com/products/powerpod*) to supply the 12V the FireWire drive needs, even if it isn't an iPod, and then hook the drive up to the USB port connected to the computer (Figure 4-18). Only the two power pins of the six-pin FireWire cable will be used; the data will go over the USB. Note that you should *not* connect the device to the computer through both the FireWire and USB ports, as the computer will be confused about which method it should use to connect to the drive.

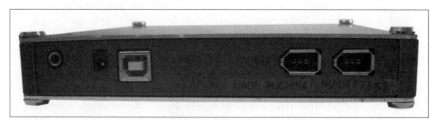

Figure 4-18. A dual FireWire/USB optical drive

See Also

- "Power Your Car PC" [Hack #42]
- "Install USB Ports in Your Car" [Hack #51]
- "Transfer Data to and from Your Car PC" [Hack #64]

HACK #51 Install USB Ports in Your Car

Installing USB ports in the front-seat area will give you the ability to easily add peripherals to your in-car PC.

Have you ever thought it would be nice if your car came with USB ports right on the dashboard? If this sort of geek chic is important to you, there are a variety of USB hubs that can fit the bill. The trick is to find a hub with a 2×2 stack of ports that is rectangular and has a narrow edge. (Your local computer store probably has dozens of USB hubs to choose from.) This will give a fabricator/installer a good unit to work with when they try to cleanly integrate it with your factory dash.

But there's no reason you must have the USB ports visible. Many vehicles have a center armrest designed to hide away CDs or other media, and this is a great place to put your USB hub. The glove compartment is another candidate, although it's a little harder for the driver to reach.

There are a couple of considerations when installing a USB hub. The primary one is power. Even with the upgraded USB 2.0 specification, every USB 2.0 self-powered hub has a 500-mA limit for each port. When the hub is bus-powered (i.e., only gets its power from the computer) that limit is lower, around 100 mA.

So, if you are going to connect a bunch of bus-powered devices, such as USB flash drives, Bluetooth adapters, flash drive readers, keyboards, and mice, you probably want to make sure that the USB hub you're installing is self-powered. Also, be sure to get a hub without an integrated USB cable. You may need to run the cable a fair distance from your computer, and integrated cables seldom have the length necessary for this.

Since USB hubs almost uniformly expect a 5V input, you're going to have to get a 12V-to-5V adapter in order to power it. At Radio Shack and elsewhere you should be able to find a cigarette lighter adapter with a variable output, like the one shown earlier in Figure 4-17. You need to run or tap into existing 12V switched or unswitched wires in the glove compartment or center armrest area, and connect these to the 12V-to-5V adapter [Hack #50]. Your best bet is to run what you need from the battery area [Hack #3].

You should probably use a switched 12V wire when powering a USB hub to make sure attached USB devices are off when your car is off. You should use unswitched wires only if you have devices that recharge off the USB port, or if for some reason you do not want the devices to lose power.

You're also going to need to run the USB cable from wherever your car computer is to wherever you're putting the hub. You'll want to lift the carpet and run the USB cable underneath so it's out of sight. You can get a 15–25' USB 2.0 cable almost anywhere computer cables are sold. I've noticed no difference in quality between the $40 gold-plated super USB 2.0 cables and the $8 store special versions.

If you're running the USB cable to the console between the front seats, your car's service manual should give you hints as to how to remove and get under the console. Depending on the vehicle, you may be able to just run the cable under the carpet and beneath the passenger seat, and then snake it into the center console from below. (Chapter 1 has more information about running wires in your car.) If you're installing the hub in the glove compartment, you can run the wires all the way to the front passenger foot area and then run it to the glove compartment through the dashboard (Figure 4-19).

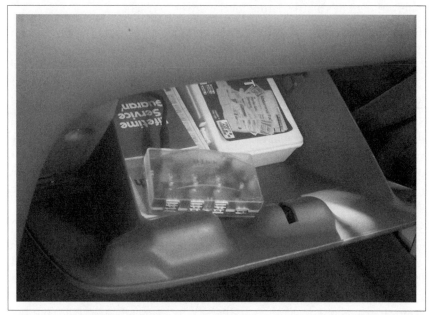

Figure 4-19. A USB hub in the glove compartment

If you know ahead of time that you are going to be using a particular higher-power device, such as an iPod or portable hard drive, it would be best to run a wire for that device now. If your hard drive takes both FireWire and USB, you're in luck—with the right wire, the FireWire portion can usually be powered straight off of the 12V.

If your drive doesn't take FireWire, that's fine too—you'll just need a second 12V-to-5V adapter to connect the drive to. However, if your USB hub's 5V barrel connector is the same as your hard drive's barrel connector, you may have a simpler option—just unplug the USB extension cable from the hub and plug it into your drive. If your USB 2.0 hard drive is designed to work on bus power (some can and some can't), there may be enough power on the bus if you disconnect the hub. If this works, you can just leave the hub there until it is needed for other devices.

Having a hub in the front is valuable in many ways. You can use it to connect keyboards and mice [Hack #55], GPS receivers, wireless remote controls [Hack #56], or Bluetooth adapters [Hack #63], just to name a few.

See Also

- "Power Your Portable Devices in the Car" [Hack #50]

Build an in-Car PC

HACK #52

Having covered all the basics, let's look at how a U.K.-based IT manager put together his car PC.

My job involves a good deal of travel, so naturally I looked into buying a satellite navigation system when I was buying a new car. But the high cost and minimal features of the factory navigation system compelled me to look at computer-based alternatives.

At first I considered using a laptop with a GPS and PC-based navigation system, but laptops are clunky copilots at best. After a lot of online research, especially on *http://www.mp3car.com*, I found that I could actually build a small PC for the car that would not only give me a navigation system, but also MP3 and DVD playback, all usable though a nice touchscreen interface. Armed with this knowledge and the cash I had saved by not opting for the factory navigation system, I began piecing together my car PC.

Choosing a Computer and Screen

To get started, I looked for a computer. Cost was a big factor here for me, and after some searching I purchased a used, preassembled 800-MHz VIA Mini-ITX system (Figure 4-20) from an online auction. The low-cost, power-efficient VIA boards [Hack #41] are by far the most popular motherboards for in-car computer use

The first version of my car PC project used an LCD composite monitor attached to the TV-out port of my video card. I thus learned that using a standard LCD TV screen (with a composite connector) will result in an unacceptably low-resolution picture for anything but watching movies. If you think using a TV for a monitor on your home PC is bad, it's even worse in the car because the screen is so small.

As far as I am concerned, the screen is the most important part of the whole system. It needs to have high enough resolution that it is readable, looks

Figure 4-20. A Mini-ITX based computer

good, and is able to cope with the resolutions needed to run computer graphical user interfaces. Lilliput's (*http://www.newision.com*) 7" touchscreen monitors [Hack #26] are by far the cheapest (less than $300) and most popular screens for in-car PC installation, so that's what I went with.

I had to do some adjustment to get the sharpest picture on my Lilliput monitor. I invested in a PCI video card with 3D capabilities and TV out, and fortunately the card I bought was compatible with a utility called TVTool (*http://tvtool.info/index_e.htm*). The Lilliput has a native resolution of 800×480 pixels, and TVTool was able to set the resolution to 800×484 or 800×480, both using the 75-Hz refresh rate. This put Windows in a true 16:9 (wide-screen) resolution and eliminated flickering on the screen. The onboard video of most VIA boards can't display 800×480, but the Lilliput can display an 800×600 image—it will just look compressed vertically, which you may be able to compensate for in your application software.

Installing and Mounting the PC and Screen

While a custom-fabricated dash installation of the screen is a very popular option, one of my goals was to have a PC that I could move from car to car. On the Lilliput units, the USB wires for the touchscreen and the VGA input are all contained in a single cable, which means that if need to I can simply unscrew the screen from the dash, unplug the cable, and quickly place the screen out of view from prying eyes.

To mount it on the dashboard I used a special mounting bracket from Dashmount (*http://www.dashmount.co.uk*) in the U.K.—the bracket needs no screws, so when I sell the car there will be no holes left in the dash. To attach the screen to the bracket itself I simply used the thumbscrew that came with the monitor, slightly drilled out the center hole of the bracket, and added some sticky rubber pads to hold the screen in position (Figure 4-21).

Figure 4-21. My touchscreen mounted to the dash

I decided to install the computer itself in the boot (that's the trunk, for all you Yanks), still keeping to the goal of minimizing the amount of modifications I made to the car (i.e., drilling holes). To wire up the computer, I needed power [Hack #42], ignition (ACC/KEY 12V), a very good ground, sound to the head unit [Hack #14], and VGA and USB extension cords. For the power I used a three-pin "Euro" mains socket and plug and a 13A main cable. I ran the power down one side of the car and the sound and video down the other, to prevent interference [Hack #17]. For the VGA, I bought a 10-foot extension cable from a computer store. Finding audio cables was easy, but I had to fabricate the USB extension cables by soldering a USB socket and plug to CAT4 networking cable.

The benefit of a trunk install is that would-be thieves are unaware of the computer's existence. However, I needed a method to stop the computer from sliding around the trunk while I was driving that didn't involve modifying the vehicle. The answer came when I was looking at my brother's new car. He was in a rush to get his stereo and amps into the car, so he had used Velcro to put them in place. This held the amp to the carpet in the back and also let him quickly remove it at night. I decided to try this myself, so I went down to the local market and bought some Velcro. Once I got it home, I laid it out on the floor in a cross and placed the CPU on top of it. Then, making sure that the plastic hooks were facing down, I measured and cut them as needed. When finished, I simply took the whole unit, with the Velcro wrapped around it, and stuck it to the carpet in the boot (Figure 4-22). Success! And although I planned to replace it with a custom-built metal case drilled into the side of the car, I have never yet had cause to change the design.

Figure 4-22. The power of Velcro

One of the questions you may be asking yourself is, "Won't the hard drive get damaged when I drive over a bump?" It's possible, but I think in the several years I have been following car computers I have only heard about this happening once or twice. Still, there are ways to minimize the possibility, two of which I have tried myself. The first is to soften the impact by placing rubber in between the hard drive and the mounts where the screw attaches to it. (I got this idea from Hewlett-Packard, who used it in some of their desktop machines that I worked on a lot a few years ago.) The second option is to use a laptop (2.5") hard drive. Although they tend to be smaller and slower, the advantage you get is that they are built to take more shock and vibration than conventional 3.5" desktop drives—and the speed of laptop hard drives today is quite sufficient to play back audio and video.

Mounting Your Car PC

Each car will pose its own challenges with regard to mounting a CPU. You have to consider ventilation, heat dissipation, access, security, removal, and what happens when you sell the car.

Facing the trunk, sedans have a nice flat seatback to which you can securely mount a 0.25" or thicker board. Any car audio shop can install the board for you if finding anchor points in the seatback proves too challenging. Measure the board to be a little bigger than your car PC, flush with all the sides except the cable side of the box. On that side, let the board extend 6". The extra space lets you secure the cables nicely for better presentation. Extend the board further if you need to mount other devices, such as power blocks or fuses. With the cover removed from the case, you can use four wood screws to penetrate the case floor (watch out for things like computer parts and wires) and mount it to the board. Using rubber feet between the case and the board can add a little vibration dampening, which will make your hard drive happier and extend its life.

Another good place for car PC installation is under the rear window, in the trunk. That deck is often made of metal, and with a few *short* screws a board can easily be fit to it. Long screws might penetrate all the way into the cabin space, and that's not a good look.

Hatchbacks are trickier, as they have fewer suitable surfaces. Depending on the size of your car PC, you may be able to wedge it behind the rear-side panels (which often house a tire jack or CD changer). You can also look in the front passenger footwell, under the dash. If the space is not overwhelmed with heating/air conditioning hardware, a small PC may fit there.

Installing your devices under a seat is a good way for them to get kicked, wet, and dusty, but this is an extremely popular option for both amplifiers and car computers. Under rear seats, heat and ventilation can be issues; however, the most popular car PCs deal with this environment just fine.

A lot of people with very customized cars use that big, inviting circle in the bottom of the trunk where a spare tire used to live. Pickup trucks often have a nice space behind the driver's seat or in an extended or crew cab, behind the back seats. That flat, tall space makes a perfect perch.

But what about the ever-present SUV or the humble minivan, with all their cubic feet of space? Unfortunately, all of that great cargo space is exposed. Finding places for a small computer in these vehicles will prove to be a little challenging. Check the usual spaces—under the passenger seats, in the rear quarters, and in the front passenger footwell—but also check right in the middle of the car. Larger SUVs often have a large center console that sits up high. There may be space under it, or in it. Alternatively, you can always create a custom box and mount it on the wall, behind the wheel wells and toward the back.

—continued—

> As there will be a different solution for every car, truck, or SUV, think creatively, and consider the materials you have and can acquire as well as the level of difficulty for each mounting place. The space you have to work with in your particular vehicle should help you decide what size and shape of computer case you purchase.
>
> —Lionel Felix

Powering the PC

After looking at the various power supply options [Hack #42], I decided to go for a highly recommended off-the-self option: the 90W supply from Opus Solutions (*http://www.opussolutions.com*). I knew that if I skimped on the power supply I could come back to my car to find it with a dead battery, or possibly even fry the machine.

Although it was slightly bigger than I expected, it was still smaller than its 150W bigger brother, and it fit very nicely in the unused hard drive bay in my Casetronic case. The Opus cost a fair bit more than many of the other options, but I felt that the extra expense was worth it because it gave me configurable shutdown options and low-battery protection for the car, as well as a clean ATX power output.

Peripherals and Controls

The primary interface for controlling the operation of my car PC is through the touchscreen and the custom skin I've made for the FrodoPlayer software [Hack #75] (Figure 4-23). I have also configured a wireless remote [Hack #56], so that my passengers can control the music playing from anywhere in the car.

Audio Connection

Once I had installed my car PC, I had to decide how I was going to connect it to my existing car audio system [Hack #14]. I tried using an FM modulator, but the sound just wasn't clear enough for me, so I purchased a Kenwood head unit (KDC-W6527) that had auxiliary audio inputs and even worked with my existing steering-wheel volume controls.

In addition to connecting my car PC to the radio, I connected a USB radio to my car PC [Hack #19]. I used the D-Link DRU100, and I installed the drivers from a program called Radiator (*http://radiator-fm.com.ru/indexuk.htm*), as they are more stable and work better with Windows XP than the ones that

Figure 4-23. My touchscreen interface

came with the DRU100. With the USB radio, I can tune radio stations and set presets via the same touchscreen interface that controls all my audio.

Networking

One of the popular solutions for getting content from your home PC into your car is WiFi [Hack #64], but this approach is much slower than good old network cable. Also, because car computers are designed to shut off soon after the car turns off (to save the car battery), if you download content via WiFi you actually have to leave your car on while your music downloads. I tried using WiFi anyway, but my house tended to absorb the WiFi signals too much. Although I could get a connection outside, when I tried to copy large amounts of data the wireless connection dropped a lot of it. To solve this problem, I installed the remote desktop program VNC (*http://www.realvnc.com*) on both the car PC and my laptop. When I need to copy content to the car PC, I simply use a crossover network cable—this solution cost me far less than buying wireless cards and a WiFi point, and it transfers the data quicker.

If you do want to connect to the Internet while you're out and about [Hack #62], you'll more than likely need a Bluetooth adapter, a Bluetooth phone, and a contract that allows you access to a GPRS data system. You may find this useful for accessing certain web-based travel data sites (such as the U.K. Traffic Master system), so you can plan your route before you leave your departure point [Hack #65]

Frontend Software

While Linux options exist, I found that most of the free frontend applications developed by and for the in-car PC community are Windows XP–based. The various car PC frontends tend to carry out the same functions, but in different ways. Most of these applications are also *skinnable*—that is, you can customize the visual look of the user interface to suit your taste. As many of them are under continuous development, I think it's a good idea to test several options before you make your choice. The main players in the freeware world that I looked at were FrodoPlayer [Hack #75] (*http://www.frodoplayer.com*) and Neocar Media Center [Hack #74] (*http://www.neocarmediacenter.com/?language=EN*) I found FrodoPlayer to offer the best options for visual customization.

After I installed all the supporting utilities, I installed FrodoPlayer and set up my preferences (such as my music and movie directories). I also placed a FrodoPlayer icon in my startup folder, so that when my PC started it would be the first application that was shown (hiding the Windows XP interface).

When choosing a skin, bear in mind that a touchscreen can be very hard to read in sunlight, so a darker skin can help the characters stand out better. I adapted one of the more well-known FrodoPlayer skins from Febsperanza (*http://febsperanza.3plast.com*), and once I'd changed the text and the "glow" of the buttons to match my dashboard color, I had an interface that looked like it came straight from the manufacturer (Figure 4-24).

GPS/Navigation

The first GPS software I used was Microsoft's AutoRoute, a quick application that supported my GPS system. Later, I switched to Destinator [Hack #71]. Destinator is one of the few PC-based systems that looks as good as factory navigation. It gives you touchscreen menus for planning your journey and excellent 3D views, just like a factory-installed system (Figure 4-25). More and more car PC applications are now supporting it.

I'm on my second GPS receiver now—my first one worked well, but it was purple and round and just didn't look good on my dash. I originally ran a single USB connection to the front of my car, with all the devices going into a nonpowered USB hub [Hack #51]. My new GPS unit is a power hog and demands more power than that USB hub could provide, though, so I ended up running a separate USB cable just for the new GPS device.

Movies and Music

Beyond navigation, the main benefit of my car PC is that I can play all of my music and digital videos in the car. I have been slowly converting all of my

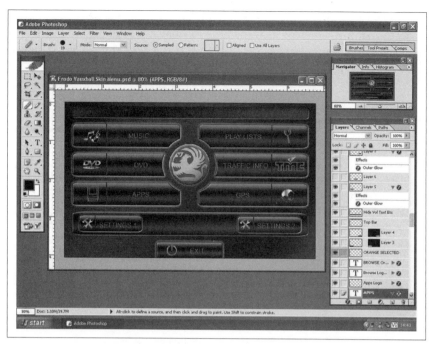

Figure 4-24. Designing my FrodoPlayer skin

Figure 4-25. Destinator's 3D navigation interface

LPs and CDs to MP3 using CDex (*http://cdexos.sourceforge.net*), and I have a collection of music videos as well. When I finally got my PC fully installed, with my entire music collection available at my fingertips, I knew it was worth all the effort.

Encoding Your Music Collection

Encoding your music collection from CD is a lengthy process that may take you months. Once you have all of the MP3/OGG/WMA files in the same place, take some time to spruce them up a little. Tag & Rename, an application from Softpointer (*http://www.softpointer.com/tr.htm*), can handle your ID3 tags one at a time or in bulk. With good ID3 tags, finding songs is much simpler and more straightforward. This app won't just help you normalize and standardize the naming conventions in your collection—it will also identify mystery albums where no names were given to tracks, and it will download and add album art to your tracks and albums.

—Lionel Felix

Conclusion

A car PC is a great thing to have, and it gives you features available nowhere else. If you put in the effort, you can create a unique, customized system that does exactly what you want and offers far better value than any off-the-shelf solution.

When you're planning and building your car PC, be sure to take advantage of the many online forums. These forums are extremely useful to the car PC community, as they enable people from all over the world to share ideas and hints, and even arrange local meetings to show off their work. I have attended a number of U.K. meets, and I've found them to be excellent opportunities for enthusiasts to meet up, see what others have done, and make new friends.

See Also

- *http://www.letscommunicate.co.uk*—Terran Brown's web site
- *http://www.pricepc.com/html/carpc.php*—A sampling of car PC installations and pictures
- *http://www.via.com.tw/en/initiatives/spearhead/Mini-ITX/car-pc.jsp*—Several more car PC installations, using VIA motherboards
- *http://www.mp3car.com*—A U.S. car PC forum

- *http://www.digital-car.co.uk*—A U.K. car PC forum
- *http://www.cpcd.de* and *http://www.car-pc.info*—German car PC forums
- *http://www.carmedia.org*—A French car PC forum

—Terran Brown

HACK #53 Build an in-Car Macintosh

Check out how one programmer used OS X and a PowerMac G4 to meet his in-car computing needs.

Several years ago I got a job in Holland, and I needed a comfortable car for almost-monthly trips to the Czech Republic. I purchased a 1993 Tatra T613-4Mi sedan with a rear-mounted 200-HP V8 engine. Ironically, although the car I purchased had been made for the Frankfurt auto show and was originally equipped with fully digital controls, a handful of computers, and features such as voice synthesis, the factory had replaced all this equipment and rewired it with more traditional controls after the show. The moment I bought it, I decided that a computer *had* to be put back in. I started to design my Tatra computer in the summer, and by Christmas I had a working installation.

The main features that I wanted my in-car computer to provide were a navigation system and the ability to play my MP3 collection—anyone who needs to make 1,000-km trips every month or has ever been lost in Copenhagen can understand the need for a lot of music and a good map.

Of course, I could simply have purchased dedicated navigation hardware (and a head unit that plays MP3s), but I was not very excited about the prospect of spending several thousand euros on a dedicated hardware solution and then having to wait for the manufacturer to release the maps that I needed of the Czech Republic. The use of a standard computer gave me much more freedom in terms of the configuration of the system and of potential software and hardware upgrades.

During the design and construction of my mobile Mac, I also decided to add some functionality that I hadn't anticipated, including communication with the engine controller and an on-board microcontroller for basic telemetric data.

Choosing a Computer and Screen

My first idea was to use an LCD iMac, and build it into the original dashboard of my Tatra. The base unit was supposed to be placed within the dashboard, and the display with its holder outside. This idea had two basic flaws: the iMac's 15" screen is really too big for most dashboards, and its

LCD screen is not designed for use in full daylight (not to mention direct sunlight).

OK, so no iMac. The second alternative was to install a separate LCD display, built into the original dashboard and connected to a computer (either a PowerMac or a PowerBook) that could be placed under the front seat or behind the dashboard. I also wanted to drive another screen that would allow rear-seat passengers to watch movies or play games. Since a Power-Book cannot easily handle two external screens, I purchased an old 450-MHz PowerMac G4 and an industrial 6.5" LCD screen (Figure 4-26) that has contrast and temperature range controls, both of which are necessary for in-car use. The native resolution of this LCD screen is 640×480 pixels, but its controller can interpolate various other resolutions. I chose 800×600 pixels, the minimal resolution required by the navigation software I intended to use (Route 66).

With the release of the Mac Mini in January 2005, Apple has created a very attractive in-car computing platform. See "Choose an in-Car PC Hardware Platform" **[Hack #41]** and "Install a Mac Mini in Your Car" **[Hack #54]** for more information.

Figure 4-26. The LCD screen in my dashboard

Installing and Mounting the PC and Screen

I soon realized that the original dashboard of my Tatra didn't have an ideal place for a fixed mount of the 6.5" LCD screen, and that a retractable screen would also cause quite a few problems. I therefore decided to rebuild the whole dashboard from scratch. This also allowed me to replace the original gauges, which were not really high-tech (almost unreadable at night, for example). Figure 4-27 is a behind-the-dash look at the rear of the LCD.

Figure 4-27. The back of the LCD screen

The placement of the computer also had to be reconsidered. There was not enough space below the front seats for a PowerMac, so I had to abandon this idea and start thinking about how to install the computer in the trunk (which, in a Tatra, is located in the front of the car). I wanted to use the least possible trunk space for the computer, so in the end I decided to install it in a rectangular case attached to the rear wall of the trunk (see Figure 4-28).

Two important engineering issues to be dealt with were heat and water condensation. The main heat source in older PowerMacs is certainly the hard disk, and the parts that are most vulnerable to condensing humidity are the motherboard and the PCI cards. Based on this knowledge, I decided to separate these two parts of the system.

Figure 4-28. My PowerMac, on a plexiglass plate

I installed the motherboard in a fiberglass case and the hard disks on a console next to this case. At first I wanted to completely seal the motherboard case, but later I found that this was not really a good idea, particularly due to temperature changes affecting the air volume inside the case. To fix this problem, I installed two Gore-Tex valves on the case (Figure 4-29). These valves are used in the automotive industry to allow air circulation in the headlight units while keeping any water on the outside.

I did not take any special measures for CPU cooling, although the CPU is mounted in a closed space with minimal air circulation—the 450-MHz G4 processor is known for its low cooling requirements, so I decided to wait and see how it went before over-engineering a solution to a problem that might not exist. This hunch proved to be correct, as even in 35° C days last summer with the computer running for 15 hours, I never had problems with CPU temperature, and the hard disks did not suffer any damage (even on the roads in the Czech Republic and Slovakia, which are not always up to civilized standards!).

Figure 4-29. A complete PowerMac G4 in the Tatra

Powering the PC

Although my final solution turned out to be simple and reliable, the power supply was probably the biggest problem I encountered during the whole installation. My very first idea was to use an uninterruptible power supply (UPS) without an internal battery, connected to the car's battery. This idea cost me two UPS units, both of whose transistors burned out. Even a 300W UPS was not able to handle the current surge that occurred when the computer started up.

My second idea was to use an inverter **[Hack #11]** and the original 220V power supply. This almost worked—I say "almost" because, while it did power the computer, there was a 50-Hz noise on the audio output of the computer that I could not eliminate.

Fortunately, my third idea, a 12V ATX power supply, did work perfectly. I used a commercial Turbo-Cool power supply (see Figure 4-30) that works with input voltages of between 9V and 16V **[Hack #42]**. The maximum rated power is only 100W, which is much less than the 250W of the original 220V power supply. However, the original power supply was designed for a workstation full of disks and PCI cards, which is certainly not my case. The only problem I have experienced so far is that the 5V output of the power supply is not capable of providing enough current for all of my USB devices, and this problem was very easy to address by using a USB hub powered by a special 5V power source [Hack #51]. The very wide range of the input voltages ensures that the power source is able to power the computer even when I'm cranking the engine [Hack #45].

Figure 4-30. The original 220V and new 12V ATX power supplies

The power supply is controlled by the power-on signal from the motherboard, which has an idle current of about 100 mA. Accidental draining of the battery is not much of an issue, since this current is comparable to the idle current of other devices in the car (such as the alarm and the engine controller).

> Motherboards usually draw more standby power—for instance, the VIA motherboards draw 300 mA without any devices attached. The drain of the PowerMac in this installation is quite low, but you might still want to invest in a startup controller [Hack #43], which will draw less than 10 mA. This is the best way to prevent battery drain, especially if the car is not driven (and recharged) daily.

Peripherals and Controls

There are several basic ways to control the computer, and most of them can be implemented using standard USB peripherals. Many people use touchscreens in similar installations. Although I also considered this option at the beginning, I rejected it pretty quickly. In my opinion, having to look at the screen while driving results in a loss of concentration that can be dangerous. Instead, I decided to use controls with fixed positions that can be used without looking at the screen.

The key control element in my installation is Griffin Technology's PowerMate rotating controller (*http://www.griffintechnology.com/products/powermate*), which is used not only for controlling the software [Hack #61], but also for starting up the computer. I also installed a row of buttons beneath the screen in the dashboard, for auxiliary functions. This is all shown in Figure 4-31

When I'm not driving, I can control all the functions of the computer using an infrared keyboard with a built in trackpoint that emulates a mouse. Rear-seat passengers can control the movie player and some other functions with another infrared device—Keyspan's Digital Media Remote (*http://www.keyspan.com/products/usb/remote*).

For convenience, I installed two USB connectors in the center console to allow ad-hoc connection of other USB devices when required (typically, a keyboard and a mouse).

Audio Connection

The sound output of the PowerMac is connected to a Sony head unit [Hack #14] that is in turn connected to two amplifiers and a total of eight speakers and a subwoofer. There is also another sound output, via a USB adapter,

Figure 4-31. The PowerMate and the buttons below the LCD screen

that provides rear-seat passengers with headphone jacks so that they can choose to listen to a different audio source than what's being played through the main speakers.

Networking

My Tatra has its own Ethernet network, with a small eight-port switch under the rear seats and a total of four outlets in the armrest and the center console (Figure 4-32). Passengers with laptop computers can connect to the network to access data on the car's hard disk or share the PowerMac's Internet connection. The PowerMac is also equipped with an AirPort card that can be used to connect to WiFi networks wherever they are available. This feature is used for smaller updates, software and data downloads from my home network, and Internet connection at places with public WiFi hotspots (such as certain fuel stations).

In places without WiFi coverage, the computer uses a mobile phone GPRS-over-Bluetooth interface for its Internet connection [Hack #62]. Of course, the

Figure 4-32. A software upload via the Ethernet plug in the rear armrest

speed is significantly lower, but it's sufficient for finding out about traffic situations, getting weather data updates, or checking email. This feature once saved me and my company quite a lot of trouble (and money), when I was able to solve a potentially very serious problem from a parking place on a highway in the middle of Germany.

Frontend Software

My Tatra PowerMac uses both standard and custom applications. I tried to use standard applications whenever possible; the custom applications mostly only provide a simplified user interface to some of the standard applications and some car-specific functions, such as the display of speed and fuel consumption.

The main application, called *Tatra.app* (*http://sourceforge.net/projects/ dash-mac*), was written by Ondra Čada. It runs in full-screen mode and hides the standard OS X menu bar, as well as the Dock. Its screen is divided into several parts. At the top of the screen, there is a space for what we call a "compass module." The middle and biggest part contains eight slots, each of which can be used by different plug-in modules to display information and user interface elements.

The user can select which modules are installed in the eight slots of the main window, but even a module that is not currently displayed or has no user interface in any slot can display urgent messages or status information, using either icons or pop-up windows. The main application also provides the modules with the ability to speak messages, through Apple's text-to-speech technology. Spoken feedback allows the user to work with the computer without even looking at the screen.

A module can optionally have a special "setup" part, which is available through the main application in its setup mode. Unlike the main window and activated modules, the user can control it only by standard keyboard and mouse input, not via the PowerMate. (Obviously, this mode is not supposed to be used while driving.)

Here's a list of the modules I currently use:

• Current speed
• Current fuel consumption
• Fuel status (consumed from last fill-up, remaining, range)
• Fuel counter (resettable, multi-instance)
• Distance counter (total)
• Distance counter (resettable, multi-instance)
• Stopwatch (resettable, multi-instance)
• Countdown (multi-instance)
• Vehicle data input (GUI-less, reads data from onboard systems)
• Temperature module (internal CPU temperature and sensors in car)
• MP3 player (controls iTunes using AppleScript)
• System (switching between apps, turning off power, night display mode)

To support all these vehicle measurement modules, I connected a separate circuit board with its own microcontroller to the car's engine and installed five digital thermometers and a distance counter on the transmission. (For the interested, the microcontroller was designed and built by Tomáš Struziak, and the schematics can be found at *http://aek4470.finalnet.cz/html/palpoc.htm*.)

GPS/Navigation

Navigation in my Tatra is handled by Route 66 (currently Route 66 Europe 2004 Professional, to be exact). Although this application was certainly written as route planning rather than navigation software, it does the job well. It has a good database of Europe, offers support for NMEA GPS devices (I use Garmin's GPS II+ receiver), and, last but not least, can receive real-time traffic information using Internet Traffic Message Channel (TMC) servers for the U.K., Belgium, Luxemburg, the Netherlands, Germany, and Italy.

On the other hand, Route 66 is not easy to control with simplified controllers. It does not use hotkeys that are easy to emulate through simple programming, and the displayed maps are not as good as those in factory navigation systems. The worst problem is that Route 66 only displays the maps "north up," while most navigation systems work with "track up" display, which is more logical and gives the driver a much better overview of the current situation ahead. With a "north up" map display, the driver must constantly pay attention to the direction, indicated by a little arrow, and make the necessary mental calculations (i.e., when driving south, right turns are left on the screen, and vice versa).

Movies and Music

In *Tatra.app*, modules can be "activated," or made responsive to the user's commands. Figure 4-30 shows an MP3 player module. In the normal state, the module displays information about the track currently being played. In the "active" state, the module displays a dialog box that allows the user to pause the playback and select the track and playlist to be played. All these functions are controllable using the PowerMate rotating controller, so the driver can cycle through the playlists without having to look away from the road.

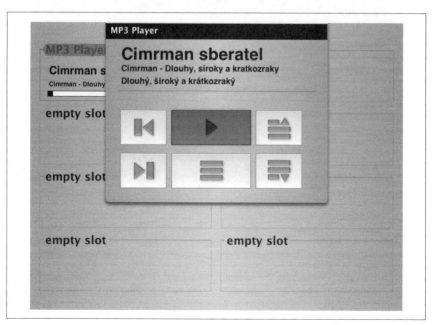

Figure 4-33. An MP3 player Tatra.app module

I had originally planned to install a DVD drive in the center console, but after seeing the high quality of DivX/MPEG movies I decided to implement a video jukebox application [Hack #70] instead of having DVDs strewn all around the car.

I wanted my computer to deliver *multi-zone* content (i.e., different audio and video in the front and back seats), so I developed another application that could play back a different movie on the second video card and reroute the corresponding audio to separate speakers or headphones. Like the main application, my movie player also runs in full-screen mode and uses a simple user interface, controllable by either the PowerMate controller or the Key-span infrared remote control. It can display the main window on any con-nected screen, so it can be used on the primary screen in the dashboard as well as on the secondary rear screen (Figure 4-34). It provides only basic play-back functions (choose a movie, play it, and pause it), but it gets the job done.

Figure 4-34. My movie-player program

Conclusion

Since the original installation, I have continued to add features to my in-car Macintosh. One change I made was to install a GPS/GSM module, prima-rily to replace the standard alarm. The one-wire bus is used for user "authentication" with a chip card (to disarm the alarm) and communication with several temperature sensors. The car heater can indeed be controlled by SMS texting, and using SMS I can also get information about the car's position, lock and unlock it, or stop the engine.

See Also

- *http://carmac.acmelab.org*—The Macintosh car integration forum
- *http://sourceforge.net/projects/dash-mac/*—Location of the open source *Tatra.app*
- *http://sourceforge.net/projects/idash*—iDash, a graphical frontend for using OS X in a car environment
- *http://www.popsci.com/popsci/how2/article/0,20967,695577,00.html*—A *Popular Science* article on the Tatra Mac
- *http://aek4470.finalnet.cz/html/palpoc.htm*—Schematics for the custom power board (in Czech)
- "Install a VGA Touchscreen in Your Dashboard" **[Hack #26]**

—Jirka Jirout

HACK #54   Install a Mac Mini in Your Car

Apple's new Mac Mini has the perfect price, performance, size, and shape for in-car computer installations.

In January 2005, Apple surprised a lot of people by entering the sub-$500 PC market. Their new product, the Mac Mini, was greeted with enthusiastic press and fanfare. The Mac Mini is equipped similarly to Apple's laptop line, with a 1.25-GHz or 1.42-GHz PowerPC G4 processor, a 2.5" laptop hard drive, and a slot-loading optical drive. It's small enough to be mistaken for an external CD/DVD drive.

For car PC enthusiasts, the most interesting thing about the Mini is its *form factor* (i.e., standard size and shape). The Mac Mini is 2" tall and 6.5" wide. For those not keeping track, the standard size of a car radio slot **[Hack #12]** is an almost identical 2" by 7"—consequently, the Mac Mini can be installed almost seamlessly in a dashboard slot. You can see a picture of a Mac Mini and a single-DIN head unit in Figure 4-35.

> On a personal note, I've been an Apple user since the early 1980s and a "Mac guy" since I bought my first used Mac 512 in 1989. I was hooked on a WYSIWYG GUI when Windows 3.0 was just a twinkle in Microsoft's eye. I'm very cross-platform, though, and although most of the software I develop targets the Windows and Linux platforms, I've written this book on a 1.5-GHz G4 PowerBook.

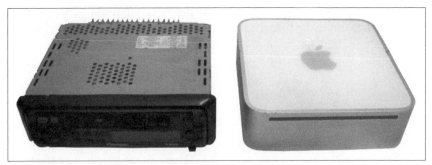

Figure 4-35. A single-DIN head unit and a Mac Mini

As soon as the Mac Mini came out, I knew I had to put one in my car. I have a young daughter who likes to watch shows on the go in her car seat. I had already set her up with a DVD player, a headrest monitor [Hack #25], and a stereo surround sound car seat (i.e., speakers built into her car seat)—she seemed satisfied, but I knew that in her heart she really wanted to see Dora the Explorer in high-definition on a VGA screen, so I installed a Mac Mini for her in our 2005 Dodge Caravan (a "MacMiniVan," if you will).

Choosing a Computer and Screen

One of the coolest things about the Mac Mini is that you don't have to assemble it—it's all there, nice and compact and already put together. Furthermore, the processor is powerful enough to do everything I want to do with my car computer. While the VIA EPIA boards do a fair job of DVD playback, the Macintosh is well known for its superior multimedia performance. Plus, DivX and other video codecs have been heavily optimized for the PowerPC G4 chips and OS X. So, although I am the only person I know of who does DivX rips of Nickelodeon shows for his toddler's in-car video jukebox [Hack #70], the Mini was a much more turnkey experience for me than any of the cheap compact car PCs I've built, hands down.

As you can see in Figure 4-36, the Mini has the standard array of ports you'd expect: two USB ports, a FireWire port, an Ethernet port, and stereo sound in and out. You can also get it preconfigured with optional WiFi and/or Bluetooth.

The Mini has a DVI port, so you can either connect directly to a digital LCD screen or use an adapter to connect to a VGA, S-Video, or composite screen. This versatility makes it easy to connect any screen you want to your Mini. Its screen capabilities are great, although its lack of dual-output video was a bit of a challenge as I usually depend on my car PC to have multi-zone (front and back) video.

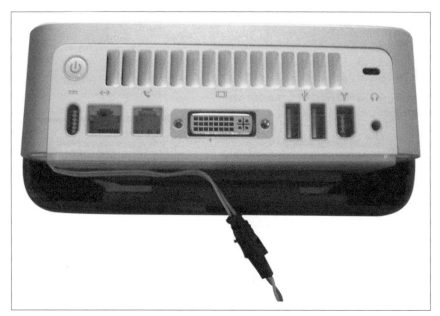

Figure 4-36. The Mac Mini's back panel

Though I had a touchscreen and a CarBot in my minivan for a while, I wanted to go back to a configuration that was a bit more "stealth." Additionally, in my pursuit of safer in-car experiences, I've been trying to get away from the "screensaver on the dashboard" look of a touchscreen and go back to just using button presses and audio feedback. Thus, I decided that I would use the Mac Mini primarily for rear-seat entertainment and music, and not try to operate it using a touchscreen from the driver's seat.

In addition to the Mini, to complete my install I needed a display. My minivan has the option for a 6" fold-down screen and DVD player from the factory, so a few months ago I called my Dodge dealer and asked how much it would cost to upgrade—$1,800 was the reply. Ouch! Consequently, part of the challenge of this Mini install was to see what I could do for a bit less than that.

The Mini had set me back $599 so far (I opted for the pricier, faster processor and larger hard drive), so I needed a cheap video solution. I went to Fry's Electronics and CompUSA, compared monitor prices, and made a selection. At first I got a $250 17" monitor from CompUSA that ran on 12V, which was perfect for in-car installation. However, the 17" monitor was actually *too big* for the car; even when it was folded up, my wife and I bumped our heads against it. So I returned the 17" and bought a 15" for $199 at Fry's.

Because I wanted the option to run my Mini to multiple composite screens, including my VGA screen, I purchased a pass-through, USB-powered

VGA-to-composite adapter from Grandtec (*http://grandtec.com/ultimateEZ. htm*). Although you can get a composite signal directly out of the Mac DVI port using a $20 adapter, you'll lose the crisp VGA high-definition output that the Mini is able to produce.

Installing and Mounting the PC and Screen

Taking apart modern cars is literally a snap. Most of the pieces of the car click in and hold in place with friction or small mounting tabs, and the main dash console is held in place with half a dozen Phillips-head screws. Getting the dashboard off (I've done it so many times that I can do it in seconds now) involves removing a few screws and then simply seizing the main dash face-plate and pulling it off. This exposes the cavernous center area that holds the radio, A/C controls, and multiple storage slots, perfect for stowing the various wires and adapters needed for this installation (such as AUX-in adapters [Hack #14], my VGA-to-composite adapter, and the Mac Mini's huge power block).

Mounting the Mac Mini was actually no challenge at all. As mentioned earlier, its single-DIN form factor makes it a drop-in installation, with only a bit of fabrication required. I took my minivan to a local install shop and explained what I wanted to do. The installer pulled out the rubber-floored coin tray (which is usually replaced with the in-dash DVD player factory option), and using a rotary high-speed cutting tool, he cut the top off the tray. This made a sort of clip to hold the Mini. To protect the Mini case's edges and to fill the space between the 6.5" Mini and the 7"-wide slot, he stuck a bit of black foamy carpet on the case's sides. He also put some plastic spacers underneath the rear of the Mini, so that it would angle down slightly to match the slope of the slot. You can see the tray in Figure 4-37.

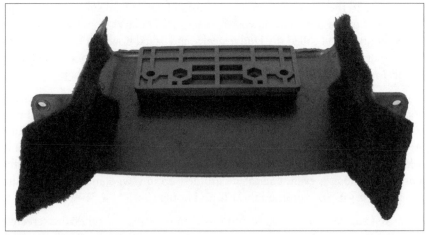

Figure 4-37. Mac Mini modified coin tray

The huge challenge of this project was not the installation of the Mac Mini, but of the screen. I tested two screens and three mounting approaches before I settled on the final install. As described in "Install a Fold-Down Ceiling-Mounted Screen" [Hack #29], a heavy screen needs to be connected to the crossbeams of the ceiling; otherwise, it will simply make the headliner sag or even rip it out. I settled on a fold-down undermounting screen support [Hack #30] (the AVF Vector LCD005) that I bought at Home Depot for $80.

Wiring everything was time-consuming but not challenging. I ran a long VGA cable from the center dashboard, along the front passenger pillar, up the column, across the ceiling under the headliner, and out near where the VGA screen was mounted. I also ran an audio cable, a three-prong computer power cord, and a 12V power cord, just to be ready for any screen I might decide to swap in later (Figure 4-38).

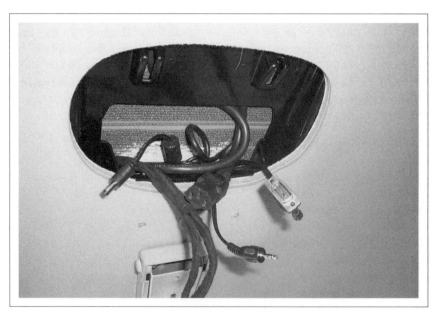

Figure 4-38. View of the headliner where the power and video cables have been run

Powering the Mac Mini was not as simple as it should have been. Unfortunately, the Mac Mini runs on an 85W, 18V DC power supply brick. Thus, you can't connect it directly to the 12V of the car. I wanted to get my Mac Mini installed quickly and easily, and I didn't feel like cutting the power cord (yet), so I took the easy route and installed an inverter [Hack #11] in the center storage bin between the front seats of the van.

I was going to have to install an inverter anyway, because my 15" screen ran on 120V AC (unlike the 17" screen I tried first, which ran on 12V). So, I ran two power cords from the center bin under the carpet and through the dashboard: a long AC power cord to the screen, and the white AC cord that plugs into the Mini's power adapter.

The only part of powering my Mac that did require some invasive surgery was adding an external power switch. The Mac does have a "boot on power loss" feature, so for a while I was restarting it by just rudely cutting power to it (by hitting the off switch on my power inverter in the center storage bin). However, I found that after a few rude reboots, the Mini gets apathetic and won't boot up. I think this has to do with powering it up and down and then up again too quickly.

So, when the Mini is off, the only way to reliably get it to turn on is to press a power button on the back of the unit, which is hidden behind and deep inside the dashboard of the car. I needed a way around this problem but didn't want to mess up the motherboard in any way, so I opened up the Mac Mini and soldered a pair of wires to the power button on the back (Figure 4-39). I then ran the wires out of one of the ventilation slots in the bottom of the Mini case, and connected them to a momentary switch (just a standard PC case switch). Once you have run these wires out of the Mac Mini, you can use any of the standard power sequencing startup controllers [Hack #43].

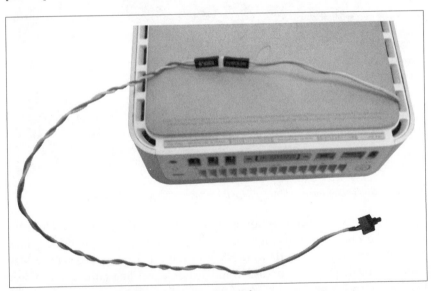

Figure 4-39. Extending the Mac Mini's power switch

As soon as the Carnetix Mac Mini power adapter becomes available (see the sidebar "Powering the Mac Mini in the Car"), I'll replace my inverter. The

Powering the Mac Mini in the Car

There are three ways I know of at this writing to power a Mac Mini on 12V. The first, and most obvious, is with an inverter [Hack #11], which is the route I initially took. Since then, I bought a Targus 90W car laptop power supply and spliced it into my Mini's power cord, and this cooler, quieter solution is working great.

Sony VAIO laptops (such as the PCG-700 series) run on 90W, 18V power supplies. You can find a car adapter for these laptops for under $50, although you'll have to cut the plug off an existing Mac Mini power supply cord and splice it on in order to get the 18V into the Mini. Some instructions on the proper splicing of the power cord can be found at *http://www.carhacks.org/macmini*.

The other solution I'm aware of is to use the CNXP1900 power converter and regulator from Carnetix (*http://www.carnetix.com/CNXP1900.htm*). This unit was just beginning to ship as I was writing this. Carnetix even offers a tidy, minimally invasive splitter wire so you can connect the Mini's inconveniently placed power button to the Carnetix. This allows the Mini to power up when the car is on and sleep when the car is off.

inverter is so well wired to the car battery (with 8-gauge cable) that my Mac survives engine cranking [Hack #45] with no problems right now, but the inverter consumes way too much power, and after about five hours of marathon DVD playback with the car off I found that I couldn't start the car again. Fortunately, I had already upgraded to a deep-cycle battery [Hack #6], so the deep discharge didn't do any damage.

Peripherals and Controls

Ever since I found the Macally KeyPoint remote (*http://www.macally.com/spec/usb/input_device/keypads.html*), I've been in love. It's my favorite of the many wireless RF remotes I've tried—it's small, has just the few buttons I need, is very programmable, and has a built-in mouse [Hack #56]. I ran a pair of USB wires from the in-dash Mini to my minivan's center storage bin so I could plug in a USB hub, and that's where I plug in the receiver for my Macally remote (see Figure 4-40). Since it is RF, it doesn't need to be in line of sight.

The Macally remote is programmable, so you can set any button to enter any keypress you want, depending on the current application. For example, it has a "menu" button that I've configured to always run iTunes, unless I'm in iTunes, in which case it runs the DVD player. Once I am in those applications, the other buttons do what they should do for those applications— seek, pause, go to the next track, and so on.

Figure 4-40. My secret USB hub

This arrangement allows me to use iTunes while I'm on the road, without any visual interface. I just put it in shuffle mode before I start driving and then hit the next track button when I want to skip songs. That accomplishes about 90% of what I want to do with audio when I'm on the road.

 Although there are many ways to achieve iPod/car integration [Hack #18], with a Mac Mini you get all the advantages of an iPod, plus CD ripping capabilities and access to the iTunes music store. If you hear a new song that you've just got to have while traveling cross-country, you can purchase it from the ITMS in just a few seconds.

The USB hub in my center console also has a Bluetooth receiver plugged into it. Although the Mac Mini had a factory Bluetooth option, I considered that having the Bluetooth receiver more centered in the car (and not stuffed into the dashboard) would give it better range for rear-seat passengers, the ones most likely to be using Bluetooth input devices.

I keep an Apple Bluetooth keyboard and mouse stashed in the Millenium-Falconesque subcompartments in my minivan, so I can whip them out when people need to use the computer for productivity.

Audio Connection

My minivan has eight speakers installed and has fantastic, enveloping sound, especially in the rear seats. To get the Mac Mini sound into my factory head unit, I needed the appropriate AUX-in audio adapter [Hack #14].

I wanted to have both XM radio and the Mac Mini as audio options when I drive, and I wanted to keep the factory head unit. To accomplish this, I actually used three different devices: an XM Direct radio receiver, an XM-to-Pioneer adapter, and a Pioneer-to-Dodge adapter. Because the XM adapters use RCA stereo jacks to connect the audio to the adapter, I was able to piggyback the Mac Mini's mini-jack (too many minis!) onto the XM AUX-in (see Figure 4-41).

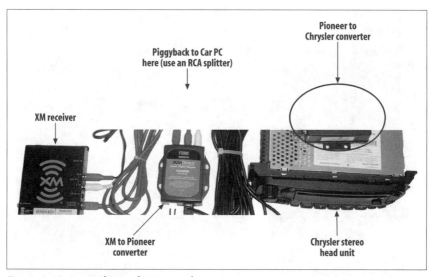

Figure 4-41. A symphony of AUX-in adapters

When I want to listen to XM radio, I just leave the Mac Mini off or mute it. When I want to listen to the Mac Mini, I turn my XM radio down to station zero (station ID), and it outputs no sound and lets the Mini's sound come out.

There's an interesting side effect to all these adapters: my car radio starts up and says Sirius, displays XM radio once the XM adapter initializes, and then starts playing music from iTunes.

Networking

Although I bought a USB WiFi adapter for my Mac Mini, I haven't even hooked it up yet. I use a Bluetooth connection to my cell phone to do most of my web surfing—luckily, my EDGE-over-Bluetooth connection runs at

60–80 kbps [Hack #62]. My minivan has a nice little mobile-phone holder on the center bin, and this is very close to the Bluetooth adapter (Figure 4-42). Since I've paired the Mini and the phone, I set up the Mini so that any time it needs to access the Internet, it just silently dials up through the phone. It can even share this connection with other WiFi laptops in the car, through Sharing → Internet in the System Preferences. This system works so smoothly that once, when iTunes needed to authenticate with the music store to play a song I had bought and copied onto the Mini, I didn't even realize it had connected until it was asking me for my password and showing me album art for the song in question. I can even stream (low-bitrate) MP3 radio stations in iTunes over the modem. Hmm…maybe soon I won't need my satellite radio anymore!

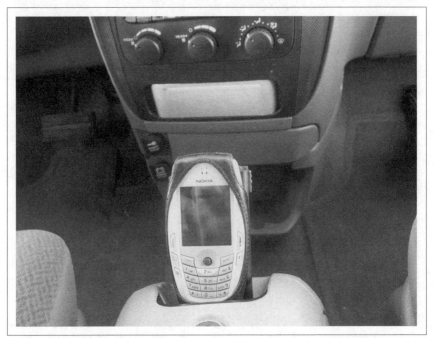

Figure 4-42. My Mac Mini Internet access point

Frontend Software

The thing about a rear-seat entertainment computer is that you don't need frontend software—for the most part, OS X works fine. That said, after having my Mini in the car for a while, I'm looking forward to having more driver-side usability. For instance, it's very difficult to switch between different functions of iTunes, and when the computer goes silent and unresponsive to my keypresses, I usually find that some dialog box has appeared on the screen and demanded interactive attention. Although such modal dialogs used to be frowned upon in the Mac OS, both the DVD player and iTunes are full of them.

At this writing the Mac Mini has only been out for a few months. There aren't any really solid completed frontends available, but that's probably going to change soon. You can find a list of a few of the current options at the end of "Build an in-Car Macintosh" [Hack #53]. I should also mention that my own company, CarBot (*http://www.carbotpc.com*), is currently porting its CarBot Player software to the Mac.

GPS/Navigation

I don't have a GPS receiver hooked up to my Mac Mini, since there aren't that many navigation options for Mac OS X. That said, I do use the Mini for navigation, and I even have features that PC navigation software [Hack #71] doesn't yet have.

For years I've wished I could access MapQuest (*http://www.mapquest.com*) or something similar while on the road, and with this Mac Mini, I finally can. In fact, Google Maps (*http://maps.google.com*) has quickly become my favorite mapping service. Google's maps are very detailed, and once you have them up in a browser window, you can disconnect from the Internet and still scroll around in them. Using Google Maps on my Mac has already saved me more than once. And if it's real-time traffic information you need, Yahoo! Maps (*http://maps.yahoo.com/traffic*) is even better than Google.

Movies and Music

I'm absolutely spoiled by the entertainment options that my Mac Mini provides. I recently downloaded the Star Wars Episode III trailer, and I've been showing that off to people who get in my van. The stereo sound is breathtaking and sounds as good as my home theater. Because I have a 2005 Dodge Caravan with collapsing seats, I can fold down the middle seats and create a capacious, three-seat in-car theater [Hack #70]. And, of course, it isn't just DVDs I can play back; I can also copy movies from a hacked TiVo (see Raffi Krikorian's *TiVo Hacks*, also published by O'Reilly, for instructions on how to do this) or download them from my computer PVR.

The Mac Mini comes with QuickTime and iTunes preinstalled, but just to make sure you can play everything I recommend that you also install all of these applications and codecs:

RealPlayer (http://www.real.com)
  RealPlayer was the first and best audio streaming technology, and many radio stations around the world simulcast their content in Real format. For in-car radio streaming, RealPlayer is a must.

Windows Media Player (http://www.microsoft.com/mac)

A large portion of the video content you're going to find online is encoded in this format, and several of the home PVRs encode in Windows Media, so it's always good to have this on your Mac.

DivX (http://www.divx.com)

The vast majority of applications for encoding video save it in this version of MPEG-4, so it's important for any video aficionado.

3ivx (http://www.3ivx.com)

In the Macintosh world, the 3ivx codecs are optimized for the Mac and play MPEG-4 content. It's best to have them in addition to DivX.

MPlayerOSX (http://mplayerosx.sourceforge.net)

This OS X port of the popular Linux player has good de-blocking (i.e., it can make DivX and MPEG-4 movies look even smoother). It's also a great app to have, just to make sure that you can play anything anyone hands you.

Future Plans

I'm planning on making a few additions to this install. So that I can still see behind the vehicle while I'm driving with the fold-down screen in use, I've just installed a rearview camera **[Hack #33]**. Once I get the rearview screen working, I'm going to connect the Mac Mini to it so that I can see a tiny (5") view of what's on the Mini screen.

I plan to get the WiFi working soon, and I'm coming up with clever ideas on how to get EVDO **[Hack #62]** working for the Mac Mini. Although the Mini doesn't have a PCMCIA slot, I'm going to use a PC laptop with a damaged screen, plug in EVDO and WiFi, run Knoppix on it to make it a wireless router (see Kyle Rankin's *Knoppix Hacks*, also published by O'Reilly), and then connect it to the Mac via Ethernet.

Heh heh heh.

See Also

- *http://www.carbotpc.com*—Porting our software to the Mac Mini
- *http://www.carhacks.org/macmini*—Mac Mini hacking resources

CHAPTER FIVE

Car PC Interface Options
Hacks 55–61

Human/computer interface design is especially important in an automotive environment. Traditional control systems such as computer mice and keyboards tend to be awkward for passengers and too dangerous for the driver to use. To make the use of an in-car computer safe and convenient for everyone, it is necessary to rethink not only the input hardware but also the computer's GUI itself. Menu-based graphical user interfaces are difficult for passengers to use and almost impossible for a driver to safely navigate, so alternatives must be found.

The car radio is a good example of an established and relatively safe to use in-car user interface. Users can select the next or prior station by turning a dial left and right or pressing a button up and down. A number of preset stations can be assigned to half a dozen buttons. The media-du-jour, be it eight-track, cassette, MiniDisk, CD, or DVD, can be shoved into a slot and will start playing automatically. Volume is usually controlled via a big, obvious dial or pair of buttons. This basic method of selecting and controlling audio entertainment has remained the same for many years.

The strength of the radio interface lies with its predictability: each button generally has an unchanging function and definitely has an unchanging position. A driver who becomes familiar with his radio can operate it without looking, and a driver who gets in an unfamiliar vehicle can usually figure out how to use that radio without a tremendous learning curve.

The onslaught of new gadgets for the car has presented a strong challenge for user-interface designers. Safely and aesthetically integrating all the new applications and functions into the car is a work in progress. But while the industry works on that, car PC hackers have worked out a few control options of their own. This chapter covers various methods and software programs car PC enthusiasts are using to control their creations.

Control Your Car PC with a Keyboard and Mouse

#55

If you're a passenger, a compact mouse and keyboard are the most familiar way to control the in-car computer.

Before we get into the various ways a driver can safely control an in-car computer, let's look at how to get the passengers going. Many in-car PCs are designed for rear-seat or passenger entertainment. In this case, there's no particular reason a keyboard can't be used to control the PC.

Wired Keyboards

In a moving vehicle, the use of any conventional mouse is difficult, due to vibration and lack of flat surfaces. Thus, a keyboard with an integrated mouse is probably best. Integrated mice on wireless keyboards usually come in the form of a small trackball or joystick. Their wired counterparts are usually bigger and come with an integrated trackpad.

If smallness is what you are after, so you can fit the keyboard in a glove compartment, the center console, or under a seat, a wired keyboard is your best bet because the keyboard manufacturer doesn't have to include room for batteries or a wireless transmitter. If you know the keyboard is going to be used, for example, in only the front passenger seat, you can run PS2 keyboard and mouse cables under the carpet from the computer to inside the dash and hide the keyboard in the glove compartment.

If the keyboard needs to be usable by passengers in the front *or* back seats, another good solution is to run a USB hub to the center console between the front bucket seats [Hack #51]. Then, you can store your USB keyboard (or other controllers) wherever it's convenient, and plug it in when you need to. Again, this solution keeps the wires hidden so your car doesn't look cluttered when everything is stowed away.

Wireless Keyboards

A wireless keyboard with an integrated mouse is the least tangled way to control the PC from any seat in the car. Fortunately, the home theater PC market has generated a variety of keyboards that fit these parameters.

A basic keyboard with a built-in mouse is shown in Figure 5-1. This unit uses an infrared receiver that plugs into the PS2 keyboard and COM ports on the back of the computer. The keyboard itself can last for months (with light use) on four AA batteries.

Figure 5-1. An infrared keyboard with a built-in mouse

One of the most popular keyboards for in-car use is the Gyro keyboard (*http://www.gyration.com*). These units are great because they use radio frequencies (RF) instead of infrared, so they don't require a direct line of sight to a receiver to work. You can get just the mouse, just the keyboard, or both together, but they're a bit expensive—over $100 for the pair. When the mouse is sitting on a flat surface, it acts like a conventional optical mouse. But when you pick it up, a gyroscope inside the mouse (hence the name) detects movement, and you can move the cursor just by moving the mouse in the air.

There are two drawbacks to using the Gyro mouse in the car: when you inevitably set the mouse down, it turns back into an optical mouse and the cursor moves unexpectedly, and to keep the mouse charged you have to mount the mouse recharging dock somewhere convenient. However, the convenience of being able to mouse in the air rather than having to find a suitable surface in a moving vehicle is a strong plus.

A good site for finding keyboards of all kinds, one of which may work for you, is *http://www.fentek-ind.com*.

HACK Control Your Car PC with a Handheld Remote
#56
Handheld remote controls are a familiar and easy way to control media playback and other applications in the car.

Before the recent emergence of home theater PCs (HTPCs), there were not many hardware options for PC remote control. Now, with dozens of personal video recorder (PVR) or, if you prefer, digital video recorder (DVR) applications available, consumer demand for computer remote controls is at an all-time high.

It used to be that all the remote controls cost over $100 and were primarily sold to business users for controlling PowerPoint presentations. Now, the average remote with an integrated mouse costs around $50.

Now, I bet you're asking yourself, "Is there one standard for PC remote controls, just like keyboards, so that any remote-controllable program can be controlled by any remote control?" Well, if you have ever seen a coffee table with 12 TV clickers on it, you'll realize that even universal remote controls haven't solved that problem. But fortunately computers, in their infinite programmability, can be taught to listen to any remote you want and, with the right software, control most of the programs you want.

Understanding Infrared

The relationship between infrared and computers is actually a bit confusing, because there are several incompatible types of infrared. Your computer, laptop, or PDA probably has an infrared port. The infrared port on a Palm handheld can act as a universal remote control, using the slow, simple language spoken by remotes, television sets, VCRs, and DVD players.

The high-speed infrared data-communication technique used by your PC, however, is designed for data transfer, not just control. *Infrared data association* (IrDA) is a networking technique that runs networking protocols such as TCP/IP over infrared signals. The infrared sender/receiver in your computer may only speak IrDA, and it probably can't listen to or speak the frequencies of many TV remotes.

Remote controls don't speak anything as complicated as TCP/IP—they have a much simpler ones-and-zeros network protocol called *ASK*. Of course, ASK is just the alphabet, if you will—each remote speaks its own manufacturer-specific dialect on top of ASK. Also, there are actually two different infrared light ranges, which is why if you look at the front of a universal remote, you'll see that it actually has two small infrared LEDs in the front (one for each "color" of infrared light used).

That's the long story. The short story is, don't get excited because your motherboard has "built-in infrared" and think that you can just connect any old IR receiver and start working. Your computer probably has an IrDA port, and you're going to have to buy and connect a separate IR receiver.

PC Infrared (IR) Receivers

IR receivers (Figure 5-2) provide your computer with the same "eye" you find on the front of a TV, VCR, or other controllable device, allowing you to use a remote to control the programs on your computer instead of a keyboard. Whereas a TV is hard-wired to respond to CHANNEL UP by increasing the channel, the software that comes with a PC IR receiver can usually translate the CHANNEL UP key to any button or keypress you want.

Figure 5-2. Irman's IR receiver box

IR receivers for PCs usually come bundled with their own remotes, but many can accept the infrared signals from the remotes you have around your house. Because they expect your computer to be on the floor or generally not in view, receivers usually come with a remote "eye" at one end of a cable. You plug one end of the cable into the computer, then place the eye wherever it needs to be to receive signals. If your IR receiver is on a PCI card, the plug is usually a mini-jack connector. Otherwise, the connector usually fits to a USB or serial port.

Irman (*http://www.evation.com/irman/index.html*) makes a great receiver box that accepts signals from almost any remote control, and a number of companies (such as Streamzap, at *http://www.streamzap.com*) sell remotes bundled with serial or USB receivers for the PC. Microsoft also offers a $30 remote bundle that has a USB IR receiver along with its new Windows XP Media Center software. While cheap, it is designed primarily to work with their own software, and because the buttons map to an unusual combination of keyboard presses, you'll need to write special software to adapt it to control other programs.

The problem with the Media Center remote and other PC remotes is the same as with TV/VCR/DVD player remotes—you wind up having several of them, each controlling a different application.

PC Radio Frequency (RF) Remotes

While IR works great in a wide-open entertainment room where line-of-sight is not a problem, it has its problems in a car. IR is not interfered with by metal or other wireless signals; however, because it requires a direct line of sight between the remote and the receiver, you have to put the receiver somewhere in the open where the user can easily point the remote at it. And unfortunately, a location that is good for one user, such as the front passenger, may not be good for all the passengers in the back seats.

Another major problem with IR in the car is that any time the sun hits the receiver, it becomes unusable—the sunlight simply drowns out the tiny infrared beam. Thus, it's important to mount the IR receiver where it won't be exposed to direct sunlight.

In contrast, RF remotes are directionless and unaffected by direct sunlight—because they use radio frequencies instead of infrared light, they work no matter where you point them. This makes them great for letting anyone control the music of the PC, regardless of where they are sitting in the car.

Figure 5-3 shows some of the remotes listed below and their receivers, along with the Microsoft Media Center remote mentioned earlier.

ATI and X10 produce excellent RF remotes. The recently released ATI Remote Wonder II (*http://www.ati.com/products/remotewonder2*) has an 80-foot range, which means your signal is strong enough to control the car PC two lanes over. I have used the original ATI Remote Wonder for both PC and home entertainment control (on my Macintosh Cube—it's cross-platform), and it has worked well in both environments. My company (*http://www.carbotpc.com*) shipped each of our first-generation car PCs with the X10 Lola media remote (*http://www.x10.com/entertainment/remote_controls.html*), as it has tons of programmable keys and is relatively inexpensive (less than $50).

SnapStream's Firefly PC Remote (*http://www.snapstream.com/products/firefly/*) is a new RF remote that has excellent support for dozens of applications in each category, from DVD players to media players to karaoke software. It also has good support for a Windows automation and scripting tool called Girder (more on this later).

Macally's compact remote control (*http://www.macally.com/spec/usb/input_device/keypads.html*), the KeyPoint, looks more like something you should have in a car, and it can be Velcroed to the dash or stashed in the center

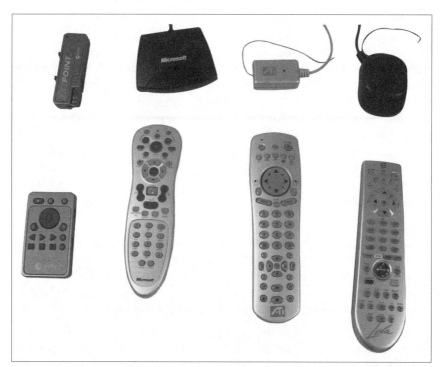

Figure 5-3. From left to right: the Macally KeyPoint, Microsoft Media Center, ATI Remote Wonder, and X10 Lola

console. The KeyPoint is bundled with simple keypress-sending software that can be configured to press different keys depending on the program that is in the front.

The one drawback of the KeyPoint is its relatively short wireless range. Unlike the Firefly or recent X10 units, its signals may not penetrate the back seats if you have the receiver in the trunk. The solution is to run a USB cable to the front area [Hack #51] of the vehicle and place the receiver up there. You'll want to install the receiver around the middle of the car, so it's close to everyone who might use the remote.

Integration and Compatibility

With all these different remotes, what are the chances that they will work with your car PC or media player application out of the box? Not good. But there are several programs that help to bridge the gap and bring understanding between remotes and the programs you want to control.

Girder (*http://www.promixis.com*) is an incredibly versatile Windows scripting and automation program that supports all the major IR and RF remotes out there and comes bundled with the Firefly. Through a plug-in architecture, it can work with any remote, including the X10 Lola, the ATI Remote Wonder, and most of the commercially available IR remote receivers, including the receivers built into video capture cards such as those from Hauppauge (*http://www.hauppauge.com*). Through various techniques such as simulated keypresses, menu selections, software messaging, and other scripting mechanisms, Girder can map remote button presses to the appropriate keys or sequences of keys or clicks that a particular program needs. Girder changes context whenever a different application comes into focus, so the control can be customized for all your applications. At $20, it is a must-have if you are doing *any* in-car software integration with a wireless remote—it just makes life easier.

On the Linux front, the Linux Infrared Remote Control (LIRC; see *http://www.lirc.org*) has comprehensive support for a wide range of IR and RF remotes, and even Bluetooth phones acting as remotes. There has been some cross-pollination between Girder and LIRC (as they address the same problems on different platforms), and many hobbyists developing homebrew IR receivers and transmitters have written support plug-ins for both programs.

If you're going to control your apps in a car with a remote control, I recommend the Macally KeyPoint for driver use, and any of the larger, many-button IR remotes (such as the Firefly, the ATI, or the X10) for passenger use. I strongly recommend that the Girder software be combined with any remote.

HACK #57   Control Your Car PC with a Touchscreen

Touchscreens are the primary way to control most of the in-car applications being developed today.

In Chapter 3, I showed you how to install a VGA touchscreen in the dashboard [Hack #26]. And for good reason—not only are VGA screens sharper and far more readable than most other screens because of their higher resolution, but with a touchscreen interface you can eliminate the need for a mouse, a remote, and even a keyboard.

As an in-car user interface, touchscreens are one of the most attractive approaches out there. They are easy to use, with the big, ATM-style menus (Figure 5-4) that characterize the state of the in-car PC software art.

A touchscreen basically emulates a mouse. The major vendors of touchscreens for in-car use are Xenarc and Lilliput. These manufacturers include software to drive their screens that can run on most versions of Windows, Mac OS, and Linux (see *http://www.xenarc.com/download.html* and *http://www.newision.com/download.htm*).

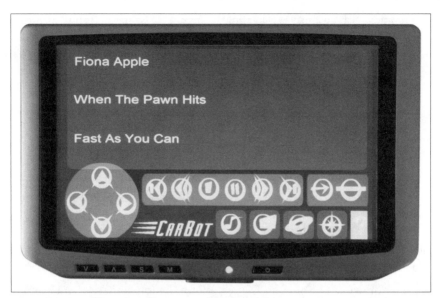

Figure 5-4. A touchscreen with an easy-to-touch interface

When emulating a mouse, touchscreens work quite well. When you touch any point on the screen, the application responds just as if the mouse pointer had been moved to that spot and the button pressed. Holding your finger down (with most of the drivers) simulates a right-click, and a contextual menu will pop up as expected. The influences of the last decade of PDA touchscreen innovation show, as even these relatively large screens can have fine, pixel-level "mouse" movement if you use a stylus or a fingernail. Touchscreens I used in the mid 1990s had calibration problems (as did my Palm Pilot) where if you touched one part of the screen your cursor was annoyingly offset, but my experience with Xenarc, Lilliput, and Pixellon monitors has been very consistent. I have never needed to calibrate any of my monitors using the software utility, even when I was using different resolutions and squishing them from a 4:3 to a 16:9 aspect ratio. Also, the different touchscreen overlays use the same technology and generally the same software drivers.

The other great feature of touchscreens is that they can act as keyboards, too. They do this by drawing the image of a keyboard on the screen, and you "type" on these virtual keys. If you've used a touchscreen navigation system or searched a wedding registry at a big department store chain, you know that you can slowly but accurately enter text on the screen via this method.

Windows actually comes with an onscreen keyboard (OSK) built in, but the buttons are designed to be clicked with a mouse pointer and are too small for general touchscreen use. You're better off using a navigation app that comes with an onscreen keyboard, such as Destinator (found at *http://www.mp3car.com*) or CoPilot [Hack #71], which has an excellent onscreen keyboard for entering addresses. Alternatively, you can Google for "virtual keyboard," "touchscreen keyboard," or "onscreen keyboard" to find a variety of configurable, large-key onscreen keyboard applications suitable for touchscreen use.

There are several drawbacks to touchscreens, and safety is potentially the biggest one. Touchscreens lack the tactile feedback that other input methods offer. Because the buttons have no recognizable feel to them (unlike radio buttons and controls), and because touchscreen menus can change position, the driver has to take her eyes off the road to use the screen.

Brightness is a problem too. The thin, plastic, touch-sensitive film used by touchscreens has a side effect of reducing LCD brightness by about 20%. Since most in-car LCD screens are already battling daylight sun, the added dimming caused by touchscreen film may be a factor in screen usability.

Another drawback is, of course, integration. The touchscreen that currently comes preinstalled with factory NAV systems is completely incompatible with car PCs. And if your car didn't come with a factory option for a screen, your dashboard will need significant (professional) rearranging to integrate one seamlessly. The other option is to make your car look like a cop car or a taxi, with a screen and a bundle of wires mounted on a functional but unaesthetic metal bracket attached to your dashboard. (Of course, you don't actually have to delve into bracketry—with liberal use of Velcro, I've had good success integrating a 7" Xenarc screen into my minivan's dashboard.)

Solutions

If you intend to use a touchscreen in your vehicle to control your car PC, there are several things you can do to make it safer and more usable. If the car PC app you are using allows you to redesign the skin, you can use a high-contrast color scheme that can deal with lots of ambient light. ("Install a VGA Touchscreen in Your Dashboard" [Hack #26] gives some additional solutions to the brightness problem.)

Another useful change to make when you're editing the skin for your UI is to put the four most often used buttons in the four corners of the touchscreen. As the late Jef Raskin (one of the original Macintosh designers) pointed out to me, you can find the corners of a touchscreen with your finger, without having to look at the screen. In some of the skins we've designed at CarBot, for example, we put the next track/last track buttons on the bottom left and right corners, so that the driver can seek and move through playlists by touch alone, just like with a normal stereo.

The fact remains that while aftermarket computer touchscreens are still a bit of a bleeding-edge gadget and are difficult to cleanly install, they are the most configurable and cool-looking additions to your car PC setup. As of this writing, both Xenarc (*http://www.xenarc.com*) and Lilliput (*http://www.newision.com*) have announced their single-DIN (standard radio size) fold-out motorized touchscreens, which will (finally!) permit easy after-market do-it-yourself installation.

HACK #58 Car-Enable Clunky Applications

You can use a scripting program to provide single-press access to application features that normally require complex menu navigation.

Many programs are difficult to use without a mouse and keyboard. For instance, most of the navigation packages for Windows are almost impossible to control without stopping the car and clicking on tiny buttons for a while. These applications are actually designed for use by a passenger with a laptop, not the driver.

A few summers ago I went on a month-long, cross-country trip with my wife and daughter ("to find America," as my friend put it). During the trip, we stopped from time to time and uploaded maps of our route so our relatives could keep track of us. We also took pictures of our daughter in front of all the "Welcome to [state]" signs we passed along the way.

Our "itinerary" was no more specific than dots on a poster-sized map of the U.S., and a printout of the addresses of our friends and family. As we had no portable Internet solution worked out for that trip except for any WiFi connection we might stumble upon, we relied on our GPS unit, our prototype CarBot, and the DeLorme Street Atlas USA program.

The DeLorme program has a sort of clunky, Visual-Basic-buttony feel, but it was pretty fast on my 600-MHz fanless VIA EPIA motherboard. I was fortunate to have a copilot who could work the clunky NAV application on that trip, though, as we quickly learned that the program is essentially unusable by the driver. Few programs are written to be used exclusively with a mouse; fewer still are designed to be used by someone with only one free hand who can't look at the screen except for fractions of a second.

Being used to MapQuest, we liked the DeLorme feature of being able to put in any two addresses and calculate the route between them, and the fact that we could switch between having the map track with the GPS unit (i.e., where we actually were) and then doing some MapQuest-like "reconnaissance" to find out where we were going.

I liked the DeLorme program, and it had all the maps and features I needed. Thus, when I later went to find the ideal NAV application for my in-car computer, I was frustrated that I couldn't just use the cheap (less than $100) app that I had already bought.

Scripting a Solution

On the MP3Car.com forums (*http://www.mp3car.com*), there is constant talk about controlling, launching, and grabbing the Windows handles of other non-car applications to make them work with car PC software. While this is a great solution for a coder (which I am, but that's not the point), I wanted to see what I could do with application scripting alone.

After a few searches, I found a freeware Windows scripting solution that, after a steep two-hour learning curve, solved my problem within a few minutes. Called PowerPro (*http://powerpro.webeddie.com*), it is a strange, non-intuitive, yet solid and versatile application. The program can do everything under the sun, including macros (sequences of keystrokes and commands), timed scripts, application launching, and pop-up and skinned menus. It seems designed to minimize the number of clicks and keystrokes you need to do any task, which is exactly what I wanted to do for my NAV program.

As mentioned in "Control Your Car PC with a Touchscreen" [Hack #57], big, easy-to-see, fixed-position buttons are far safer for a driver to use than pop-down menus. In PowerPro, you can create a menu full of clickable command buttons, known as a *bar*. You can specify the color, text size, and a background for these buttons. You can also tell the bar to be always on top and to position itself in all sorts of fixed and variable locations, related either to the main window or to the frontmost screen.

Navigation software tends to have two basic modes: route planning, and simply showing a map of where you are. In the case of my road trip, all of the basic routes were planned in advance (i.e., "Drive from Tacoma to Boise on this freeway"), so I didn't need the route-planning functionality in my application. What I *did* want to be able to do while I was driving was:

- Zoom in and out on the map, so I could see the forest or the trees
- Toggle pan-to-GPS-location, so I could glance ahead on the map and then snap back to showing where I was

Showing you how to set up these two functions should give you a feel for how PowerPro works and enable you to create your own custom uses. Setting up zooming was simple, because zoom in and zoom out functions were already enabled in the DeLorme application, using the keyboard shortcuts of Page Up and Page Down. Toggling pan-to-GPS-location was more difficult.

To get PowerPro to control Street Atlas, I had to learn its simple scripting language. After a while, I figured out that the syntax for sending Page Up and Page Down keystrokes to the window of a running program were the following (for up and down, respectively):

```
*Keys {to *USA*} {pgup}
*Keys {to *USA*} {pgdn}
```

The *Keys command tells the button to send keypresses; the {to *USA*} sends them to a particular window of a running program, identified by the text in its titlebar (in this case, "USA"). The titlebar of the running Street Atlas program contained the text "startup.sa9 – DeLorme Street Atlas USA." In my matching string, the * wildcards before and after USA basically say, "Find a window with 'USA' somewhere in the title." I first tried the string DeLorme, but I ran into problems I couldn't debug; once I changed it to *USA*, it worked fine. If I were going to run another program that had "USA" in the window title, though, I would need to change my search string to something more specific.

PowerPro allows you to set a few button preferences, including the button transparency, the button size (I made it 80×80 pixels), and the font and position of the button text. The results were plain, but functional. I created two large, easily visible buttons on the righthand side of the screen that held their positions no matter what I did and allowed me to rapidly zoom in and out.

Toggling pan-to-GPS-location off and on was slightly trickier, as the checkbox option in the menu can't be run with a single keypress. As you probably know, Windows menus usually have accelerator keys assigned to them. When you press and hold the Alt key, various letters on the menu become underlined. When you press those letters in combination with the Alt key, the corresponding menu item is selected. The PowerPro code for the Alt key is a %. Using that piece of information, I was able to use the following command to launch the menu item that was accessible with the Alt-A-G key combination:

```
*Keys {to *USA*} %ag
```

I experimented with putting a one-second delay between the two letters, but I found it wasn't necessary, and the option toggled without even showing me a pop-up menu. I wasn't finished yet, though. I had corny-looking buttons—functional but way uncool—and I wanted to improve them a bit before I called the project done. So, I did a screen grab of Street Atlas, selected the tiny zoom buttons and a GPS button off the top of the screen, resized them, and pasted them into a rudimentary stack of three buttons.

Then, I simply configured a background for my button bar in PowerPro, and voilà—my big, iconic, touchscreen-friendly buttons were in place (see Figure 5-5)

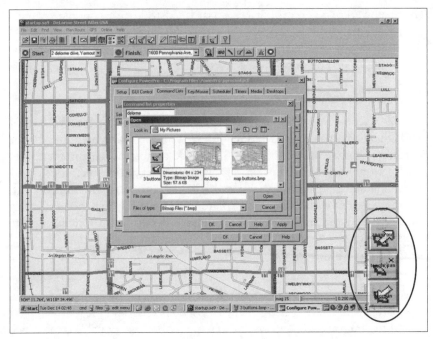

Figure 5-5. Stylish PowerPro DeLorme buttons

In addition to everything else, PowerPro gives you 12 virtual desktops that you can instantly switch between with a button press. Using this feature, you can create a fixed-position button bar along the bottom of the screen, containing nothing but one-sentence "scripts" (which are just keypresses) that switch between your various virtual desktops. On each virtual desktop, you can run one in-car PC application, such as your navigation software, iTunes, a movie player, a video game emulator, and so on. Not only that, but using the facilities available with the {to NameOfWindow} command, you can configure buttons to operate on apps that are on different screens, so that, for example, your music controls (play, pause, rewind, fast forward, next track, shuffle, etc.) all appear on whatever screen you're looking at. You can then use whatever media player you'd like, whether it's "driver-friendly" or not.

With an image-editing program, a few solid hours spent learning the Power-Pro program, and a couple of days to play, you can put together your own custom in-car PC application to automate your favorite programs, without having to "program" at all.

See Also

- "Control Your Car PC with a Handheld Remote" [Hack #56]

Listen to What Your Car Computer Is Saying
HACK #59

Your computer may be talking, but is it really saying anything? With the right application, it could be.

When I first started researching in-car computing trends, I tried to determine what the biggest obstacles were to launching a successful product that large numbers of people would buy. What I learned from reading a lot of market research, analysis papers, and expert opinions was that *safety* was the number one concern of millions of potential consumers.

To be fair, price, standards, ease of installation, ease of use, cost of operation, form factor, performance, and supported applications all impact a product's sales potential as well. But if car computing products aren't made safe enough to begin with, anti-car-computer legislation could stop the whole market, at least in the very litigious United States.

I thought the problem through and decided that one of my design goals was to be able to operate every function of our CarBot software using only button presses and computer voice responses, without requiring a screen—and thus the CarBot Player software was born.

Text-to-Speech

TTS is the acronym often used to describe any system where a computer attempts to read text or speak command results to the user. There is a control panel called "Speech" in Windows that allows you to configure which voice you want the system and programs to use by default, and to test that TTS is working on your system. The Windows Speech Application Programming Interface (SAPI) comes with a few built-in Microsoft voices and allows third-party developers to add additional higher-quality voices to a system. Any program that uses TTS can use the high-quality speech from these additional voices.

TTS has many useful applications in in-car computing. For example, many of the laptop navigation programs have a mode where they can read turn-by-turn directions to you [Hack #71].

The CarBot Player Software

The CarBot Player software was designed to allow the driver to easily and safely control any function that an in-car computer could possibly do, including controlling video for rear-seat entertainment, activating games, sending and receiving email, receiving instant messages, activating an in-car webcam...you name it. Yet I still had the goal of preserving the lowest common denominator of buttons available on remotes and stereo head units: fast forward, rewind, last track, next track, and perhaps five or six numbered preset buttons.

To accomplish all this, I tried to map everything to a CD player control methodology. For instance, while a DVD has a complex menu system, I wanted to make it as easy as possible to just start playing the actual movie. As a recent dad, I have a simple need: I want to be able to put in a Dora the Explorer DVD, press next next next, and have my daughter contentedly eating goldfish crackers while watching the show from inside her surround-sound car seat within moments.

Another application I really wanted was email. I used to have the privilege (thankfully, I love driving!) of driving 35 miles from a suburb to my office in downtown Los Angeles each day—a commute that averaged 1 hour and 15 minutes. Though I could have listened to music or books on tape/CD, what I really wanted to listen to were the hundreds of emails I got every day that didn't actually require responses, and the Slashdot headlines and blurbs from that morning.

So, using the same interface my company was already using to control DVDs, we implemented an interface for navigating through email messages just like tracks on a CD—the next, back, pause, fast forward, and rewind buttons moved me through the messages in my Inbox, and the CarBot software read each message to me. One of our staff figured out that he could email himself chunks of text, or even long articles, and have them read to him during his commute.

Can I Have a Screen with That?

While the market research we did while preparing for this project may have been valid for millions of potential future consumers, I soon learned that it wouldn't necessarily help us sell in-car computers *today*. As I mentioned earlier, our market research said safety was the most important issue. But in fact, safety was actually what was on the minds of all the people *not* buying in-car computers. To sell our computers, we had to "give the market what it wants." And what was that?

Almost every one of our conversations with the customers that called for information about the first version of the CarBot (which was screenless) went something like this:

> Customer: Hello, I'm interested in your CarBot. Does it come with a screen?
>
> Me: No, it speaks to you, and you control it with a wireless remote control unit.

Customer: **Oh you mean it has speech recognition?**

Me: **No, it speaks to *you*; you control it with a wireless remote control unit.**

Customer: **But can it work with a screen?**

Needless to say, you can imagine what my response became:

Me: **Absolutely! CarBot can work with or without a screen. You can run any Windows application, because it's a full-fledged PC...**

Dance, sales guy, dance.

Questions such as "Can I check Outlook when I'm on the road?" and "Can I connect to my VPN?" indicated the real needs of the *actual market*—i.e., the people ready to actually pay money and buy the product. They weren't interested in safety (how could a populace addicted to driving while using mobile phones be worried about safety?); they were interested in *applications*. I don't even know if most of our buyers were worried about price or even standards, except for the standard "Does it work with my car?"

Voice/Button Interface

The well-established human interface for audio in the car is the car radio, which has remained essentially the same for many decades. One of the benefits of radio buttons is that they stay put and always have generally the same function, or at least the same function depending on what mode you're in (FM1, FM2, AM, CD changer, etc.).

One successful manufacturer of a Linux-based (but closed source) in-car computing platform is PhatNoise (*http://www.phatnoise.com*). Their digital media player started out with one main function: playing large MP3 libraries. To solve the problem of navigating through these libraries, they actually designed and even filed a patent on a method of using the CD changer buttons on factory stereos to reshuffle MP3s based on artist, album, title, genre, and so on. Early in the design process, I knew that we wanted to have excellent TTS software. Not being limited by the small CPU power of a handheld, we looked for a system that took advantage of the ample hard disk space and computational power of our in-car computers. We tried out the ViaVoice voices from IBM (*http://www.wizzardsoftware.com/products/IBMttssdk.php*) as well as some other Anglo-centric companies, but we finally decided to use the voices from a French company, Elan Sayso, now part of the largest European TTS company, Acapela Group (*http://www.acapela-group.com*).

My goal was to feel like Tomb Raider's Lara Croft (picture Angelina Jolie or the anatomically implausible video game character of your choice) was reading my email to me. And it worked! The Lara voice we chose, with her French-tinged British accent, actually made listening to some of my spam enjoyable.

Listening to Your Apps

The original CarBot Player had several user interface methods, all completely usable without a screen. Our design started with voice feedback and basic buttons that did not require the user to look at a screen. Then we built the visual interface, which is just a Flash movie. The user or installer can customize it to taste, making it as simple or complex as desired (or as permitted by the laws in their region).

When using the music playback features, the titles of the songs, artists, and folders being navigated are read to the user, who can navigate through them quickly without looking at the screen. Since the user can memorize the locations of the relevant buttons on the controller, navigating can become an automatic action—there's no need to hunt around on the screen for the right button, song, or folder name.

Figure 5-6 shows a screen capture of one simple skin for our email application, which displays just the sender and title. Simple, huh? Listen, the last thing I want is people reading emails on a monitor while they're driving; I do have to share the road with these people!

Figure 5-6. Screen capture of the CarBot Player software

Control Your Car PC with Voice Recognition

HACK #60

You can use software to make your car PC's navigation system and other functions voice-operated, just like the cool cars in the commercials.

My initial inspiration for implementing voice recognition in my car PC came because I kept seeing commercials for voice-activated navigation systems, like those in Hondas and Acuras.

Speech recognition requires the computer to accept spoken words as input and interpret what has been spoken. To make the job of understanding speech easier for the computer, a method of speech input called *command and control* is used. With command and control, a limited number of voice commands are specified and listened for by the computer, which greatly decreases the chances of errors in interpretation.

If you install Microsoft's Speech API (SAPI) and my NaviVoice (*http://www.whipflash.com/vamr/routisvoice.htm*) program on your Windows computer, you can configure it to respond to voice commands. The text commands that you can use are stored in an XML (eXtensible Markup Language) file. In the XML file that comes with NaviVoice, each command is next to a number; when a command is uttered, the corresponding number is sent to NaviVoice, which then executes the command that is associated with that number. NaviVoice itself responds to the number that it receives from SAPI by executing commands stored in INI files. These INI files specify what should be done to respond to the recognized voice command (e.g., launching a file or executing a macro).

NaviVoice implements a macro system so that it can control closed source applications for which no documentation or programming API exists. Basically, the macros are series of emulated user commands (such as menu selections) that are executed very quickly and automatically.

Controlling Routis and iGuidance

Routis and iGuidance are popular in-car computer navigation programs [Hack #71], but neither of these programs provides a way to access their commands from software, so I had to develop a workaround. NaviVoice emulates the keyboard and mouse inputs a user would normally give to the program. When you want to enter a destination, you speak a voice command and NaviVoice "presses" Alt-F, Enter, Enter, Enter in the NAV application on your behalf. When you then spell out an address and say "Enter" twice, NaviVoice enters the information in the host NAV application for you and has it perform a search for directions.

The process of accessing favorite locations is even easier. Enter your desired favorite into the configuration program, and add the desired voice command and its corresponding number into the XML file. When you want to go to that favorite, speak the voice command you associated with it, and NaviVoice will do all the typing for you. Then you can just follow the directions to your destination.

Currently, NaviVoice voice-enables *almost* every function that either Routis or iGuidance can perform, including access to some nested commands, such as automatic speed warnings, map orientation, map size, 3D map view, point of interest icons on/off, map or guidance view, route mode, and so on.

 Ninja Monkey (from the *http://www.mp3car.com* forums) has developed another popular navigation program based on the Destinator engine, called Map Monkey. NaviVoice controls this version of Destinator just as well.

In earlier versions of NaviVoice, the application was always listening, leading to erroneous command recognition when the driver spoke to passengers or talked on a mobile phone. The solution I implemented was to give Navi-Voice a trigger word that, when spoken by the user, opens up a user-configurable "window" (in time) in which the user may speak all of his commands. Each successful command recognition resets the window, so you won't have to say the trigger command constantly. This way, NaviVoice listens constantly just for the trigger word, and only when it hears it will it then listen for other navigation-specific commands. If the user needs to close the window early, there is a "done" command; there is also an infinite time window command to eliminate the need for a trigger word. When Navi-Voice is listening for commands, the system tray icon will indicate this by changing from a globe with headphones to a microphone.

Problems Caused by Standby or Hibernation

SAPI has an unfortunate tendency not to resume after Windows comes out of either standby or hibernation, both of which are often used with in-car computers. However, I've noticed that if I pause the recognition before the system goes into either standby or hibernation, SAPI *will* work when I resume after I click on resume recognition. So now, NaviVoice monitors system power events and pauses recognition before going into standby or hibernation and resumes recognition after resumption.

Another problem that was fixed by monitoring the system power events was a bug in which Routis/iGuidance did not recognize USB GPS receivers when the computer resumed from standby or hibernation. In *NaviVoice.ini*, you can configure NaviVoice so that when resumption is detected, NaviVoice will dismiss the GPS error dialog and command either Routis or iGuidance to recognize the GPS receiver.

Text-to-Speech Output

Text-to-speech (TTS) is another technology offered by SAPI. The speech is totally synthesized in software, and additional voices are available in your favorite dialects and languages [Hack #59].

Routis, iGuidance, and many other navigation applications use prerecorded voice prompts instead of generic voice synthesis. This is because they have a standard set of 50 or so phrases that they say a lot (e.g., "turn left"), which are recorded by a voice actor instead of being synthesized. However, it can be unsettling to have multiple voices in the car (one for general TTS and one for prerecorded navigation prompts). With help from Frodo (the author of FrodoPlayer [Hack #75]), I added a feature to the NaviVoice configuration application that uses the SAPI 5 engine to output the navigation text prompts into WAV format, suitable for replacing the prerecorded prompts in Routis/iGuidance and providing a more consistent listening experience.

SAPI Hints

Here are some useful hints for using the Microsoft Speech API:

- Update to the latest version of SAPI (6) included with Microsoft Office 2003.

- Increase the "Pronunciation Sensitivity" and "Accuracy vs. Recognition Time" settings (Start → Control Panel → Speech → Settings).

- Disable the "Background Adaptation" setting (Start → Control Panel → Speech → Settings). Do you really want SAPI learning from what it hears? Probably not.

- Use a noise-canceling microphone.

- Training seems like an obvious requirement, but most people seem to skip this. The original SAPI training session is not the means by which a properly configured SAPI learns to understand you. The more you train, the more accurate SAPI will be.

Further Development

For future versions, I would love to enable album and artist selection of MP3s using voice recognition. I know that this is possible; it's just a matter of figuring out how to add voice commands after SAPI has initialized. Also, I would love to add support for PhoneControl.NET [Hack #63], with the goal of being able to say things like "call home" and have your home number automatically dialed.

See Also

- "Car-Enable Clunky Applications" [Hack #58]
- "Choose Your in-Car Navigation Software" [Hack #71]

—David Burban

HACK
#61

Find More Ways to Control Your in-Car Computer

On the horizon are several new integrated control methods that will make in-car PC control even easier.

Some people in the car PC world like to claim that auto manufacturers are a decade behind the technology curve. True, it took years before a single car had MP3 support, and even today almost no new cars support it.

The automotive industry has two strong drivers for its technology: the need for minimal price per unit and the need for maximum safety. Thus, expensive computer gadgets that add to driver distraction are the first to get cut in any design effort, and those features that *do* make it through this powerful filter of cost and litigation-consciousness have to be designed to be cheap and as safe as practical.

To a user-interface designer, arguably, no user interface is inherently intuitive. Even the mouse is not intuitive; rather, every desktop computer uses it, and it's a good control method, so people can adapt to new programs easily because they know how to use a mouse.

If you have new functionality to add to a car, you have a few choices: use a familiar interface (be it good or bad), or start from scratch and design a new one that, once learned, will be safer and easier to use.

Rotating Knobs

At a recent automotive trade show I visited the booth of a very, very cool company, Immersion Technologies (*http://www.immersion.com/automotive*), which designs and builds *haptic* (touch) interfaces for a variety of technology fields, including automotive. In fact, they partnered with BMW to design the iDrive interface. With iDrive, you have a single haptic rotating knob in the center console. The cool thing about it is that it can take on different qualities to allow you to control various applications: it can act like a click knob with hundreds of small angular increments, or with just five positions; it can be an infinitely rotating knob, or rotate around four times and then stop, or it can be configured through the car's embedded software to feel like it only turns 180 degrees and stops hard at 3 and 9 o'clock.

As a result, the user can look at the road while operating a complex set of menus, each of which has its own unique feel. You can control all the deep, layered functions of the car, such as climate controls, the radio, and the navigation system, by pressing and rotating just this one knob.

Now, there is definitely a learning curve to using the knob. While it is some-what intuitive, in the sense that people are familiar with using knobs (e.g., to control the volume, tuning, and fade and balance settings on a car radio), we haven't really experienced morphing knobs before.

After getting you all excited about Immersion's knob, I have to say that in single-unit quantities these units are prohibitively expensive. I tried to buy one at a trade show, and for the price they quoted me I could buy a Segway. Nonetheless, you can control your media with a much simpler dial at a much lower cost. Contour Design's ShuttleXpress (*http://www.contourdesign.com/shuttlepro/shuttlexpress.htm*), pictured in Figure 5-7, is a sub-$100 device designed for film editing but applicable to any rapid-scrolling application. It has five configurable buttons (ideal for mapping to CD controls) and two scrolling wheels. The outer, ridged wheel is a shuttle-wheel—it can rotate to the right or left, but not all the way around, with the degree of twist indicating how fast it seeks through selections. The top jog-wheel with a recessed finger hole can rotate around and around indefinitely—excellent for spinning rapidly through thousands of songs. Like handheld remote control programs [Hack #56], the software that accompanies the ShuttleXpress changes the key mappings when you switch applications, so you can customize how different applications react to the shuttle input.

Another even smaller, cooler looking device is the Griffin Technology PowerMate (*http://www.griffintechnology.com/products/powermate/features.php*). The PowerMate is a brushed aluminum or black metal jog/shuttle-wheel with a glowing blue programmable light. Although the pretty lights are less useful for in-car applications, the wheel has five "buttons": twist left, twist right, press, press and twist left, or press and twist right. Originally conceived as a huge volume and mute knob, it can be configured to scroll through large media collections, like the ShuttleXpress.

Both of these devices, which connect via USB, are small enough to mount between the driver and passenger seats, giving a nice clean look compared to a clunky remote control and requiring less button pressing.

Car PC/Head Unit Integration

One of the most obvious but difficult control options for car PCs is head unit integration. Almost every stereo head unit manufactured today has at least an eight-character display and an array of buttons including up, down, left, right, and preset buttons 1 through 6. The display is used for showing CD text, station identifications, and song names sent by terrestrial and satellite radio stations.

Figure 5-7. The ShuttleXpress

XM has released a new model of their XM receiver, called XM Direct (*http://
www.xmradio.com/xm_direct/*). This unit is universal, costs only $50, and
connects to another device, a "digital adapter," that converts it to the proprietary OEM or aftermarket protocol for a variety of head units. Depending on
the satellite-ready capabilities of the head unit, the XM Direct unit either
displays a simple channel number, like a CD changer, or displays the full
text of the channel when possible.

Many hackers have figured out the XM Direct protocol, allowing computers to talk to the XM receiver, making the car PC the head unit and allowing it to change stations on the XM radio through the car PC software.
This connection can also be reversed, with the car PC connecting to the
satellite-ready head unit through the digital adapter. In this configuration,
car PC software developers can receive the button presses from the head
unit, and send text to be displayed on the head unit, for any application
they want! My company (*http://www.carbotpc.com*) has developed the
hardware and software implementing this feature for inclusion in our next
car PC, but we are by no means the first or only one. I know of a number
of adapter manufacturers (such as In-Dash PC, at *http://www.indashpc.org*)

and individual hackers and car PC frontend developers (such as Frodo, author of FrodoPlayer [Hack #75]) that are working on the same sort of things, and I'm confident that several of them will be available before this book hits the shelves.

Future Controls

Members of the car PC community are working on several control methods to improve your interaction with your in-car computer. Even though these hacks aren't done yet, they are natural extensions of other hacks in this book and are left as an exercise for the reader. Here are a few of the options that are being developed:

Steering wheel controls
> The Pacific Accessory Corporation, mentioned in "Get Computer Audio into Your Head Unit" [Hack #14], makes a unit called the SWI-X (*http://www.pac-audio.com/products/swi.htm*), which is a sort of universal learning infrared remote control for your steering wheel. It connects to the wires connecting the steering wheel controls to the factory head unit (it supports almost every model built after 1986) and can learn and imitate codes from another remote control. The use here is obvious—since you can teach it your own codes, the natural thing is to teach it to send IR codes to a receiver such as the one made by Irman [Hack #56].

Shift knob controls
> Pacific Accessory Corporation also makes a line of performance shifters with four programmable buttons on top that extend through wires to an infrared transmitter. If you aren't already in love with your existing shift knob, you can program this learning IR transmitter to control your in-car computer so that you can switch tracks between shifts.

Bluetooth mobile phones
> A lesser-known feature of Bluetooth mobile phones is that they can serve as wireless controllers for your computer. For PCs, Zoran Horvat's PhoneControl (*http://zoran-horvat.de/private/CarPC/*) enables the use of certain Sony Ericsson, Siemens, or Motorola mobile phones to generate keypresses or mouse movements. Likewise, Jonas Salling's Salling Clicker (*http://homepage.mac.com/jonassalling/Shareware/Clicker/*) allows a wide variety of Bluetooth mobile phones to control applications on a Macintosh. The Salling Clicker has won numerous awards, and its iTunes integration is fantastic.

CHAPTER SIX

Wireless Connectivity and in-Car Internet
Hacks 62–68

It's a fun and promising time for wireless Internet access. 802.11 Wireless Networking, or *WiFi*, is growing at an explosive rate, and metropolitan-area networks are being deployed with new technologies such as *WiMax*, a proposed wide-range evolution of WiFi technology. Mobile phone providers are also beginning to deploy their own broadband wireless networks, using solutions under the banner of *3G* (third-generation wireless).

Wireless technology allows data to flow freely between the car PC and its surroundings. Wireless technology already lets cars pass through tollbooths without stopping, and future trials have been announced to download movies directly to the car as it pulls up to a gas station. But while it may be years before we can purchase an audio book, movie, or song at the pump, the technology to get the information we need into our cars today is already at our fingertips.

From real-time traffic updates to videoconferencing to auto-downloading MP3s to the car, this chapter will cover some of the fantastic features that are available when you bring wireless networking and the Internet to your car.

HACK #62 Get Online in Your Car

You have several options for how to rig your car PC for wireless Internet connectivity so you can surf the Web, download email, or transfer files while on the go.

In the old days, there were only a few ways to get online wirelessly, each of them slow and expensive. Recently, that has all changed. This hack will help you understand your options and choose your wireless connectivity solution.

In the era of analog cell phones, you could pay upwards of a dollar per minute for a modem connection of between 2,400 and 9,600 bits per second (i.e., up to 9.6 kbps). Not only was the connection slow, but it usually took a minute or so to connect as well, making even a failed attempt at getting online a costly affair. The conversion to digital cell phone standards opened the door to faster connect times, but for a long time it did nothing to increase connection speeds, which were still pegged at 9600 bits per second.

For many years the U.S. market had its own handful of cell phone standards, including analog and early transitional digital standards, while Europe had standardized on *GSM* (Global System for Mobiles). In the last five years GSM has gained popularity in the U.S. market (through T-Mobile, AT&T, and Cingular), and now the two major standards in the United States are GSM and *CDMA* (Code Division Multiple Access, describing how the signals travel).

Both GSM and CDMA have basic digital transfer and fax capabilities, being digital protocols. But these so-called 2G (second-generation) cellular standards max out at modem speeds (i.e., up to around 50 kbps). Higher-speed data protocols build upon these standards.

Wireless Internet Options

The broad set of aims for wireless evolution with all the features anyone could want falls in the scope of *3G* (the third-generation wireless protocol; see *http://www.3gpp.org* for GSM and *http://www.3gpp2.org* for CDMA). What has been deployed so far is only part of this grand vision, and these transitional standards have been dubbed *2.5G*.

In addition to the GSM and CDMA standards, there are a number of technologies that seek to push data-transfer speeds into the broadband range. These include GPRS, EDGE, 1xRTT, and EVDO.

GPRS (20–40 kbps). At the bottom of the speed barrel is *GPRS* (General Packet Radio Service). While the top speed of GPRS is theoretically over 150 kbps, in practice it consistently offers only the speed of a 28.8-kbps modem. However, unlike with traditional dial-up-over-cellular solutions, the connection times with GPRS are so short as to seem instant, and the connections are *very* durable, handling the transition between cell towers well so that your connection is not dropped.

GPRS service is relatively cheap—T-Mobile provides it for an additional $20 per month on your existing Bluetooth phone or for $30 per month on a PC card for unlimited data transfer. It has a very wide coverage range (pretty much anywhere you get GSM cellular reception, GPRS will work), and you can use it to surf the Web (slowly) on your car PC. For general telemetry applications, it is a cheap, solid solution.

T-Mobile and Cingular (which has absorbed AT&T) provide GPRS service in the U.S. market. There are two major ways to use it. One way is to get a dedicated GPRS PC card. T-Mobile provides a Sony Ericsson combination WiFi and GPRS card, so that you can transition between a T-Mobile WiFi hotspot and their GPRS service. The other way is over a Bluetooth connection to your mobile phone.

EDGE (60–80 kbps). *EDGE* (Enhanced Data Rates for GSM Evolution) is an upgrade path for GPRS speeds. It has a theoretical maximum connection speed of 128 kbps or 384 kbps, depending on the configuration. In the U.S. it actually provides about 60–80 kbps. Since Cingular recently absorbed AT&T, Cingular and T-Mobile are now the two leading GSM phone service providers in the U.S. Right now, Cingular/AT&T has EDGE, and T-Mobile is about to deploy it.

EDGE networking works in the same way as GPRS. You can use either Bluetooth or a PC card to get it in your machine, and EDGE access cards are backward-compatible with GPRS networks, so you get wide coverage. In my experience, it delivers a sort of choppy enhancement to normal GPRS. When fetching large emails or downloading files, the raw throughput is fantastic. However, the latency of the connection is high, and while you're surfing the Web this can mean lots of failed connections or 20-second waits while switching towers. Once established, though, EDGE connections, like GPRS, are very solid.

CDMA2000/CDMA 1xRTT/W-CDMA/EVDO (40–60 kbps/80–144 kbps/300–500 kbps). As this list of confusing acronyms shows, the marketing hasn't really caught up with the technology. Within the CDMA standards used by Verizon and Sprint, the terms *1xRTT* (1 pair of channels, Radio Transmission Technology), *W-CDMA* (Wideband-CDMA), and *1xEVDO* or just *EVDO* (1 pair of channels, Evolution, Data Only) describe the new higher-bandwidth data protocols that are available. While 1xRTT only goes up to 144 kbps, EVDO operates at up to 25 times the bandwidth of traditional CDMA, with a theoretical maximum connection speed of 2 Mbps and an average of between 300 kbps and 500 kbps. The upload speeds are considerably slower, at 60–80 kbps.

Sprint provides the bandwidth for the very popular Treo (Palm OS) handhelds, but their network, as of this writing, only offers speeds of up to 144 kbps, and their pricing is not that competitive. Verizon, on the other hand, offers the fastest flat-fee bandwidth available. Their NationalAccess plan offers only modest speeds of 40–60 kbps, but it lives up to its name with coast-to-coast availability in the U.S. Verizon's BroadbandAccess, however, provides what you can truly call broadband speed at 300–500 kbps, and it is available in a dozen major city markets. Reviews I have read report sustained speeds as high as 800 kbps, with spikes of up to 2 Mbps. At this speed, live audio streaming (e.g., via *http://www.live365.com*) and even video streaming are possible.

WiFi (802.11) (1500–50,000 kbps). *WiFi* is the consumer marketing term for a group of wireless networking technologies that you must have heard of by now. Most WiFi signals run at the frequency of 2.4 GHz. WiFi speeds range from 11 Mbps (802.11b) to 54 Mbps (802.11g), and newer standards run into the 100-Mbps range. However, because of protocol overhead, interference, and bandwidth sharing, you are guaranteed to get less than half of the theoretical throughput in the best case.

WiFi was not originally designed as a wide area networking protocol, but the emergence of open wireless hotspots and the workability of WiFi at driving speeds have made it a viable option for mobile Internet access. Mind you, this does not mean that you can drive down any highway and have guaranteed high-speed WiFi access—WiFi will not let your passengers surf the Web unless you are near a hotspot, or driving slowly in rush hour through a WiFi-saturated neighborhood.

What it does mean is that a number of vendors, such as T-Mobile (*http://www.tmobile.com*), have installed WiFi access points at many popular retail locations (such as Starbucks), and that the same WiFi adapter you use to access the Internet at home and work can seamlessly "roam" onto these networks. For uses that can be batched, such as downloading email and news feeds [Hack #21], synchronizing MP3 collections [Hack #64], or uploading GPS logs to a web site [Hack #67], this high-bandwidth but intermittent connectivity works perfectly.

Getting Online with 3G

To connect to one of these mobile phone wireless networks, you'll need a new network card. Your existing WiFi cards won't work on the 3G networks (although your Bluetooth-equipped laptop can communicate with these networks through a Bluetooth-equipped mobile phone).

Normally, wireless PCMCIA cards are sold as part of a service contract (like mobile phones) by the wireless provider. To get a better picture of all the available wireless options, try looking up the hardware first, rather than going directly to the service providers.

Sierra Wireless (*http://www.sierrawireless.com*) is one of the best starting points, because they make wireless PCMCIA cards (their AirCard series) for almost all of the major wireless networks. Another good hardware provider is Novatel Wireless (*http://www.novatelwireless.com*), with their Merlin series of wireless cards.

You can improve the reception of these cards by using an external antenna. The best vendor I've found for a wide array of antenna products is Hyper-Link Technologies (*http://www.hyperlinktech.com*). My own company, Car-Bot, buys all its car-mount WiFi antennas from HyperLink, and we've been very happy with the reception using their 5dB antennas. (Decibels, or *dB*, are a measure of signal strength; more is better.)

Because of a lack of early standards, there are literally dozens of possible connectors for WiFi antennas. HyperLink takes care of that, because they provide *pigtails* (short wire adapters) that convert any WiFi card or access point you have into an N-female ending, which can then be connected to any of their antennas.

HyperLink's 19" pigtails also provide stress relief for the tiny connector needed for the most popular PCMCIA WiFi cards (see Figure 6-1). Wavelan, which became Orinoco, which became Proxim (*http://www.proxim.com*), makes the most popular and best-supported WiFi cards. Most of their 802. 11b and 802.11g cards come with an antenna port, which is a rare thing for PCMCIA cards.

Although you can get online with a PCMCIA card, another way to do it is by connecting through a Bluetooth-capable phone [Hack #63], which you may already own. The cool thing about the Bluetooth modem feature is that it works just as fast as a PCMCIA card and connects very rapidly. It only takes a few seconds to get connected, and your phone can be sitting anywhere— you don't have to point it at the computer or even take it out of your pocket—although I usually put it on the dashboard or clip it to the ceiling so I ensure that it has a good signal.

On-Road Experience

I've traveled from Los Angeles to San Jose, California via Interstate 5 and maintained a GPRS (modem speed, about 20 kbps) connection most of the way, with some interruptions in the Grapevine (naturally). While going through a canyon on the 152 (which takes you inland from Interstate 5 to the 101 Freeway near San Jose), I lost my connection completely for an hour; however, my mobile phone didn't work in that canyon either.

Once I upgraded to my Nokia 6620 with EDGE (60–80 kbps), I continued testing. When I repeated my LA-to-San Jose mobile connectivity test, the EDGE connection lasted just as durably, with the same Grapevine and

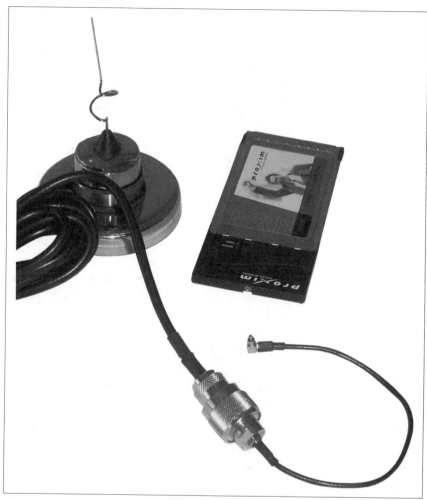

Figure 6-1. Connecting a car-mount antenna to your WiFi card

Route 152 interruptions. One of my passengers was downloading programs and doing extensive Google searching while we went at freeway speeds up the Interstate 5. Another friend of mine was even programming in the car, using a remote desktop connection to his home PC.

Making Your Car a Mobile WiFi Hotspot

If your car PC is configured to connect via WiFi, and your laptop has a 3G card, you can get your car PC online using your laptop. Conversely, if you have passengers who need to get their laptops online while they ride in your car, and your car PC has a 3G card, why not make your whole car a WiFi hotspot?

Since I got my new PowerBook with built-in Bluetooth, I've used it frequently to give my WiFi-equipped CarBot an Internet connection. Since my PowerBook is already paired with my Nokia 6620, I just click "Connect" in Internet Connect on my PowerBook, which rapidly brings up a Net connection via AT&T/Cingular's EDGE network and then, using Connection Sharing (System Preferences → Sharing → Internet), shares it as a WiFi hotspot. My CarBot and any passengers with laptops (including passengers in other cars in the same vicinity!) then get the benefit of my WiFi connection.

I mention my Macintosh because that's what I use, and I find it very simple. However, there is similar software available for PCs that turns them into real WiFi access points. PCTEL (*http://pctel.com/softap.php*) makes a software access point product for around $20 that can be installed on a car PC with a PCI WiFi card (their site lists supported cards).

If you have a permanent 3G wireless connection set to auto-dial on your car PC, you can use the PCTEL SoftAP to make your car PC into an access point. If you happen to be in, say, a restaurant near your car and you need to get online, you can just turn on your car PC remotely [Hack #46] and then connect to the Internet through your car PC access point.

HACK #63 Make Your Mobile Phone Hands-Free with Your Car PC

Your car PC and car speakers can act as a hands-free unit for your mobile phone, using Bluetooth wireless networking.

Bluetooth is a low-range, low-speed, and low-power radio frequency transmission protocol designed for attaching peripherals to computers. You can think of it as a sort of wireless alternative to USB, just like WiFi is a wireless alternative to Ethernet.

One of the "killer applications" of Bluetooth technology is making mobile phones hands-free, either through a wireless headset or by direct integration with your vehicle. And while only a few of the newest cars come with Bluetooth hands-free capabilities built in, your car PC can speak Bluetooth and integrate with your mobile phone, no matter what kind of car you drive.

In order for your car PC to act as a Bluetooth hands-free speaker, it needs to make a wireless connection to your mobile phone. To enable this, you need a Bluetooth interface (a.k.a. a *dongle*; see Figure 6-2). The most common interface used for Bluetooth dongles is USB. Some manufacturers have a serial (RS232) interface, but this is unusual. For a car PC, the tiny USB form factor is excellent.

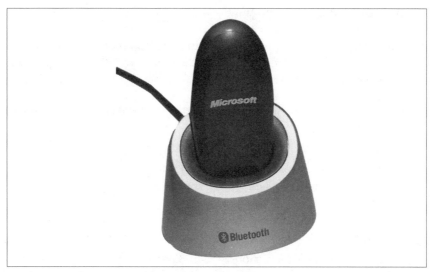

Figure 6-2. A Bluetooth dongle

Bluetooth is fairly standard. Most of the dongles are based on a Cambridge Silicon Radio (*http://www.csr.com*) Bluetooth microchip. Pretty much any standalone dongle you purchase should work with your phone (the adapter that comes with the Microsoft Bluetooth wireless mouse and keyboard is a notable exception).

Each Bluetooth dongle is equipped with driver software for your operating system, which contains the so-called "protocol stack." This stack implements the Bluetooth *profiles*, which are the services you can use with your Bluetooth dongle (such as Dial-up Networking, Serial Port, or Headset/Hands-Free). When ordering a Bluetooth device, be sure it comes with the latest version of the protocol stack (post-1.1). Early versions don't include the Headset Profile and thus don't support hands-free use.

Most of the Bluetooth driver software comes from a company called Widcomm (*http://www.widcomm.com*), which was recently acquired by Broadcom (*http://www.broadcom.com*).

Installing Bluetooth on Windows

Installing Bluetooth hardware consists of sticking the Bluetooth dongle into a free USB port, either in your car PC or in a USB hub connected to the PC, and then inserting the CD that came with the dongle and running the setup program. Follow the steps shown on the screen and reboot your computer if you're asked to.

If you're using the Microsoft Windows XP operating system with Service Pack 2 (SP2) installed on your PC, however, start the setup on the CD first, and don't plug in the Bluetooth dongle until the setup program instructs you to do so. This is important because SP2 has its own Bluetooth protocol stack, which is not compatible with the Widcomm stack and will inhibit accessing the dongle with the Widcomm stack. The Microsoft protocol stack doesn't implement the Headset/Hands-Free Profile as of this writing, so you shouldn't use it.

After the setup is complete, you'll have a new icon on your desktop called "My Bluetooth Places" and a new applet in your System Tray. This applet should show a white B, signalling that your Bluetooth dongle is initialized and ready to use. A red B signals that the device hasn't been started yet (check whether your dongle is plugged in correctly). As soon as you've established a connection to any Bluetooth device, the B turns green.

Right-click on the applet and choose Open Bluetooth Settings from the pop-up menu to display the Bluetooth configuration dialog (Figure 6-3).

Figure 6-3. Bluetooth advanced configuration

In this dialog, you have all the configuration settings categorized and grouped by tabs. The first tab (General) is important because it shows the currently installed version of your software. Below the version, you can give a name to be used by your car PC when it establishes a Bluetooth connection to other devices.

The Local Services tab contains a list of services this computer provides that can be used with other Bluetooth devices. Double-click the Headset Profile in this list to see its properties. Make sure that both checkboxes ("Startup Automatically" and "Secure Connection") are ticked.

On the last tab (Hardware), you can check the hardware you're using. You'll see some internal information, such as the device address and the Host Controller Interface (HCI) version. If the HCI version is less than 1.1, you might have problems when using this device.

Searching for Your Mobile Phone

After you've checked your installation, you have to let your car PC search the Bluetooth Neighborhood for all devices in range. Before you start this search, make sure that your mobile phone is in range and has Bluetooth switched on.

Double-click the Bluetooth icon on your desktop to open a new window displaying the Bluetooth Neighborhood. The menu on the left displays several Bluetooth tasks. Click "Search for devices in range," and after a while, your phone should appear in the area on the right. Don't be surprised if you find more devices than just your mobile phone, though. Each device will be listed with its individual name and its device class (e.g., Laptop Computer, PDA, Cellular Phone).

Pairing with Your Mobile Phone

Before you can use any Bluetooth services on your cell phone, you have to *pair* your computer and your phone. This is like introducing your devices to each other. To pair the devices, right-click the mobile phone icon in Windows and select Pair Device. This opens a dialog where you'll be asked to enter a new four-digit PIN number.

When you click OK, your phone will come up with a dialog stating that some device is about to connect over Bluetooth and asking whether or not you want to allow the connection. If you confirm this request, you'll be asked to enter the PIN code you just created on your car PC.

Once you've entered the code, your phone will acknowledge this action, and the icon in your Bluetooth Neighborhood will show the state of the paired device by displaying a check mark.

If you accidentally enter the wrong code on your mobile phone or you wait too long before confirming this action, the Bluetooth Neighborhood will raise an error message and you will have to start the process over.

Setting Up Your Phone

Even after you've paired your mobile phone with your car PC, some mobile phones will require you to tell your phone that there is a new head-set/hands-free device available that you'd like to use. This is especially true for Sony Ericcson phones. For instance, on the Sony Ericsson T610, you'll need to select the car PC Bluetooth connection in your phone, and then select "Service list." A window will appear listing all the services provided by the car PC that the mobile phone itself can handle, which hopefully includes your headset.

If your headset is not on this list, click the Refresh button. After a while, you'll see an updated list. If the headset still doesn't appear, turn your phone off and then back on and repeat the procedure.

If you can see your headset in the list, go back to the Bluetooth menu and select Handsfree → My Handsfree → New Handsfree. Click Add, and your phone will display the name of your car PC.

If your phone starts searching for new headset devices, this is a signal that something has gone wrong—for example, your car PC may already be in your list.

Initiating a Call

Now it's time to test the work you've done so far. Dial a number on your phone. As soon as the call is established (i.e., the phone is ringing on the other end), a bubble will appear over the Bluetooth applet in the System Tray of your car PC.

This tooltip is labelled "Bluetooth Authorization Request," and it appears because you set the "Secure Connection" option for the Headset Profile (see "Installing Bluetooth on Windows," earlier in this hack). As long as this option is set, you'll always have to click on the tooltip and then click OK in the resulting dialog to establish the connection. (If you want the connection to be made automatically in the future, open up the Headset Profile and

PhoneControl.NET

PhoneControl.NET is a software application that helps you to control your mobile phone from your car PC. If you've been envying the address book/mobile phone integration offered by some of the newest cars, you should definitely check it out.

PhoneControl.NET lets you control your mobile phone and place calls through your touchscreen monitor, but it also reads the address book out of your mobile phone and displays your contacts and their phone numbers in a large, readable font on your screen. It will automatically mute your car PC's music when a call comes in, identify the caller for you, and even display a picture of the caller if one is available. You can also import vCards and Outlook contact databases into PhoneControl.NET, so that you can access all your contacts on the road.

PhoneControl.NET works with several of the popular car PC frontends, such as FrodoPlayer [Hack #75] and CENTRAFUSE [Hack #73], and even some home theater PC apps, such as Meedio [Hack #70].

check the "Always allow this device to access this service" box.) Once you press OK, you should be able to hear your phone call through your car's audio system.

If you have an active (phone) connection and you open the Bluetooth Neighborhood to view your "Local Services," you'll see that the My Headset icon has changed to green to signal ongoing traffic.

The Widcomm drivers use your car PC's sound settings for voice input and output. If you can't hear the caller on your speakers or the caller can't hear you talking, you'll need to take a look at your system configuration settings. Go to Start → Control Panel → Sounds and Audio Devices Properties, and check whether your settings in the Voice tab are set to your phone. Then use the Test Hardware button to confirm that the configured devices are up and running.

Choosing the Right Phone

Not all cell phones support the Headset Profile, which means they are not all suitable for use with this hack. Some phones, notably those made by Nokia and Symbian OS, have a Hands-Free profile, but unfortunately this is not compatible with the Widcomm drivers' Headset Profile. If you're interested in this hack and you're planning on buying a new phone, you should check which of the profiles it supports for wireless audio (Headset/Hands-Free) before making your selection. A great resource for these types of questions is the Bluetooth forum at *http://www.jonsguides.com/bluetooth*.

—Zoran Horvat

HACK #64   Transfer Data to and from Your Car PC

USB flash drives, portable USB/FireWire hard drives, and WiFi are a few of the ways to get data onto and off of your car PC.

One of the things you should know before you get an in-car computer is that you are going to have to feed it. Car computers are *multimediaivorous*, subsisting primarily on digital audio, video, and GPS coordinates for roughage.

Seriously, though, you are going to want to get your media into the car, and probably update it from time to time. Some people prefer to perform a one-time dump of their entire MP3 collections into their cars and leave it at that. Others want to be able to listen to daily music feeds from Podcasts (*http://en.wikipedia.org/wiki/Podcasting*), books on tape (*http://www.audible.com*), or their own email and documents converted to MP3 using computer text-to-speech synthesis (*http://www.nextup.com*).

Although wireless is sometimes touted as the holy grail of car-computer synchronization, 802.11a/b/g may be too slow for routine large media transfers. Also, any WiFi solution depends on your car being parked close enough to your home network to get a decent signal and requires your car PC to run when you aren't in the car, which can potentially drain your car battery.

Table 6-1 compares various ways to transfer data to your computer. Which method you choose comes down to how much data you have to transfer.

Table 6-1. Network transfer speeds

Technology	Theoretical speed (in Mbps)	Maximum (in Mbps)	Minimum (in Mbps)	Expected time to transfer a 700-MB CD (in minutes)	Expected time to transfer a 4.3-GB DVD (in minutes)
802.11b	11	5	< 1	19	117
10-MB Ethernet	10	9	3	11	63
USB 1.1[a]	12	9	4	11	63
802.11g	54	20	12	8	49
USB 2.0 flash drive[a]	480	80[b]	24[b]	4	N/A

Table 6-1. Network transfer speeds (continued)

Technology	Theoretical speed (in Mbps)	Maximum (in Mbps)	Minimum (in Mbps)	Expected time to transfer a 700-MB CD (in minutes)	Expected time to transfer a 4.3-GB DVD (in minutes)
100-MB Ethernet	100	90	70	<2	6
FireWire[a]	400	400[b]	80[b]	<1	4
USB 2.0[a]	480	350[b]	80[b]	<1	4
1-GB Ethernet	1000	500	160[b]	<1	4

[a] Technically, you should double the time, as you need to copy the data twice (once from your desktop to the portable device, and then again to the car PC). However, portable hard drives and flash drives don't require you to move the content onto your car PC's hard drive.

[b] Typical hard drive data rates will vary a lot and will be the limiting factor on these speeds.

Flash Drives

Flash drives (Figure 6-4) are small, cheap, and possibly the easiest way to get your media into the car. Priced at around $100 for a 1-GB drive, and less than $20 for a 128-MB drive, these USB devices are smaller than a cigarette lighter yet can store up to several gigabytes of data.

Figure 6-4. A USB flash drive

Flash drives have several car-related benefits. As they have no moving parts, they are essentially shockproof, and their low power consumption makes them ideal for in-car use. Most USB ports [Hack #51] are limited to less than 500 mA of power. Though many portable USB hard drives require more power than this, USB flash drives usually don't. This means you can plug a USB flash drive into a bus-powered USB hub (i.e., a hub that gets its power from its USB connection to the computer), and you shouldn't have any problems powering the drive.

The important things to check for when purchasing a USB flash drive are that it can run on a bus-powered hub and that it supports high-speed USB 2.0

(480 Mbps, not 12 Mbps, which is known as "full speed"), so that your media will copy and play quickly.

> If you've been looking for an excuse to get an iPod, the new iPod Shuffle makes a great USB flash drive.

A review of USB flash drives can be found at *http://www.arstechnica.com/ reviews/hardware/flash.ars.*

Portable Hard Drives

Laptop hard drives are only 2.5" wide and are designed to withstand more vibration than 3.5" desktop hard drives. Over the last few years, compact USB 2.0 enclosures for these hard drives have made it very easy to port hundreds of gigabytes of data in your pocket. You can purchase a hard drive/enclosure combo or, if you have an old laptop drive sitting around, you can find the enclosures themselves for less than $20 at places like *http:// www.compgeeks.com.*

The best hard drives and optical drives are bus-powered and can run right off the computer's USB or FireWire connection. However, if you are using a long (more than 15-foot) USB or FireWire cable to connect a PC in the trunk to the dashboard, chances are that your hard drives, optical drives, and other mechanical devices will not have enough power to run, especially if they go through a hub. In this case, the solution is to provide them with power directly [Hack #50].

> If you don't want to copy your media onto your car PC but just want to play it, that's easy to accomplish. Most of the car PC frontends (discussed in Chapter 7) can easily, if not automatically, switch to the media on an inserted removable drive.

iPods and Other Portable Media Players

Apple's immensely popular iPods are also high-capacity, portable, self-powered USB 2.0 and FireWire hard drives, so they can be used to transfer anything you want—video included—to your car PC.

The nice thing about iPods is that iTunes automatically synchronizes the MP3 collection you have in iTunes and the collection on your iPod. Thus, it's simply a matter of plugging your iPod into your home PC for long enough, and you'll always have all of your music with you.

If you install iTunes on your car PC and plug your iPod into it, you'll be able to see your iPod in iTunes and play any non-copy-protected songs. To play songs purchased from the iTunes Music Store, your in-car copy of iTunes will need to be *authorized*, which requires you to have an Internet connection, at least temporarily. Click Advanced → Check for Purchased Music, and type in your iTunes Music Store name (Apple ID) and password. The copy of iTunes on your car PC will connect to the store, authenticate itself, and permit you to play your purchased music on that machine as well.

If you have other media besides music, you're in luck, because the iPod also doubles as a large portable hard drive. With a 20-GB iPod, you can carry five full DVDs' worth of video, or 40–80 hours of video if it's been compressed with a video compression format such as MPEG-2 or MPEG-4.

With its compact design and high storage capacity (and the fact that you may already own one), the iPod is a great tool for getting music and video from your desktop computer out to the car.

As fantastic as the iPod is, though, most of the third-party portable media players out there are just as good, if not better, at moving audio and video to your in-car PC. You can load most of them with music by just copying a directory full of music, without having to use some other music-management program.

The best portable media players for in-car use are *self-* or *bus-powered*, meaning they are powered or recharged by the USB or FireWire connection on your computer. Most flash solutions and small hard drive solutions meet this requirement. As long as they use the newer USB 2.0 standard, you should be able to play audio and video right off the device without having to copy it to your in-car computer's hard drive.

Portable Media Synchronization

If you're the type of user who transfers your entire media library onto your car PC once and then rarely needs to update it, auto-synchronization probably isn't that essential to you. However, if you're an avid fan of Podcasts or are constantly adding music, TV shows from your PVR, or movies to your in-car jukebox [Hack #70], you'd probably like your car PC to pull these files from your portable hard drive or desktop PC automatically.

Some brands of USB flash drives come with synchronization software. Flash drives from Iomega (http://www.iomega.com) come with Iomega Sync, which is designed to automatically keep files and folders synchronized between the desktop and the drive. It can even be configured to keep two computers in sync, using a single drive moved back and forth between them. Naturally, this software only works for Iomega drives.

Most of the synchronization apps I have found are pretty useless for the kind of automated synchronization you'd need for a car (i.e., no dialog boxes popping up). The best I've found so far is ZincSync (*http://www.zincsync.com*). It has a nice feature for automatically "backing up" an inserted flash drive or other removable hard drive to a specified directory (without overwriting what is already there). I made my "backup" directory the "My Music" folder in *My Documents*, inserted my flash drive, and voilà. It immediately began syncing just like I want it to when I plug it into my car PC—*without asking*. A very nice utility.

WiFi/Lan Synchronization

Using a program by Karen Kenworthy called Karen's Replicator, you can automatically sync your car PC with your home media library over WiFi. This program (including Visual Basic source code!) can be found at *http://www.karenware.com.*

To make synchronization automatic and seamless, you need connectivity between the two computers, which means you need a wireless network set up in your house that you can access from your car when it's parked in the driveway or garage. The faster the network the better, because media files (especially video files) are big [Hack #70]. If the distances involved are great enough, you may need to get a wireless network extender or put a wireless base station as close to the driveway as possible (maybe even in your garage).

> If you really need fast transfer, you can park in your garage and plug an Ethernet cable into your car PC—kind of like filling it up with gas, but filling it up with digital media instead.

Once you have your network extending to where your car is parked, you need to configure networking so that your car PC can see your home file server, where your media files are stored. On the car PC, you should map persistent network drives to the server directories you want to sync with (check the "Reconnect on login" box when creating the share in Windows), so that they will automatically reconnect when the computer is rebooted. (This is a feature of Windows, not of Karen's Replicator.)

Once you can access the file shares, it's time to set up Karen's Replicator. Run the program, and go to Edit Settings → New Job. Browse for the file folders you want to sync, and create any filters or extra rules you want to apply (for example, exclude *.asf*, but sync *.mp3*).

Click Schedule, and set all the timer options except minutes to 0 (I recommend setting minutes to 2). Make sure you set the beginning time to something soon, so you won't have to wait long for it to go into effect. Click Save, then Save Job, name the job, and click Close and Save.

Here is the cool part: with these settings, your car PC will attempt to sync every two minutes; if it doesn't find the network, it will fail silently. This means that when you pull up to your house, within two minutes it will find your network and automatically synchronize the folders you've selected!

If you set up your computer to stay on for a while when you go in the house [Hack #43] or boot up on a schedule [Hack #47], you can simply park, go into your house, and trust your computer to sync unattended and shut off shortly afterwards.

If you prefer to do the synchronization manually, don't schedule automatic syncs in your jobs. Instead, choose a job and click "Run Highlighted Job Now" when you want to sync.

FrodoPlayer [Hack #75] comes with a special version of Karen's Replicator with large, touchscreen-compatible buttons (see Figure 6-5). If you are running FrodoPlayer, you can simply click on the main menu and choose "SYNC".

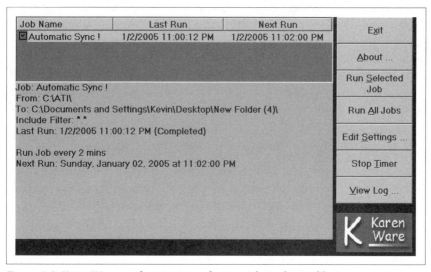

Figure 6-5. KarenWare synchronization software with Frodo-sized buttons

You can set up additional jobs to synchronize multiple folders, if you like. I think it's a really cool way to keep a car PC up to date, and it certainly beats burning CDs full of media that must be manually uploaded to the car computer. One thing to remember, though, is that wireless networks aren't very fast, so you may want to transfer the bulk of your media to your car PC by directly connecting the drive to your server or using higher-speed Ethernet or FireWire networking.

See Also

- "Get Online in Your Car" [Hack #62]

—Kevin "Frodo" Lincecum, Jacob Riskin,
and Damien Stolarz

HACK #65 View Real-Time Traffic Data on the Road

If you have a wireless Internet connection for your car PC, even a slow one, you can get real-time traffic information for any major U.S. city.

Even with all the nifty PC enhancements that you can put in your car, you probably still don't want to sit in traffic on a hot summer day sweating and wasting your time, gas, and money. There are several ways to interface with traffic data so that you can avoid bad traffic and get where you need to go before you or your car overheats.

The easiest way to access traffic data is not via a navigation program, but simply via a web browser. One of the best sites is *http://www.traffic.com* (see Figure 6-6). This service has sensor networks measuring traffic speeds for most major U.S. cities, and their web site provides an interactive, color-coded map showing the state of congestion of all the major thoroughfares in a particular city. If you register for their free membership (i.e., trade your email address), you can get even more information, such as the current traffic speed on each freeway segment.

Information on how Traffic.com works can be found at *http://www.traffic.com/Mobility/faq.html* and *http://www.traffic.com/Mobility/data.html*.

Traffic.com even provides an RSS feed, updated with close-to-real-time traffic incidents. (If you use this service with the CarBot Player software [Hacks #21 and #59], you can even have the feeds read to you while you drive.)

Traffic.com is not the only good provider of traffic-related information. Not only are there other traffic sites, but the same or similar traffic information is actually available from the national, state, and city Departments of Transportation (DOTs) on their respective web sites. However, the problem with these sites is that there is no standard for how that information is provided or accessed.

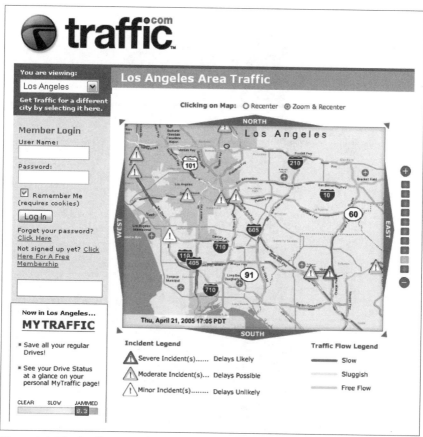

Figure 6-6. The Traffic.com web site

Almost all of the traffic sites render traffic conditions as static GIF/JPG images. Some cities report only traffic incident information, while others provide complete real-time traffic flow information. Incidents are useful to know about, but their reports are delayed by the time it takes for the DOT to acknowledge them. Real-time reporting of traffic flow requires special hardware on the streets, and not all cities currently have this equipment. Real-time conditions almost always include incident reports, too. This inconsistency in freely available information has created a market for Traffic.com and other real-time traffic condition data aggregators.

I live near Seattle, and free public access to the city's traffic data is provided through the Washington State Department of Transportation (WSDOT) system. Their web page (*http://www.wsdot.wa.gov/traffic/seattle*) renders their traffic data and includes a lot of other useful information (Figure 6-7).

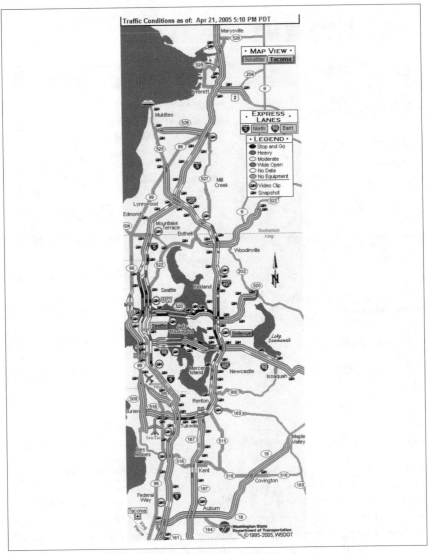

Figure 6-7. The WSDOT's Seattle Traffic web page

On this web page, you can:

- Click on any traffic still/video camera at any major intersection and see a live image of the actual traffic conditions. Some cameras even provide a five-second AVI video of the traffic flow.

- Click on some suburbs of Seattle and view details of city street traffic conditions.

It is all very well organized and accessible to the average user, and I have not found another home-grown metro traffic site that provides this much detail. Information on how the Seattle system works can be found at *http://www.wsdot.wa.gov/traffic/seattle/questions/*.

While you can access web-based traffic information directly from your web browser without having to develop any code, you will be limited to the web site's interface and access to information. Furthermore, many of these user-interface factors are not conducive to a car PC environment, especially when you're the driver.

My Traffic Viewer Application

The relatively low resolution of in-car PC screens makes accessing a web-based map (with its large borders and banner advertisements) while on the go inconvenient and distracting. I decided that a better way to view traffic data would be to embed a browser into a custom application that gave me more control over the user interface.

To demonstrate my idea, I wrote *Traffic.exe*, a C# application that polls Seattle's traffic data via FTP or HTTP and renders that data. You can download the application and its source code at *http://www.oreilly.com/catalog/carpchks*. As with any C# application, you'll need to have the .NET runtime installed to use it.

> Unfortunately, this application (as well as my demo code) is only directly applicable to hacking Seattle's traffic data. However, it should provide valuable insight when it comes time to hack your own city's traffic web site.

Traffic.exe first pulls down an uncolored freeway map that is not populated with any congestion data (Figure 6-8, left). When you click the Process Data button, *Traffic.exe* retrieves the up-to-the-minute traffic information, decodes it, and appropriately color-codes the map (Figure 6-8, right).

Using Seattle's Raw Data

Custom traffic-monitoring applications would flourish if the information they provided was more standardized. Alas, there's little indication that a nationwide open traffic standard for all cities will be developed anytime soon, so the next best thing may be to directly use the web pages from the existing traffic web sites. Fortunately, a lot of traffic information is freely available on the Web, and with a bit of work it can be formatted for your car PC any way you want—that's what I did with my *Traffic.exe* application

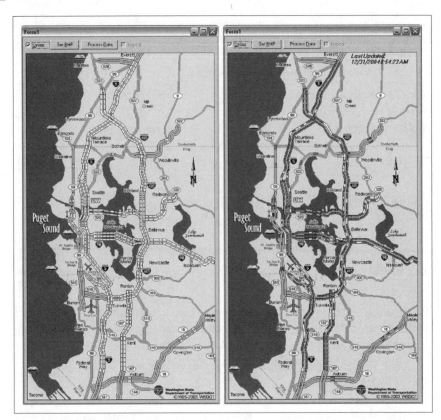

Figure 6-8. Traffic.exe in action

and the raw data I was able to pull down from the WSDOT web site. This section tells you a little about this data, to help you understand how my program operates, and to help you write your own traffic program.

Seattle's raw traffic data is presented in a proprietary, albeit simple, format. The files can be accessed via either *http://images.wsdot.wa.gov/nwflow/wireless/* or *ftp://webflow.wsdot.wa.gov*. Both of these URLs contain the following identical data files:

webflow.dat

    Contains the "occupancy" information for a certain set of *loop detector* stations. Loop detectors are wire loops, about a meter square, embedded in the road. They are used to detect whether a vehicle is present over that patch of road. This file is an older data file that is about 6 KB in size.

wirelessxxx.dat

    Contains the "occupancy" information for a slightly different set of loop detector stations. *xxx* is a version number that the WSDOT increments from time to time. This file is a newer compressed data file that is about 0.2 KB in size. The basic source code to decompress this file can be found at *http://www.wsdot.wa.gov/PugetSoundTraffic/palmflow/huffman.c.* (This code will need to be modified a bit before it can be used.)

webflow.sta
> Describes each loop detector in *webflow.dat.*

wirelessxxx.sta
> Describes each loop detector in *wirelessxxx.dat.*

/WebFlowUpdates/SysVert.bmp
> A bitmap of the loop stations in *webflow.dat.*

/WebFlowUpdates/SysVert.XY
> (X,Y) polygon coordinates of the loop stations in *SysVert.bmp.*

webflow.msg
> A text file that describes relevant current information (incidents, construction, etc.).

As you can see, *wireslessxxx.dat* is much smaller than *webflow.dat*; however, Seattle does not provide *.bmp* or *.XY* files for *wireslessxxx.dat*, so if you want to use *wirelessxxx.dat* you will have to create your own *.bmp* and *.XY* files. For simplicity's sake, the example *Traffic.exe* application uses the larger *webflow.dat* file and the relevant *.sta*, *.bmp*, and *.XY* files.

You can use these data files to create your own traffic application. To get the raw data, all you have to do is open an anonymous FTP or HTTP connection to one of the data URLs and download the latest data file(s).

—Paul Peavyhouse

Videoconference from Your Car

#66 With mobile broadband Internet connections, car PCs will soon achieve James Bond–style videoconferencing.

I think it was 1998 when I first started trying to set up a webcam in my car. I have a Nash Ambassador, and in addition to putting a screen in the center console, I hooked up an X10 camera facing the driver, with the eventual goal of letting people keep tabs on me. For several years I tinkered with a number of low-speed, expensive Internet solutions, such as analog cell phones connected to 14.4 modems, while searching in vain for an affordable flat-fee service.

Fast forward several years, and wireless connectivity has matured a lot. GPRS (and more specifically, EDGE) networking has brought the bitrates into ISDN range (64–128 kbps), and pitiful but recognizable streaming video has become a viable option for in-car use.

Since two of my cars (my 1950 Nash and my 1998 Malibu) already had X10 cameras in them, I wanted to find out if I could finally realize my dream of a James Bond (or Austin Powers, depending on your pop-culture exposure) in-car videoconferencing experience. This hack will take you through my attempts to get videoconferencing working between my home PC and my car.

Choosing Your Conference Software

The best conference program I've used is the Mac-only iChat. It has a very good codec and smooth full-screen display, and with my Apple iSight FireWire camera, the picture is very clean. AOL recently made their Instant Messenger product (AIM) compatible with iChat, so my first thought was that I could use AIM on my CarBot (which runs Windows XP) and iChat on my Mac in the house. Unfortunately, as I soon found out, iChat had set my expectations too high.

To get video into my CarBot car PC, I decided to use a USB 2.0 video capture device. Since I was using an X10 video camera, which outputs composite video like a TV (instead of an integrated USB webcam), I needed a composite video capture device. I went for the cheapest thing I could find at Fry's Electronics, a $59 USB video capture dongle. For my initial tests I used WiFi networking, which depends on the car being parked near an access point.

Figure 6-9 shows a diagram of a vehicle and the various parts of the videoconferencing setup.

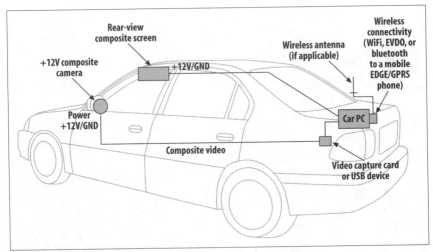

Figure 6-9. Videoconferencing car PC setup

The good news is that my setup worked cleanly and perfectly. The bad news is that AIM's chat program has *no* full-screen mode. Thus, although my conferencing buddy on the Macintosh in my house was able to see a full-screen image of my face, the AOL chat program only showed me a small-screen image of my partner. This, on an already small 7" touchscreen in the car, was not what I was after—I wanted to be able to have a full-screen video chat with the other party.

> Today's instant messaging programs quite reasonably make the assumption that you are going to type a lot and read a lot, both things you should not be doing while driving.

My next step was to check out several other chat programs to see which would give me the video experience I was looking for. I looked at Yahoo! Chat, but their model is more suited to a webcam than a two-way conference. I then tried MSN, but it has the same drawback as AIM—you can't do full-screen chats.

I finally tried out Trillian (*http://www.trillian.cc*). With perfect timing, they had just come out with Version 3, which supports the videoconferencing protocols of all the major IM apps (AIM, MSN, Yahoo!) *and* offers full-screen video.

For my testing, my CarBot was using an Orinoco PCMCIA WiFi 802.11b card, installed in a 1-GHz VIA EPIA M2 motherboard, with 256 MB of RAM. One of the things I quickly learned about Trillian is that it takes a lot of CPU power. I'm guessing that's because they've just implemented the codecs for each of the major IM apps, and they're pretty unoptimized at this point. On my desktop 1.6-GHz Athlon it only took 15 seconds or so to start a chat with my 1.5-GHz Apple PowerBook, but it took more than twice as long to negotiate a chat with the CarBot.

Going Wireless

Although the new Verizon EVDO network offers broadband speeds [Hack #62], I had already signed up for an AT&T Wireless EDGE networking phone. I wanted to see how well I could conference with just the 60–80 kbps EDGE provides. People video-chat and webcam on modems all the time and get a few frames per second, which I would have been happy with.

I plugged a Bluetooth adapter into my CarBot so that it could get online through my phone, and then I paired the phone and the computer [Hack #63] and set up dial-up networking so that the CarBot would dial up through the phone. I tried repeatedly to get the conferencing going over this connection, but the combination of high latency, low bandwidth, and an underpowered car PC brought Trillian to its knees—I could never establish a connection, and it simply timed out repeatedly. However, when I used the same Bluetooth-to-EDGE connection on my faster desktop PC, I *was* able to get connected, so the speed of the machine clearly has a lot to do with it. Later, I tried EVDO from Verizon, with similar results.

Not Quite There Yet

My endeavor showed me that while we're right on the cusp of in-car videoconferencing capabilities, it's going to take a little more software and hardware development to pull it off.

One frustration I had with all the IM apps, Trillian included, was that I could not get them to auto-accept chat requests. The Accept button is just big enough for me to hit it on a touchscreen, but I can't really do it when I'm using my non-touchscreen setup. However, I know I can solve that problem with a scripting program [Hack #58], so I'm not overly worried about it.

After playing with various apps, I think Yahoo! Messenger would be a decent way to set up a one-way webcam, where your car uploads a shot of you once a second so that people can see you when you drive—this would work well on even the slower modem-speed connections available with base-level GPRS.

In conclusion, while my PC teleconferencing setup has enough speed to do voice chat and basic webcam delivery, my dreams of full-screen, one- or two-way videoconferencing in the vehicle will have to wait until faster broadband wireless comes about 20 miles north in Los Angeles county to meet me, or until someone writes conferencing software specifically for the car that's optimized for wireless 2.5G (40–80 kbps) connections.

One lesson I learned from this attempt is that the current low-power VIA processors popular for in-car computers are just too underpowered for videoconferencing. I've also learned that without custom software development, nothing less than wireless broadband (or WiFi while the car is stationary) is sufficient for conferencing.

HACK #67   Use GPS on Your Car PC

With GPS, your car PC can always know where on Earth it is, and with wireless Internet, it can also tell the world.

The *Global Positioning System* (GPS) provides fairly accurate (to within a few meters) location coordinates for anyone who has a GPS receiver. GPS receivers come in a variety of shapes and sizes, from standalone units with LCD screens showing your location in latitude and longitude, to units with a little map and an "X" marking where you are. The GPS hardware and antenna can be made smaller than a matchbox, and you can purchase tiny CompactFlash-sized GPS receivers for PDAs, or small USB dongle receivers for PCs (see Figure 6-10).

Figure 6-10. A USB GPS receiver

Knowing exactly where you are can be useful for many different applications, and recording everywhere you've been can be even more useful. Maybe you run a business with a fleet of automobiles, and you want to be able to store your routes on a daily basis and improve efficiency by examining exactly where you went. Or maybe you're going on a cross-country trip and you want to keep a journal of your travels. Why not include the coordinates of the path you take?

Even better, you can upload your coordinates to a web page as you travel, so others can keep track of your vehicle in real time. This feature can be used for people to monitor your progress while you're making a trip, so you can keep track of someone who borrows your car, to monitor the positions of company vehicles in real time, or even for stolen vehicle recovery (assuming your car PC always runs when the car is driven).

GPS is standard, well documented, and easy to program for, and while you can simply purchase navigation software [Hack #71], none of the navigation programs on the market are designed with all the features I've mentioned. In this hack, I'll briefly explain how to understand the language GPS units speak and then provide several example programs (available for download at *http:// www.oreilly.com/catalog/carpchks*) that illustrate the features I've mentioned.

The term *telemetry* describes the action of remotely communicating with a device for measurement, be it a Mars rover or a gas meter. *Telematics*, however, is a term that has recently come into use to describe all the technologies (and businesses) involving GPS, wireless data, and vehicles.

How GPS Works

The basic way that GPS works is that satellites in known locations in space transmit radio signals with embedded timestamps to Earth. Your GPS receiver measures the time that it takes for four or more of these different satellite signals to reach your location, and compares that information to the current time. If you've ever heard of "triangulating your position," it's like that, but with GPS you're "quadrangling" or "sextangling" your position—the more GPS satellites your receiver can get a signal from, the more points of reference it has to calculate a more accurate position.

When you first power up a GPS receiver, it has to spend a while getting a "lock" on the satellites, and it has to find at least four signals that it can use to calculate a position. If your GPS receiver has been powered on recently (a "warm start"), it will remember at least which hemisphere it is in, and perhaps the general latitude and longitude, and so will be able to get its bearings in a matter of seconds. However, when you turn on a GPS receiver for the first time (or when you turn it on after its batteries have been removed and it has "forgotten" everything), it has to literally figure out where on Earth it is, which can take a few minutes.

The GPS represents coordinates in the same way that the Greeks originally used coordinates. The sky is divided into 12 regions, which are further split into 30 one-degree segments (12 * 30 = 360). Locations in GPS are represented using the standard trigonometric system of Degrees, Minutes, and Seconds, such as:

```
47 Degrees 38 Minutes 12.372 Seconds North Latitude
122 Degrees 7 Minutes 58.8 Seconds West Longitude
```

On a computer, Minutes and Seconds are often mathematically combined to one decimal fraction. For example:

```
47.63677 Latitude
-122.13300 Longitude
```

North is positive latitude, and east is positive longitude; south is negative latitude, and west is negative longitude.

Most GPS receivers communicate their current location coordinates to the computer using the *NMEA 0183* protocol. (Make sure the GPS receiver you purchase conforms to this format.)You can find out more information about this standard from the National Marine Electronics Association (NMEA) web site, at *http://www.nmea.org/pub/0183*.

Most GPS devices for the computer run at a nice, mellow speed of 4,800 baud (for comparison, modems run at 56,000 baud) and speak in ASCII characters over a serial port or USB port. If you plug a GPS unit into your serial port, run a terminal program (e.g., Hyperterminal on Windows), and set the baud rate correctly, you'll see what the GPS device is saying.

The NMEA protocol is fairly simple. Once connected, the GPS device will output a string every second or so containing its latitudinal and longitudinal data. While the GPS unit is still figuring out where it is, it will not output location coordinates, but it may report which satellites it sees and what it is currently doing.

Writing a program to process GPS information is as straightforward as reading data sent to the serial port and processing some text. This is easily done in any programming or scripting language.

Reading and Understanding GPS Sentences

Assuming that you have your GPS device attached and configured (though usually not much configuration is necessary, other than making sure that the port and speed settings are correct), reading information from it is very easy, since it talks in ASCII and provides data that is close to what is necessary for this hack. The device outputs comma-delimited *sentences*. The beginning of each sentence is a code that explains what is in the rest of the sentence. The sentences that tell you your current coordinates start with $GPGGA. These will probably be the only sentences that you are interested in, but you can check the NMEA 0183 standard if you want to know more. The most interesting parts of the sentence are listed in Table 6-2

Table 6-2. Some useful NMEA codes

Field number	Description	Example
1	Time that the position was calculated. (hhmmss.ss)	180432.00
2	Latitude (ddmm.mmmmmm)	4738.2062
3	Direction of latitude (N=north, S=south)	N
4	Longitude (dddmm.mmmmmm)	12207.98
5	Direction of longitude (W=west, E=east)	W
6	GPS quality (0=invalid, 1=GPS fix, 2=DGPS fix)	1

Table 6-2. Some useful NMEA codes (continued)

Field number	Description	Example
7	Number of satellites used for calculation	07
9	Altitude above mean sea level	212.15
10	Units for altitude (M=meters)	M

For information on the other fields, check the NMEA 0183 reference.

Creating a Record of Your Travels

I've written a handful of Perl scripts to illustrate how easy it is to work with GPS information. You can download the source code for each of these examples at *http://www.carpchacks.com/gps/*. The programs were developed on a Windows XP machine running Perl. You can get Perl for Windows from ActiveState (*http://activestate.com/Products/ActivePerl/*). The second two code examples require an additional script to be running on an Internet-based web server running Perl. These scripts require IIS or Apache, Perl, and write access to a file so they can store GPS locations.

Each of the Perl scripts running on the car PC will be storing locations to a file. Like any log file, this can get very large over time. Whatever method you use to get the data off your car PC, you should have some mechanism for moving and storing it all.

These scripts are examples, so if you want a more secure solution that isn't viewable by the whole world, you may want to password-protect the script on your web server. Making a robust, secure version of a GPS tracking web service is left as an exercise to the reader.

Example #1: Record Your Travels to a File

My first code example runs on the car PC. It reads the GPS sentences from the GPS receiver, decodes them, and writes a simple travel log of latitude, longitude, and timestamp to disk. The text file generated by this script can be manually parsed later on your desktop PC and displayed on a map (see the next section in this hack, "Displaying GPS Data on a Map").

When you get home and your car PC can connect to your home network [Hack #64], you can transfer this file off of the car PC and start over again with a fresh file.

Example #2: Upload Your Current Position to a Web Page in Real Time

My second code example is a pair of client/server Perl scripts. The client script is almost the same as the first code example, except I've added a few lines that post the GPS data to the web server script at an interval (I have mine set to every four minutes). It depends on you having always-on Internet access in your car, but the bandwidth requirements are so low that any persistent wireless connection will do. (T-Mobile offers a $20/month GPRS plan, as of this writing—see "Get Online in Your Car" **[Hack #62].**)

The server-side script collects the location data (latitude, longitude, and timestamp) from the car PC and stores it to a file. The same script that receives data from the car PC also returns an HTML page linking to a map of the current location (see Figure 6-11). There are two versions of the server-side script. One of them only keeps track of the current location, so viewing it from a web page will simply show the last uploaded location of the vehicle. The other version of the script keeps a path for the last 24 hours (this is user-configurable, depending on how much history you want to keep). This allows viewers to observe the migratory patterns of your car PC for as far back as you'd care to store it.

Example #3: Use MapPoint to Generate Maps on the Car PC

This third code example can deal with intermittent Internet connectivity (for instance, relying on WiFi hotspots **[Hack #68]**). It also adds code to produce a map that's visible in the car, if MapPoint 2004 is installed on the car PC. The site I used to learn how to control MapPoint with my Perl scripts is *http://www.mp2kmag.com/a100--perl.automate.Win32-OLE.mappoint.html.*

This code uses MapPoint's ability to generate a graphic file with the GPS map coordinates drawn on it. It then uploads that image and the HTML code displaying that image to the web server (see Figure 6-12). Using MapPoint on the client machine simply moves the map-generation code from a web service to the client and allows for local viewing of the generated map file.

Displaying GPS Data on a Map

All of this tracking information is great, but without pretty graphical maps at the end, there's little payoff for all the hard work. Unfortunately, high-quality, high-resolution mapping software costs money, and the terms of service of most online mapping sites do not necessarily permit you to generate free, real-time illustrations of your car PC's travels (i.e., they'll want you to pay for that functionality). A great site that *does* allow this (and which I've included

Figure 6-11. A real-time position map using http://mapper.acme.com

in my sample code) is Acme Labs (*http://mapper.acme.com*). Another useful site with few restrictions on its use is *http://terraserver.microsoft.com*.

MSN Maps, Yahoo! Maps, MapQuest, and Google Maps can all display graphical maps of your location information if you learn how to generate the right URLs, and depending on the license agreements of these sites, you may be able to link to them with your location (but always check the site's acceptable use policy before doing so).

Google Maps (*http://maps.google.com*; see Figure 6-13) is growing in popularity for projects like this, and they tend to be more flexible than their competitors when it comes to terms of service.

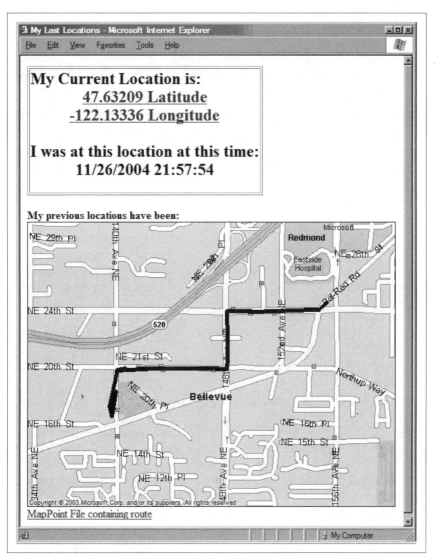

Figure 6-12. A map generated with MapPoint 2004

As mentioned in the description of Example #3, you can also run MapPoint (or a similar mapping product with an API) to generate the maps on your car PC and then simply upload them. This uses more bandwidth, but yields potentially better-looking results than a free online mapping service can provide.

Each of the major search engines is in the process of adding a local search capability, and this is causing them to revamp, enhance, and solidify their online mapping technologies. At the same time, improved mobile Internet

Collecting GPS Location Data

The script that runs on your car PC to collect GPS coordinates can fill an entire hard drive in time if the information is not managed intelligently. The script will generate data once a second, as long as the GPS device has a fix on your location. If you are just blindly storing data to the disk and you wind up sitting at a red light or stuck in traffic for a few minutes, that can add up to a lot of unnecessarily recorded data points. By keeping track of the distance traveled between data points, you can determine whether a new data point is different enough (i.e., whether the car has moved) and thus whether it should be saved to disk.

To determine the distance between two GPS points in decimal form, you can use the Great Circle Distance Formula:

```
r * arccos[sin(lat1) * sin(lat2) + cos(lat1) * cos(lat2) * cos(lon2 - lon1)]
```

However, that's rather complex and really only pertains to measuring long distances on the curved surface of the Earth. For my own approximations (since in each case the distances traveled will probably be only a few meters), I have used the following equation:

```
Sqrt([4774.81 * (lat2 - lat1)2] + [2809 * (lon2 - lon1)2]) = distance
in miles
```

In my program, I use this equation to determine how far I have moved from the last recorded data point.

Another thing that I have found about GPS is that while it's *fairly* accurate, it does have a tendency to jitter—that is, if I'm sitting still, it will show me moving around slightly. Since I don't want all those random changes to be saved in my log files, I decided to specify a certain minimum distance that must be traveled before a new point is recorded. I chose 45 feet, or about 0.00852272727 miles, as my minimum distance to travel. I can now calculate the minimum required difference in GPS coordinates:

```
Difference in GPS = Sqrt((0.00852272727)2 / 7583.81)
```

The result of this calculation is around .0000978, which I then further rounded to 0.0001. (See why 45 feet is not so random?) You can use these calculations to easily come up with your own threshold, in the manner that I just described.

Just to make my data even tidier, whenever I read a data point that is within the threshold that I defined, instead of throwing it away, I simply average it with the previous value that I was comparing to. This helps focus in on my location when my car is sitting still for a while in traffic.

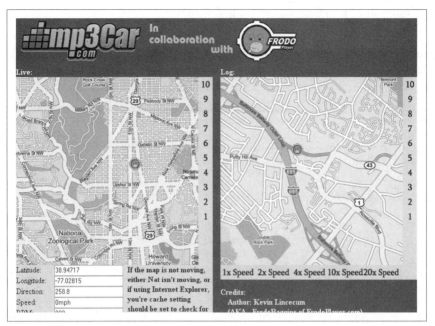

Figure 6-13. A car PC location using Google Maps

connectivity is becoming available. It's a great time to be tinkering in this area, as the raw materials for some really innovative telematics hacks are now readily available.

See Also

* "Choose Your in-Car Navigation Software" [Hack #71]

—J.P. Stewart

HACK #68 Find WiFi Hotspots on the Road

WiFi is the best friend of the well-connected commuter and traveler.

Early last spring I sold my business, moved into an RV, and took off traveling. I have been on the road for six months now, cruising from the east coast of the U.S. to Alaska. During this time I've managed to access the Internet nearly as often as I like, staying in touch with friends and family via email and maintaining an active web site. I also use an Internet telephone account to make and receive phone calls through my laptop whenever I'm online. For anyone contemplating long-term travel and wanting to stay "connected," perhaps some of my own experiences and discoveries of late may prove useful.

Staying Free and Connected on the Road

Once I hit the road, I discovered a variety of ways and means for getting online. I should mention here that although more and more commercial RV parks are offering Internet connections to their overnight guests these days, I have never once stayed in such a place. I prefer the roads less traveled and the places less visited: free, secluded campsites along National Forest back roads and streams, in the countryside, and on empty beaches.

Still, I manage to get online quite often. For example, whenever I visit a friend with broadband access, I just bring my laptop in and connect it.

> With a compact WiFi access point such as Apple's AirPort Express (*http://www.apple.com/airportexpress/*), you can also use that network connection to quickly create a WiFi network accessible by your car PC. Simply plug your WiFi router into an open Ethernet jack on your friend's Internet router and plug in power, and in most cases you'll be able to connect.

It's also possible to connect through a cell phone [Hack #62], and this may be the best solution for many travelers. Unfortunately, a cell phone connection was not an option for me. I was planning to hang out in the northwestern U.S. National Forests, where cell phones generally don't work; in western Canada, where there is no cell phone service at all outside of a few big towns; and in the wilder parts of road-accessible Alaska, where coverage is sparse to nonexistent.

Public libraries are a good place to look for an emergency Internet connection, although it is rarely wireless. A few I've come across are set up to allow visitors to plug in their own PCs, and one on Orcas Island off the northwest coast of Washington actually provided WiFi in addition to cable connections. That was the exception, however.

Many coffee houses today also offer Internet connections (cable, wireless, or both). Some of them charge; some don't as long as you buy something while you're there. These cozy Internet cafés are a pleasant alternative to sitting alone in my RV, and I use them from time to time.

However, I much prefer to download incoming email onto my own laptop to read and file at my leisure, and I usually compose and answer emails when I'm camped out in the woods, to be sent the next time I log on. In addition, I often want to upload files from my laptop's hard drive to my web site, which I can't easily do using someone else's computer.

Finding WiFi

Of course, the RV PC holy grail is a free WiFi hotspot, and finding these on the road can become an art and an obsession. A WiFi hotspot is an area where an Internet connection is available through localized radio waves rather than through a hard-wired cable hookup. As long as your computer is set up to receive these signals and you're within their (typically limited) broadcast range, you can get online without plugging in.

My laptop came ready-made with a built-in WiFi card and antenna to access wireless signals. Computers without this feature can usually be upgraded with a plug-in wireless PC card and a small external antenna. For the RV vagabond, the appearance of the screen message "One or more wireless networks are available" is always welcomed—it's kind of like finding money on the street.

If you're already online, you can often locate some local hotspots simply by doing a search at web sites that list them, such as *http://www.jiwire.com*. However, these sites often don't list all of the hotspots in a given town, and sometimes they don't list any at all where they actually do exist. New WiFi hotspots spring up all the time, as anyone with a broadband Internet connection and a hundred-dollar Linksys access point can create one.

One tactic I use to find hotspots is to set up my laptop on the passenger seat of my RV and slowly cruise through a town or city, watching for that heart-warming "One or more wireless networks are available" message. Not all of the signals are useful, however. The provider of a WiFi signal can, if he chooses, block access to it so that only those who know the password can log on. These protected signals are obviously intended for the benefit of members or paying customers only and are therefore of no use to me. It's the free, unblocked WiFi signals I'm looking for.

When I come across an accessible hotspot, I pull over and see if I can spot the source. Whoever is transmitting a wireless signal gets to name it, and the receiving computer displays that name. Sometimes the network name will indicate plainly that it's coming from this office or that café. Others bear cryptic names that have no obvious meaning to anyone besides the owner. If I can't guess the signal's source, I might move around a bit in an effort to home in on it, but regardless of whether or not I ever actually locate the signal source, once I've got a strong connection I'm in hacker's heaven. I can then sit in the comfort of my motor home with a hot mug of tea on the table and Mozart on the stereo, sending and receiving emails and surfing the Web to my heart's content—for free! I also make all my phone calls then, which I'll tell you more about later in this hack.

During these months traveling in my RV, I have found WiFi signals in some interesting and unlikely places. Once I pulled off Interstate 40 at one of those exits where a bunch of motels, gas stations, and chain restaurants are clustered together—a commercial oasis in the middle of nowhere. On a lark, I booted up the laptop, and bingo! There was a good signal coming from a Best Western motel. So I parked discretely in a corner of their parking lot and spent a happy hour sending email from the Texas prairie while tumbleweed rolled across the road two blocks away.

On another occasion, I had parked way out on a beach point near a town on Vancouver Island. I had already searched the small community for a WiFi hotspot without success, yet when I fired up my laptop to do some writing a strong WiFi signal magically appeared. I was surrounded by ocean, sand, and city parkland, yet I sat chatting with friends back east through my laptop as though I was next door. My best guess was that the signal emanated from the high school's administration offices on a hill nearly a mile away, but I never really knew (and it never really mattered).

Most recently, I've been using a WiFi signal I found on the town docks in beautiful Seward, Alaska, broadcast by one of the tour boat operators there. I park my RV a stone's throw from their cabin-like ticket office and surf and email and make phone calls while gazing at glacier-clad mountains across the bay, where bald eagles fly and bears fish for salmon in the streams.

Improving Reception

Capturing strong WiFi signals is the key to happy RV PC hacking. I bought a 4' long, fiberglass-encased antenna to increase my signal quality, but erecting it outside the RV each time I wanted to use it was usually more hassle than the slight improvement in reception was worth. In the end, I tended to leave the antenna up more often than I should have, projecting several feet above the roof of my RV (which already stands 10' above the road). One day, while I was hunting for WiFi signals in downtown Kamloops, British Columbia, I pulled up to a curb to park, failed to notice an overhanging tree branch, and snap! There went my expensive external antenna. I'd like to try out a directional antenna, but I haven't gotten around to it yet. For the time being, I manage to find enough WiFi signals to carry on just using my laptop's built-in antenna. (For more on WiFi reception, see "Get Online in Your Car" [Hack #62]).

Internet Telephone over WiFi

In addition to staying connected via email with my RV PC, I also have an Internet telephone account with Vonage (*http://www.vonage.com*). This is

Wardriving

Wardriving is the act of driving around and seeking out and recording the locations of wireless networks. It is derived from *war dialing*, the act of randomly dialing phone numbers in the hopes of finding a computer modem to connect to (an act made popular by the movie *War Games*). Wardriving is possible because the transmissions of wireless networks seldom stop at the boundaries of house or yard. By intercepting these transmissions as you drive by a wireless network, you can often learn the name of the network, the IP address of the wireless access point, and a little bit about the makeup of the network (e.g., whether it requires encryption to access and what channel it is broadcasting on).

The most popular program for finding WiFi networks is NetStumbler (*http:// www.netstumbler.com*). Not only does it monitor names of networks and their signal strengths, but it works with your GPS receiver **[Hack #67]** and records the geographic locations of the WiFi hotspots.

NetStumbler uses the combination of location information (from the GPS receiver) and signal strength (from the WiFi receiver) for each access point it finds to pinpoint where the hotspot is. This allows you to quickly zero in on open hotspots (the ones you want).

There are also several web sites where you can upload the data that you have captured for the benefit of others. Some of these sites will draw a map of your discovered access points, and many will let you view the discoveries of other people. Here are just a few of these sites:

- *http://www.gpsvisualizer.com/map?form=wifi*
- *http://www.wifimaps.com*
- *http://www.wigle.net*

If you'd like to learn more about NetStumbler and finding WiFi networks, Rob Flickenger's *Wireless Hacks* (O'Reilly) is your best resource. Have fun wardriving!

one of the relatively new, groundbreaking Internet telephone companies that are, I believe, heralding the end of home and office telephone service as we know it. Rather than using traditional telephone systems for phone calls, these companies use the Internet to carry voice communications. This technology, called *Voice over IP* (VoIP), enables the calls to avoid expensive switching fees and a host of petty taxes that drive up "normal" phone bills every month.

You can even cut the last cord tethering you to your permanent residence: your home phone number. If you haven't already ditched it for a mobile phone, you can transfer your traditional landline number over to Vonage, and keep the phone number you've had at your home for so many years.

Unfortunately, Vonage's standard package and service do require a bit of hardware (which they give you) and a hard-wired (Ethernet) connection to the Internet. They also offer a "SoftPhone" package, which works directly through a laptop computer and a wireless connection, without the extraneous hardware; however, they would not sell me the SoftPhone package alone. I had to first sign up for the Residential Basic 500 plan, which I cannot use, and then add on the SoftPhone package for an additional $10 (plus tax) per month. Also, the SoftPhone package doesn't offer "all you can eat" flat-fee calling, like their equipment-based plans do.

Still, I am paying less than $30 (including tax) a month to have wireless Internet telephone capability, including voicemail that is accessible both by telephone and online. I can park my RV (or just myself with my laptop) in any hotspot, plug my operator-style headset and microphone into the computer, and chat with friends and family as if I were calling from a landline.

> Note that with the Vonage system you cannot make or receive phone calls except when your computer is actually online. The voicemail service, however, works all the time. People can leave messages whether you're online or not, and you can retrieve them anytime via Internet or telephone.

While it wasn't ideal for my purposes, as it happens, the Vonage hardware limitation can also work to your benefit. While "Get Online in Your Car" [Hack #62] showed you how to use your dial-up connection to make your own WiFi hotspot, with Vonage you can do the opposite—use your laptop or car PC to turn a WiFi connection into a hardwire connection for your phone.

On Windows XP, there is a feature called "Internet Connection Sharing." Once your laptop or car PC is connected to the WiFi connection you want to use, you can share this connection through your Ethernet port. Go to Control Panels → Networks → Wireless Connection (whatever it is named on your PC), click Properties → Advanced, and check the "Share this Internet Connection" box. Once you've done this, you can connect the WAN port of your Vonage equipment to the Ethernet port of your PC. After a few moments, the LINE 1 light on your Vonage adapter or hub should glow, letting you know that an Internet connection has been found and you can make a call.

To accomplish the same thing on a Macintosh, just go to System Preferences → Sharing → Internet and share your AirPort (WiFi) connection over Ethernet.

It gets better. I plan to be on the road in New Zealand soon, but Vonage treats all my phone calls as originating in the United States, no matter where in the world I happen to be when I log onto the Internet. Thus, when I log on over there, I'll still be able to use my Internet telephone system to call anywhere in the U.S. and Canada, and I won't have to pay any overseas charges!

Conclusion

As computers and the Internet continue to evolve, people are finding new ways of applying these tools to suit the way they live and work. Footloose travelers like me can now stay as connected as they want to be—well, almost. I foresee a day of omnipresent, broadband WiFi signals worldwide, so that we'll be able to log onto the Internet while parked in an RV in the deepest forest or sailing a boat in the middle of the ocean. In fact, the beginnings of that technology are already available, but that's another story altogether.

—Tor Pinney, J.P. Stewart, and Damien Stolarz

In-Car Applications

Hacks 69–75

The majority of this book has focused on the hardware side of car PCs, with very little discussion of the software you will actually run on your computer. At first blush you might think that you can run any software you want on your car PC. And though this is technically true, as Chapter 5 points out, most software is designed to be used with a mouse and keyboard and is not easy or safe to use while driving.

For this reason, several clever hackers have designed special software to run on your car PC. This software acts as a frontend to your operating system and applications, and provides a simplified interface with large "touchable" buttons so you can launch an application with a brush of your finger. This chapter covers three of the most popular frontend programs: CENTRAFUSE, Neocar, and FrodoPlayer.

However, your car PC is not limited to the features provided by these frontends. There is plenty of software that is suitable for use in an automobile, especially by passengers. These range from navigation systems, to game emulation software, to video jukeboxes. This chapter has several hacks that cover these possiblities.

HACK #69 Plug into Your Car's Built-in Computer

If your car is less than a decade old, you can hook into a wealth of real-time information through its on-board diagnostic port.

If you say "car computer," most auto repair shops will assume you mean one of the various electronic control units, or *ECUs*, built into your car. Almost all modern vehicles are computerized in the sense that they have computers that read inputs from various sensors and use that information to control the engine, transmission, and other electronic systems. Most car users are not even aware of the existence of these computers (until they break, at which point they become very aware of the expense of replacing them). However, people who modify their cars with aftermarket performance parts sometimes need to provide new software to the computers in order to take maximum advantage of the new hardware they've installed. This process, known as *chipping*, is often as simple as replacing a single *EEPROM* (Electrically Erasable and Programmable Read-Only Memory) chip.

> ECUs are not monolithic computers that control everything in your car. In fact, cars have many different ECUs, such as the Electronic Control Module (ECM), which controls smog emissions through engine tuning; the Powertrain Control Module (PCM), which controls the transmission and engine; and the Vehicle Control Module (VCM), which oversees a number of non-smog-related functions, including antilock braking systems.

Almost all new consumer vehicles conform to a standard called *OBD-II* (On-Board Diagnostic System II). A vehicle that supports OBD-II will provide real-time readings for dozens of engine parameters, such as fuel temperature, oxygen temperature, coolant temperature, fuel pressure, RPMs, speed, and throttle position, in addition to decoding all the fault codes that cause a "check engine" light to go on or stay on.

OBD-II describes both a physical plug in your car's computer and the network protocol you can use to communicate with the car. Using the information in this hack, you will be able to connect to your car's built-in computer and have it tell you everything it is seeing and doing.

While OBD-II defines a standard set of data that has to be made available by all cars, each car manufacturer also uses the OBD-II port to access additional codes. Sometimes they also use higher-speed protocols to speak directly to (and even reprogram) the various ECUs in that car.

Entire in-car networks and related hardware standards and protocols have been developed so that the various ECUs can talk to each other. The *Controller Area Network* (CAN) bus is a standard used throughout Europe and in some U.S. cars to connect everything from brake systems to engine management systems to seatbelts, windows, and door locks. However, there are several standards for in-car interdevice communication, and more than one network system may be used in a particular car design—one for essential real-time engine control and another for audio and lighting, for instance. A great summary of various automotive networking protocol standards can be found at *http://www.interfacebus.com/Design_Connector_Automotive.html*.

If you're just trying to get the standard set of OBD-II readouts, which are quite numerous, you can get a simple, inexpensive generic adapter that works with your general make of vehicle. If, however, you'd like to do exotic things such as engine tuning, you'll want to get an adapter and software designed specifically for your make and model of vehicle—these are most likely to be found on the fan sites relating to your specific car model. Before you can buy an adapter to talk to your vehicle's OBD-II port, though, you have to figure out which of the versions of OBD-II your car speaks.

On-Board Diagnostics Version II

In the 1980s and 1990s, automobile service centers started needing to employ "computer guys" to deal with the ECUs and fuel computers of modern cars. However, most shop technicians, with a little training, could still do smog inspections. All they needed was a DOS program running on a greasy Intel 286 computer wired into a long sensor stuck in the car's tailpipe and a tachometer sensor clipped to a spark plug wire. Decades later, these systems have been replaced with much more sophisticated test computers that connect directly to the car's ECU, assess its smoggyness, and then immediately phone home to the DMV mother ship. This provides more accurate and honest smog-test information to the DMV. Notably, it will also give vehicles a means of receiving orders when, in the not-too-distant future, they become self-aware and rise up against us.

As U.S. state governments worked to increase the sophistication of their tests and cut down on fraud, they pushed for a standardized interface for accessing the ECU diagnostic and engine information needed for smog-testing cars. The early version of this on-board diagnostic standard (*OBD*) was not universally installed, but the second version (*OBD-II*) became a requirement on all U.S. passenger cars from 1996 onward, and on most European cars from around 2000 onward.

The Four Flavors of OBD-II

The OBD-II port (Figure 7-1) is a 16-pin, trapezoidal-shaped connector found somewhere in the driver's-side dashboard area of modern vehicles.

If you're familiar with computers, you know that just because the plug fits, that doesn't mean it will work. The same applies to the OBD-II interface. This hardware plug is actually an interface to four different possible connection protocols—it's sort of like if you had a serial port, a USB port, and a PS2 keyboard port merged together into a single connection socket.

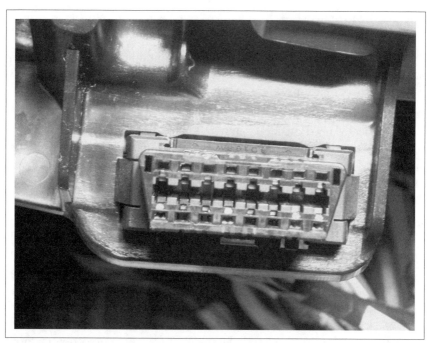

Figure 7-1. An OBD-II connector

The functions of the different pins in the OBD-II connector are shown in
Table 7-1.

Table 7-1. The OBD-II port pinout

Pin	Purpose
2	SAE-J1850 (VPW/PWM) bus positive line
4	Chassis ground
5	Signal ground
6	CAN high (J-2284)
7	ISO 9141-2 K (data) line
10	J1850 bus negative line
14	CAN low (J-2284)
15	ISO 9141-2 L (initialization) line
16	Battery power

See *http://www.obdii.com/connector.html* and *http://www.auterraweb.com/obdiipinout.html* for more information about
the pinouts.

The unassigned pins (1, 3, 8, 9, 11, 12, and 13) are all available for use by the manufacturer for things such as airbags, alarms, remotes, and so on.

OBD-II is actually a software layer on top of multiple hardware interfaces. Society of Automotive Engineers (SAE) standard J197 defines the communication protocol that runs on this hardware (sort of like how TCP/IP runs on top of Ethernet).

You practically need an R2D2 unit to speak all the different languages, protocols, and electrical standards that this innocent-looking port can speak. The following list describes the four different wire protocols crammed into the OBD-II port (and thus the four types of adapters you might have to purchase):

ISO (International Organization for Standardization) 9141-2 and ISO 1430
ISO 9141-2 is the electrical connection method used by European, Asian, and Chrysler vehicles and is electrically similar to a serial port. ISO 1430, or *KWP2000* (Key Word Protocol 2000), uses the same physical interface but speaks a different language. The ISO protocols use pins 5, 7, 16, and sometimes 15.

VPW (SAE J1850)
Variable Pulse Width (describing the electrical communication method) is used by most General Motors vehicles. This uses pins 2, 5, and 16.

PWM (SAE J1850)
Pulse Width Modulation (describing the electrical communication method) is used by most Ford vehicles. This uses pins 2, 5, 10, and 16.

CAN (SAE J2284)
Controller Area Network (described in ISO documents 11898/11519/15765) is slowly replacing the three buses above, and it should be the one standard OBD-II interface method by 2008. This uses pins 4, 6, 14, and 16.

There are dozens more acronyms where those came from, but this list should allow you to wade through some of the morass and figure out what kind of adapter you'll need to connect your PC to the OBD-II port in your car. A good list of car makes and the protocols they support for each year of manufacture can be found at *http://www.etools.org/files/public/generic-protocols-02-17-03.htm*.

Access Your Car's OBD-II Data

Some vendors make standalone devices that plug into the OBD-II port and are primarily designed to read vehicle fault codes. To use your computer to take readings, you will need an OBD-to-serial or OBD-to-USB adapter.

There are too many OBD-II adapters out there to mention them all, but a couple of popular adapters used by car PC hackers are the BR-3 from *http://www.obddiagnostics.com* and the Elmscan from *http://www.scantool.net*. While both have free software available for Windows and Linux, the Elmscan has more third-party application support (*http://www.scantool.net/software/scantool.net/*). You can download the software for both of these units and check them out before you buy.

Once you get one of these adapters, you're going to need to figure out where to plug it into your car. Depending on your vehicle, the physical interface may be with the fuses, under the steering wheel to the left or right, or in some other inconspicuous and car-specific location. A great resource for finding this location is at *http://www.autocenter.weber.edu/OBD-CH/vehicleoems.asp*. If your port is right under the steering wheel, you may want an adapter that folds over nicely. Since you're probably going to be leaving your OBD-II interface plugged in all the time, you don't want to have a big plug hitting your knees as you try to drive.

Once you have plugged the unit into your OBD port, you'll simply need to plug the serial connector into your car PC or laptop, and inform the OBD-II software which COM port you've connected it to.

One of the most popular uses of live OBD-II data is for a computerized dashboard display. The software that comes with the BR-3 has a built-in gauge function, which you can see in Figure 7-2

Although the Elmscan software does not come with a gauge display, I went onto the OBD-II forums at *http://www.mp3car.com* and found a skinnable real-time gauge designed to use the Elmscan hardware (Figure 7-3).

As I write this, both FrodoPlayer **[Hack #75]** and CENTRAFUSE **[Hack #73]** are adding support for OBD-II data streams directly into their applications.

Going Beyond OBD-II

OBD-II will give you an interesting set of data and may even help you diagnose engine troubles, but it's only the beginning of in-car interfacing. Beyond the sub-$100 hobby interfaces (which are perfectly adequate for most users), there are professional *scan tools* that understand the unique dialect of your make of vehicle and can interface more intimately with your car than ordinary OBD-II can.

There are aftermarket products dedicated to the specific make (or even model) of most popular vehicles. Some of these products are designed for tuning the vehicle and improving its racing performance, and to facilitate this they can tap into the car's real-time sensor networks (as opposed to

Figure 7-2. BR-3 gauges

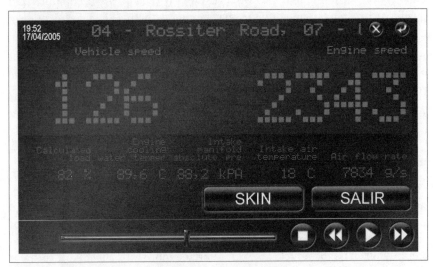

Figure 7-3. OBD-II gauge from MP3Car.com forums

the slower, once-a-second readouts of OBD-II). Examples include *http://www.tweecer.com* (for Mustangs), *http://www.ecutek.com* (for Subarus), and so on for every other make of car you can think of. Combining the OBD-II data with other sensors can allow for some very accurate measurements of engine performance. For example, for $239 Auttera (*http://www.auterraweb.com*) offers a unit that combines all four OBD protocol standards, and also includes an accelerometer. Combining the speed and RPM measurements from the OBD-II with the accelerometer readout, the device can accurately estimate horsepower and torque, acceleration times (0–60, quarter-mile, and so on), and fuel mileage.

You have to spend a bit more for the ultimate in ECU measurement and interfacing. Vehicle Spy (*http://www.intrepidcs.com/vspy/*), which uses a highly sophisticated (and very expensive) hardware interface, can simultaneously record information from a number of your car's ECUs in real time and correlate them to location data from a GPS unit. Designed primarily for engineers at auto manufacturers, it has APIs and programming interfaces so you can get at the data any way you want. Although this tool is total overkill for most car PC hacking, I've listed it here because there's little it can't do.

See Also

- *http://www.obdii.com*—This site provides a great introduction to OBD-II and is sponsored by AutoTap (*http://www.autotap.com*).
- *http://www.andywhittaker.com/ecu/obdii_software.htm*—This site provides a good tutorial, sells OBD interface hardware, and links to other useful OBD programs.
- *http://www.mp3car.com*—The MP3Car.com forums are the best place to see what cheap, open, functional adapters are most popular amongst car PC hackers.

HACK #70 Put a Video Jukebox in Your Car Theater

Use home theater software to provide a great multimedia experience in your car.

Home theater personal computers (HTPCs) are pretty leading-edge stuff, but if you want to go to the real bleeding edge, you'll need a car theater PC (CTPC). Imagine all the rear-seat entertainment you could provide with a few hundred gigabytes of movies, music, photos, and games [Hack #72], all of which you can take with you anywhere you drive!

The good news is that there is a lot of choice in HTPC software; the bad news is that it varies from very beta to fairly mature, and most of it was not designed for in-car use. I've isolated a handful of good candidates, though, and to help you narrow down the choices I'll go over the caveats of using these programs on a car PC.

Table 7-2 shows a sampling of the HTPC software available today.

Table 7-2. HTPC software snapshot

Availability	Program name
Free	MythTV, Mini MythTV, WinMyth, myHTPC, OpenHTPC, Freevo, GAM, GB-PVR, Media Portal, VDR
Commercial	SageTV 2.1, SnapStream Beyond TV 3, ShowShifter, Windows XP Media Center Edition, Meedio, DirectTivo
Xbox	XboxMediaCenter
Mac	EyeTV, MythTV (viewer only—requires a Linux machine as well)

For the purposes of this hack, I'll assume you have video in digital form (on a PC or on CD/DVD) that you want to get into your in-car PC. I'll avoid most of the PVR applications—such as Frey Technologies' SageTV (which I think is one of the best in-home PVRs), SnapStream's Beyond TV, and Home Media Networks' ShowShifter—because the main focus of these PVR programs is on scheduling, recording, pausing, and playing back live TV. Importing content, which is needed for a car theater, tends to be an afterthought.

Most HTPC applications are written with a remote control in mind, and they assume you don't have access to a keyboard or a mouse. ("Control Your Car PC with a Handheld Remote" [Hack #56] covers the use of remote controls for in-car computing in detail.) However, I find that having some sort of mouse (such as a touchscreen [Hack #26]) is still essential. If you are using Windows, there is nothing more annoying than a pop-up that you can't get rid of with the remote control or having no way to recover from an application crash.

As you can see from Table 7-2, other operating systems (such as Linux or Mac OS X) can also be used for this project, as can alternative hardware (such as an Xbox). However, setting up Linux can be a real chore, Macs tend to be a bit pricier for the hardware you get (though the Mac Mini [Hack #54] is changing this), and the Xbox requires a bit of hacking to get it to work well in the car and make it home-theater-ready. For most uses, the easiest, cheapest solution with the best third-party support is Windows (XP or later).

Hardware Requirements

While VIA's EPIA motherboards are the most popular in-car computing platform [Hack #41] today, even their fastest processors are a bit anemic for all the different video compression standards used currently. A true Pentium or Athlon processor of at least 1 GHz is a requirement for smooth video playback with all the video codecs you're going to run into.

I recommend the following system specs:

- A 1-GHz or faster processor to handle all forms of video playback
- A DVD optical drive to play DVDs
- A large hard drive (60 GB or above) to store media files
- A DirectX 9–compatible graphics card to play the latest video games

A two-hour movie compressed to MPEG-4 typically takes up either 700 MB or 1400 MB (i.e., one or two CDs, depending on the compression). With that kind of compression, you can fit 40–80 movies on an empty 60-GB drive. If MP3 music files average 5 MB per song, just 20 GB of your space will hold over 4,000 songs (that's 11 days of no-repeat music!). Live TV content recorded with a hardware MPEG-2 encoder such as the Hauppauge line of PVRs (150/250/350) is typically recorded at much higher data rates. A typical 60-minute program in MPEG-2 may be 2–4 GB or more, which means you can store less than 50 hours of television on a 60-GB disk.

Some people like to keep their DVDs uncompressed on their hard drives (better quality, and no time-consuming compression to do). These files will be 4–9 GB per movie, so plan on getting a monster 400-GB drive if you want to do this!

Software Requirements

Since you will probably be transferring media files [Hack #64] from your hacked TiVo (Raffi Krikorian's *Tivo Hacks* tells you how to do this) or other in-home HTPC, your CTPC needs the correct codecs to play back the various video formats.

While Windows XP comes with the Windows Media codecs, to play DVDs you need a software decoder such as InterVideo PowerDVD, CyberLink PowerDVD, or the drivers that came with your DVD player. Once you've installed any of these programs, you'll be able to play DVDs in any of the HTPC applications I mention here. Note, though, that there may be some MPEG-2 or MPEG-4 encoded formats that you'll need additional codecs to play back. DivX (*http://www.divx.com*) is the most essential codec to install; after that, *http://www.free-codecs.com* should help you get any others you need.

When you install codecs in Windows, they become available to every application on the system. Thus, once you have the right codec installed, you should be able to play back your media in any HTPC application. A quick test to make sure everything is working is to try playing back the media in Windows Media Player first. If you can play back your DivX movies, your MPEG-2 movies, your MPEG-4 movies, and your DVDs in Windows Media Player, chances are all the HTPCs listed later in this hack will play back your content, too.

Just about every piece of software I tested requires the latest versions of both DirectX 9 and .NET 1.1, both of which are available from the Microsoft web site.

If you want to transfer media to your CTPC, one option is to directly rip content off your own CDs and DVDs. The main advantages of this approach are that it is legal (depending on who you talk to) and that many of the ripping tools download metadata (such as cover art, artists' names, release dates, and so on) automatically. This metadata can be imported into and used by many HTPC applications. A presence or absence of accurate metadata really shows up when you're using these applications—if you have a large collection of audio and video that you've imported from many different sources, you'll want a way to have the content show up with album art, movie posters, and all the other eye-candy that these HTPC applications can provide. Though downloading media from the Internet will save you the time of compressing and ripping it yourself, you'll likely need to add metadata information manually to make these files truly useful.

HTPC Comparisons

I tested half a dozen of the HTPC applications that I thought might be appropriate for in-car use. For the reasons stated earlier, I did not test all of the PVR-centric applications. In the end, the programs covered in this section were the strongest candidates for in-car use.

Windows Media Center Edition ($150 OEM). Windows Media Center Edition (MCE), shown in Figure 7-4, is by far the most well-polished of the HTPC applications, with stunning 3D visuals (and hardware requirements to match). Almost Mac-like in its ease of use, it was unfortunately not Mac-like in its importing ability and compatibility with my media library.

I found that the application did a good job of collecting metadata (such as artwork and DVD information) from ripped content, but didn't do so well with media downloaded from the Internet. I don't know how it manages to guess which CD is which, but with downloaded content it was more miss than hit. When displaying metadata, I liked how as a fallback it will generate preview icons for videos by displaying an actual video frame (although with CDs you just get a generic icon).

Meedio ($59.99). Meedio (Figure 7-5) has an interface remarkably similar to Media Portal's MCE skin and, obviously, similar to MCE itself. At first, it seemed like an ideal solution (if at a cost). The interface is as clean as Windows MCE's, the menu sound effects are easily the best of the bunch

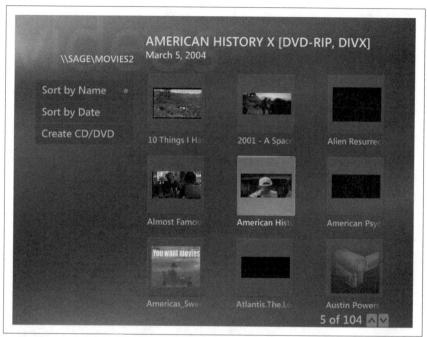

Figure 7-4. Windows MCE

(very TiVo-like), and the onscreen menus for playing back media are all top-notch. It does a fine job of playing back DVDs, videos, and music, and of displaying photos. Meedio also has more plug-ins than any of the other applications I tested, giving it compatibility with a wide range of remote controls and allowing it to download tons of information, ranging from movie listings to weather forecasts to top-10 music lists (just to name a few).

Since I'm big on metadata support, I was eager to test out how well Meedio handled gathering information from both ripped content and stuff I downloaded from the Internet. Though Meedio did find some of the cover art for my music, it couldn't make use of any of the textual metadata. It performed similarly poorly with videos—in fact, a little worse than MCE, since it didn't create preview icons for them.

Media Engine (free). Media Engine (Figure 7-6) is the only software I looked at that was actually designed as a car PC application. The bad news is that it's the most difficult to set up and has the worst user interface of all the applications I tried. The setup dialogs are daunting, the menu options are usually not clear, and the buttons take time to learn and aren't always obvious.

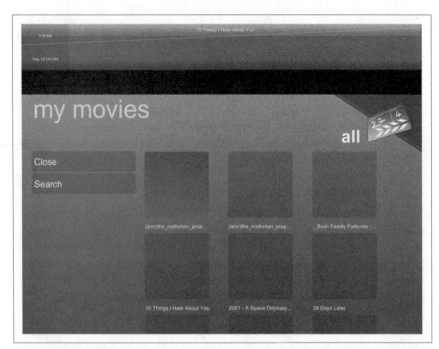

Figure 7-5. Meedio

Figure 7-6. Media Engine

On the positive side, it has a few features that may make it a must-have for some users:

Synchronization
You can point it at a directory to automatically sync up with your media directory [Hack #64].

Dim at night
You can set a time of day for the display to automatically dim the look of the interface.

XM and radio tuner support
Media Engine supports USB-connected XM and FM radio receivers.

External application launcher
It comes with buttons to help control external applications.

Windows GUI replacement
It can completely replace the regular Windows interface, to save memory and prevent its use while driving.

Media Engine is also the most tenacious of the applications about keeping itself on top, and it doesn't use pop-up windows. This is great, because with some of the other apps I had to reboot just to get back to a menu that had been obscured by some dialog box that I couldn't get rid of without a keyboard. A major downside, however, is that the limitation of a single media folder prevented me from managing my media the way I prefer, with separate volumes and folders for my music and videos.

Media Portal (free). I really was impressed when I ran Media Portal (Figure 7-7) for the first time. The setup is almost as easy as that for Windows MCE, and the menus are almost as polished. The only bad news is that it is brand new and was a little unstable. However, development is proceeding at a rapid pace, and as the program is open source, if any of the programmers drift away there should be others to pick up the slack. There also seem to be quite a few plug-ins in development, and the message boards are very active.

The setup for Media Portal runs you through several wizards for music, pictures, DVDs, videos, and TV. These wizards allow you to specify as many music, picture, and video folders as you want, as well as which external players and MPEG-2 codecs to use, and all the typical options expected of a media player. Once inside Media Portal, you can get back to the setup panel or the wizards from the main menu (which isn't visible in full-screen mode), or you can hit F2 to open the setup menu (whether it's in full-screen mode or not). The video playback function could use a bit of polish, but it was very solid and got the job done. My only complaint is that the onscreen menus were a bit sloppy and occasionally flickered.

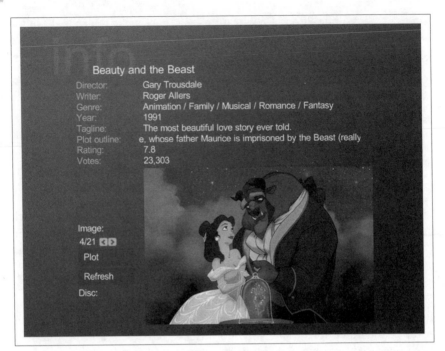

Figure 7-7. MediaPortal

I also love the media information setup. While MCE is good about meta-data when working with ripped media, it falls flat on its face with down-loaded content. Media Portal can use the same metadata that Windows creates, but it also builds on it by using the Internet Movie Database (*http://www.imdb.com*) for video metadata and another online database for music metadata. In my experience, the music section was good, but the video section was amazing. With movies, you can hit the Info button on your remote (or select Scan from the main menu), and Media Portal will attempt to search the IMBD based on the filename. It then presents you with a list of results you can choose from. If it gets it wrong, there is a manual setting where you can put in your own search terms. Once you've made a match, it downloads the complete cast information, artwork, and a synopsis of the film. I love it!

Another very nice feature is that when you turn off your car PC, Media Portal remembers the position you were at in any video files that were playing. This means your kids can pick up watching *Finding Nemo* at the same spot they were at when you turned off the car to fill up the gas tank! Unfortunately, this doesn't currently work for remembering DVD positioning, but I have a feeling that this is on the to-do list.

Overall, Media Portal gets my vote for the in-car HTPC application of choice. It's free, it has good support, the interface is excellent, the setup was easy, and the player is solid.

—Jacob Riskin

HACK #71 Choose Your in-Car Navigation Software

With a car PC you have access to cutting-edge navigation features, and you aren't locked into using the expensive and limited system that came with your car.

In-car navigation used to be a status symbol of the elite, reserved only for those who could afford a Lexus or an Infiniti. Now, however, anyone with an in-car computer (or handy laptop) and a GPS unit can have a navigation system. This hack will describe some of the PC navigation software that can give you a near-MapQuest-like experience with your car PC.

Before we start, let's make one thing entirely clear: you will never get after-market integration as tight as you would with a factory-installed navigation unit (at least, not without spending a lot of money). Factory-installed units offer such niceties as spoken directions and automatic lowering of the radio volume so you can hear those directions. They also generally present a cleaner interface (steering-wheel controls rock) and better integration with your dash (have you ever tried to shoehorn a 7" screen into a Honda Civic?). But navigation still isn't a common factory option on vehicles below $20,000, so if your budget doesn't stretch to a more expensive car, chances are you'll have to either go aftermarket or roll your own with a car PC.

Once you've decided to add in-car navigation, there are several routes you can take (no pun intended). You can combine a Palm or PocketPC with a CompactFlash-based GPS unit and some software for a quick and highly portable solution. You can also get a dedicated navigation unit, such as a TomTom GO (*http://www.tomtom.com*), for around $900. If, like me, however, you happen to have an old laptop (or two or three) lying around the house, why not put it to use? More adventurous souls will install specialized PCs in their vehicles [Hack #52], complete with dash-mounted touchscreens [Hack #26]. The software described in this hack will work with both.

Regardless of the computer you use, you will need a device that can capture GPS information and send it to the computer. Many external GPS units are available for PCs. Garmin (*http://www.garmin.com/mobile/*) and DeLorme (*http://www.delorme.com*) are two of the big names out there. You can spend anywhere from $70 to $400 on your GPS hardware. The most expensive options come with Bluetooth or external antenna jacks. Just make sure that whatever unit you purchase, there's enough cable to run it to the windshield or the rear window, because GPS units don't work very well if they can't see the sky. (This is where the newest Bluetooth units come in handy, as there are no cables to run.) Nicer units have magnetic backings so you can attach them externally (e.g., to your roof or the top of your trunk). Fortunately, most GPS units adhere to the NMEA standard, which means that you should be able to buy a GPS unit from one vendor and use it with any other piece of software.

So, you have a computer, and you have a GPS unit (serial, USB, or Bluetooth). Now the only thing you have to decide on is software. More than likely, your GPS unit came with some form of navigation software, such as Garmin's nRoute, DeLorme's Street Atlas, Microsoft's Streets and Trips (*http://www.microsoft.com/streets*), ALK's CoPilot Live (*http://www.alk.com*), or one of a dozen lesser-known navigation packages. All of these programs have their strengths and weaknesses, and most are intended for passenger use, as the buttons and interface are usually too small to be used on a 7" touchscreen (for a way around this, check out "Car-Enable Clunky Applications" [Hack #58]). If you usually drive solo, you need to use a software package that can be used safely and won't distract you.

One such navigation program is CoPilot Live (Figure 7-8), which offers a stripped-down Driver mode. At about $199–299, depending on the maps you get with it, it is a bit expensive, but it's very polished. Many car PC resellers consider it the best navigation software out there for in-car computer use. It borrows several of its features from a sophisticated truck fleet management package from the same company. It offers a powerful navigation feature set, and if you have a wireless Internet connection in your vehicle [Hack #62], it even has various telematics features, such as the ability to receive text messages and real-time updating of your location over the Internet [Hack #67].

The interface is clean and well designed, and it even has a text-to-speech (TTS) engine to read back directions to you. Be forewarned, though: trying to edit your route while driving is a sure way to get yourself into an accident. Let your passenger do the work, or at least pull off to the side of the road to do it.

Having used CoPilot Live extensively on a road trip through Napa, San Francisco, Monterey, and Santa Barbara, I can testify that the software works pretty well (better, at times, than my weary traveling companions!). Here are some items of note:

• Just like with MapQuest or any other computer-based routing system, you will occasionally get bum information—for example, sometimes CoPilot will tell you to turn left off a street that has "No Left Turn" signs liberally applied at every intersection.

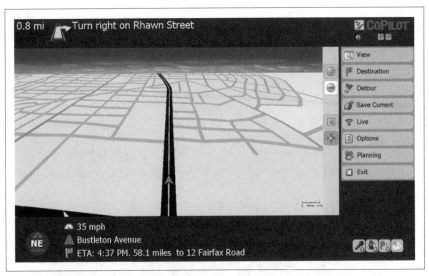

Figure 7-8. CoPilot Live (3D view)

- CoPilot's Planning mode will give you a MapQuest-like interface to build your trip. It's much easier to deal with this interface than it is to add waypoints (places to go) on the fly in Guidance mode, which is intended for use once you start moving.

- If you don't get all the way to a waypoint on your planned route (perhaps because the parking structure is a couple of blocks away), you'll have to delete that waypoint in order to move on to your next destination. Failure to do so will keep you running around in circles until you realize what the software's trying to do.

- The Driver mode gives you the simplest display possible, showing only your next turn/instruction and basic information such as your speed and ETA. Switch to Passenger mode to see more of your mapped surroundings.

- The software automatically changes views when you're stopped. Get up to 10 mph, and it switches back to Driver mode. This is to keep you from looking away from the road and tinkering with settings at high speed.

- Not getting a GPS fix? You might be in an area where high terrain features (hills, tall buildings, etc.) are blocking your view of the sky. Also, the software generally will not give you a good fix until you start moving.

- Feel like giving back to the company? You can send back your GPS tracks to help ALK refine its mapping data.

Another very popular package is Destinator (*http://www.destinator1.com*). Although current versions of Destinator only run on PocketPC, the company that makes Destinator (*http://www.hstcglobal.com*) offers a software development kit (SDK) that others can use to produce PC-based applications.

Using the Destinator 3 SDK, the user Ninja Monkey on the popular MP3Car.com site has developed a completely touchscreen-compatible navigation app. Ninja Monkey's frontend, called MapMonkey (*http://www.mapmonkey.net*), is designed to work with a VGA touchscreen and let the driver control everything (see Figure 7-9). As far as I know, it is the only aftermarket navigation app designed specifically for car PC use.

Figure 7-9. Ninja Monkey's MapMonkey navigation software

MapMonkey is a popular add-in to various car PC applications, such as FrodoPlayer [Hack #75], Neocar Media Center [Hack #74], and CENTRAFUSE [Hack #73]. Because it's under development, you can get a beta version of the software for free right now, but you'll need to purchase the maps and SDK for your country and city from Destinator. Although most of the NAV apps use maps from the same vendors, Destinator maps use a special compression format that takes up a lot less hard drive space—useful for handhelds, but not as essential when you have a large car PC hard drive.

You can use CoPilot or Destinator with a laptop, but if you're going to use them with a car PC you'll want a VGA touchscreen [Hack #26]—a low-res composite LCD TV screen isn't going to work well. Since Destinator 3

(MapMonkey, specifically) is under continuous development, it's probably the car PC product most likely to add the features you want. Just hop on the message boards at *http://www.mp3car.com* and discuss your needs. Maybe Ninja Monkey will like your idea and add it to the program.

Having in-car navigation is like having high-speed Internet access: once you've got it, you'll never want to go back. It beats carrying around a bunch of paper maps that may or may not give you the level of detail you need to get to your destination—and you'll never again have to worry about refolding them.

—Jason Tokunaga and Damien Stolarz

HACK #72 Play Thousands of Games by Emulating Video Game Consoles

Here's a creative way you can get inexpensive, interactive in-car entertainment.

Perhaps the most common in-car entertainment device after the radio and a DVD player is a game console, such as an Xbox or PlayStation 2. Though you can easily install a game console in your car, many car computer enthusiasts get shivers up their spines (and down their checkbooks) at the thought of having yet another ominously power-hungry box hidden under a seat. Thankfully, a solution exists that is far less costly (free, even!) and requires no additional power, video, and audio cables to be run. This hack will show you how to emulate popular game consoles on your car PC, which means you can provide a wide variety of games to all of your passengers from a single machine.

Emulation is quite simply the act of getting one piece of software to imitate another piece of software or hardware. In the case of video game emulation, a program is making your PC imitate the hardware of your favorite console. To make this work, the game information is sucked off the original game pack or CD, using special hardware and/or software. The game images are then stored in either *ROM* format (for game packs) or *ISO* format (for CDs). (Note that the use of a ROM or ISO file for a game you do not actually own could be illegal.)

Emulators

There are many emulators for practically every game system, and I've picked out the ones that I think have the best features for in-car application. I should note, however, that I've only covered emulators that run on Windows machines. If you have Linux or some other OS, or want to emulate a system I haven't covered here, check out Zophar's Domain, at *http://www.zophar.net*—this site discusses pretty much any emulator for any system you could desire.

Nintendo emulation. The Nintendo Entertainment System (NES) is an old-school machine from the mid-1980s with some real classic games. While they don't provide snazzy 3D action, NES emulators will run easily on car PCs with processors as slow as those found in the Mini-ITX systems, and they can do so without interfering with your MP3 listening. Out of all the available NES emulators, I would recommend NNNesterJ (*http://www.emulation9.com/nnnesterj/*) as your mobile NES choice, due to the easy setup, wide range of controller emulation (including the Zapper—Duck Hunt, anyone?), and IP-based net-play (in case you have multiple computers in one car). However, you should probably get it from *http://www.zophar.net/nes.html* instead of its own web site, due to the fact that the Emulation9.com site is mostly in Japanese. NNNesterJ is showcased running Super Mario Brothers in Figure 7-10.

Figure 7-10. NNNesterJ running Super Mario Brothers

The Super Nintendo Entertainment System (SNES) is, somewhat obviously, the successor to NES. The graphics are far superior to NES but will still run smoothly on somewhat low-end systems. The best SNES emulator, hands down, is ZSNES (*http://www.zsnes.com*). This emulator is incredibly full-featured, with countless customization options, and it runs fast. Also, you can emulate the SNES mouse and Super Scope (the SNES light gun, or rather, light-zooka). If you pair those features with a touchscreen and a Super Scope game such as Battle Clash or Metal Combat, you'll have super robot-poking fun for your passengers. You can see ZSNES in action in Figure 7-11.

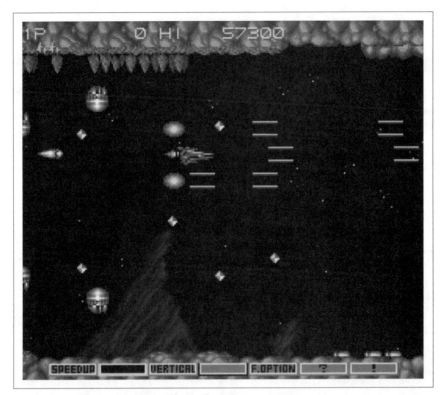

Figure 7-11. ZSNES in action, with Gradius III

Nintendo's next big thing was the Nintendo 64 (so named because it was a 64-bit system). However, with this and more recent systems, you're probably going to need at least a 1.5-GHz Pentium 4 or comparable machine and a decent gaming 3D video card. For N64 emulation, NEmu (*http:// www.nemu.com*) is the most compatible emulator available. I won't sugar-coat it, though; it's a pain in various places to get running, and the ROMs are typically hidden somewhere in a web page labyrinth of endless "VOTE FOR ME AT TOP 5000 ROM PAGES" loops and cartoon breasts. I wish you luck if you do set out on this endeavor.

Sega emulation. The SNES's main competition was Sega's Genesis; however, a few lesser-known Sega systems were released before and after the Genesis, including the Sega CD and the 32X. Those didn't do too well, but there are still some good games for them, and running an emulator won't take much processing power.

Kega (*http://www.eidolons-inn.de*), shown in Figure 7-12, is what you want for Sega Genesis/CD/32X emulation. It's great, aside from the fact that you have to have your colors set to 16-bit for it to run.

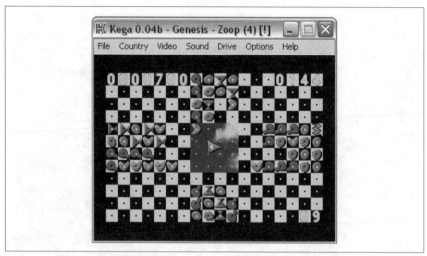

Figure 7-12. Kega playing Zoop

The Dreamcast was Sega's final system, and it had some excellent four-player games (which could be just the right thing for a road trip with a full minivan, provided that the emulator runs smoothly and supports four players, and you have enough input devices). There's only one Dreamcast emulator that's currently capable of playing commercial games at a decent speed, and that is Chankast (*http://www.chanka.org*). The recommended processor speed is along the lines of 2 GHz, though, so make sure your in-car computer has decent specs.

PlayStation emulators. Sony originally just made TVs and other home electronics, but when they released their own game system, the PlayStation, it was massively successful. If it's a PlayStation you want to emulate, then ePSXe (*http://www.epsxe.com*) is the program of choice—it does everything you could want and runs fast on any gigahertz-class computer. However, you need to separately download the plug-ins for things like graphics, sound, CD reading, controller support, and netplay. You can find all the needed plug-ins and instructions on how to use them at *http://www.ngemu.com/psx/index.php*.

Other game emulators. If you want to emulate any arcade game, MAME32 (*http://www.classicgaming.com/mame32qa/*) will be your best friend. There are about a zillion unofficial versions of MAME with all sorts of little tweaks, but I recommend MAME32.

If you're looking to find a way to play all the latest console games without actually buying a PS2, an Xbox, or a GameCube, chances are you're not going to find all of what you're looking for in an emulator just yet. There's one Xbox emulator (Xeon, no web site) that is running Halo, and a PS2 one named neutrinoSX2 (*http://nsx2.emulation64.com*) that can run Blade 2 and Mortal Kombat 5. The most developed GameCube emulator is Dolphin (*http://www.dolphin-emu.com*), which is running Zelda: The Wind Waker. Check back in a couple of years, and you should be able to play a lot more games on these brand-newish emulators.

Game Controllers

Of course, all of these games require some type of controller in order to play. It can detract from the head-to-head gaming experience if everyone has to share one keyboard for game input, and even for single-player use you may want a more intuitive or convenient input method than a keyboard. Here are a few creative control solutions for your gaming pleasure, so you don't have to run all your game-craving passengers through the tutorial of "Okay, here's the keyboard, now W is up, Enter is start," and so on.

Probably the simplest approach is to use a standard USB controller/joystick for your computer, and simply map the buttons on it to the controls on the emulator.

If you've already made a large investment in console controllers, you may be able to use one of those with your PC by using an adapter. Figure 7-13 shows one of the many adapters you can buy that will allow you to plug original SNES, NES, and other controllers into USB ports. To find a wide selection of these adapters for any system imaginable, go to *http://www.lik-sang.com* and head over to the SmartJoy page.

Figure 7-13. A SmartJoy SNES controller-to-USB adapter

You can also use a touchscreen for some games—playing light-gun-based games with a touchscreen is pretty darn close to cheating, but it's still amusing to kill time on the road by tapping ducks, robots, zombies, or what have you.

I tried to find some way for a standard X10 Lola RF remote (which integrates with car PC frontends) to control ZSNES so that you could use the same remote you use for your music programs on your emulators, but my efforts proved fruitless. First I tried using Girder (*http://www.proximis.com*) to turn the button presses on the remote into keystrokes [Hack #56], but, it turns out emulators are very stubborn about only taking commands from a real keyboard. Then I tried pairing Girder with PPJoy (*http://www.geocities.com/deonvdw/Docs/PPJoyMain.htm*) to turn the faked keypresses into faked joystick button presses, but it turns out that either PPJoy would only talk to real keyboards too, or ZSNES would only talk to real joysticks.

Although I couldn't make the X10 work for me, there's an indication on the Firefly PC Remote web page (*http://www.snapstream.com/products/firefly/*) that their remote can control ZSNES. I'm not sure to what extent they mean—i.e., whether you can actually configure the keys for the remote in the menu—but you might want to look into that option if you want to successfully control everything on your PC with one device.

—Adam Stolarz

Use CENTRAFUSE as Your Car PC Frontend
#73   CENTRAFUSE integrates media playback, navigation, and hands-free mobile phone control in a clean, sharp-looking interface.

When I first installed a computer in my car, there wasn't any software available that did exactly what I needed it to do. That's when I decided to write CENTRAFUSE. What originally started out as a small project quickly grew into a large one. My main focus was to build a touchscreen-friendly music player, but it became much more than that. Just like any other car PC owner, I soon wanted navigation, video playback, and radio control capabilities, and I wanted it all integrated into one application—and hence, CENTRAFUSE expanded into what it is today (see Figure 7-14). This hack will tell you a bit about how CETRAFUSE works and the features it offers.

Installing CENTRAFUSE

To get started, visit *http://www.fluxmedia.net* and download the latest version of CENTRAFUSE. While visiting the site, it is also a good idea to download the latest user manual. If you plan on using any third-party applications (such as PhoneControl.NET [Hack #63] for phone integration or Radiator [Hack #19] for hardware radio control), I recommend that you install and set up these applications *before* running CENTRAFUSE. This will simplify the configuration process, because you will already know the locations of

Figure 7-14. The CENTRAFUSE music manager

your external applications. If you plan on using GPS, you should install your GPS software and verify that it is functional before attempting to embed it within CENTRAFUSE.

Once you've downloaded CENTRAFUSE and installed any helper applications you intend to use, simply run the setup and follow the onscreen instructions. When the installation is complete, click the CENTRAFUSE icon to launch the program, and the configuration will start automatically.

Integrating External Programs

You can integrate external programs into CENTRAFUSE by embedding them. One of the problems with Windows for car PC use is that you don't want or need Windows Explorer (the Windows GUI, not the web browser). And when you run other applications, you don't want to have to switch to them using the Alt-Tab or a mouse—you want them all to look and function like one integrated application.

To embed any external application into CENTRAFUSE, you'll need two important pieces of information:

- The name or "title" of the external application, as listed within the application's title bar
- The location of the executable file you wish to embed

Using GPS as an example, here is how you can embed a program in CEN-TRAFUSE. First, visit the CENTRAFUSE support forums at *http://forums. fluxmedia.net*, and navigate to the Installation subforum to view a list of commonly used GPS window titles. This list includes only verified and tested applications and is updated as new information and software become available. If your GPS program is not listed, don't worry; you can determine this information on your own. To do so, run your application and write down the exact title listed within the main title bar across the top of the program window. Once you have this information, open the CENTRAFUSE configuration utility and enable GPS support. Next, key in the correct location of the executable file for your GPS program, and enter its window title in the "GPS window name" field.

When you click the GPS button in CENTRAFUSE, it will now launch your selected GPS program and embed it within the main window (see Figure 7-15). Once the GPS window is loaded, you can toggle to a full-screen mode by clicking the song title display across the top of the window (which happens to be one of my favorite features—being able to use your GPS software and still have easy access to your music controls is awesome!).

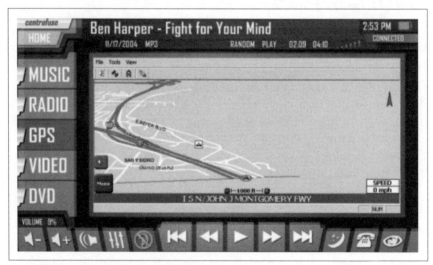

Figure 7-15. An embedded GPS application

For the curious programmers amongst you, I first get the GPS application's window handle by using FindWindow (*user32.dll*), and then I used SetWindowLong (*user32.dll*) to attach it to a .NET panel. I designed it this way so a user can plug in any GPS application. Also, through the use of Set-WindowLong, I am able to remove the border and client edge. When I first saw how good it looked, I couldn't believe it.

Changing CENTRAFUSE's Appearance

CENTRAFUSE is completely customizable and skinnable, which means anyone can customize its appearance. I added skin support because I love being able to easily change the look and feel of the application. Creating custom skins is not difficult. Open the installation folder where you installed CENTRAFUSE, and locate the *skins* folder. Here you will find a folder for each skin included with CENTRAFUSE. Each skin folder consists of many images that represent different states of the skin. All the buttons and icons are stored in JPEG files, and the action for each button is defined by a *hot spot*, a user-defined zone that is specified in the *skin.xml* file. Hot spots are rectangular areas defined by specifying the location of the top-left corner and then providing a width and a height. The ability to edit the skin files gives you control over almost all aspects of the application's look and feel, including text, fonts, and sizes. So if you decide you want to change a font size or don't like the way a font looks, don't worry—you can customize this in the skin file.

Setting Up the Radio

To use the radio mode within CENTRAFUSE, you need to install an application called Radiator (*http://www.flesko.cz*). (I also have links to the latest version of Radiator on the CENTRAFUSE support forums.) After installing Radiator, you should verify that it works with your current hardware setup. Then you need to enter the CENTRAFUSE setup utility, enable radio support, and provide the location to the Radiator executable file (*rc.exe*). Now, through the use of the Radiator external application, CENTRAUFSE will have full control over your radio hardware.

Adding Support for New Audio and Video Formats

CENTRAFUSE supports any audio or video format your system supports. The audio and video file formats are determined by a list of file extensions within the *config.xml* file, which is located in your CENTRAFUSE system directory. By default, CENTRAFUSE supports all the most common audio and video extensions. However, if you install any extra codecs, you will need to edit the *config.xml* file to instruct CENTRAFUSE to support these new file types. The following code is a segment from the *config.xml* file, which shows the default list of supported audio and video file types:

```
<APPCONFIG>
    <MUSICEXT>wav|mpa|mp2|mp3|au|aif|aiff|snd|wma</MUSICEXT>
    <VIDEOEXT>avi|qt|mov|mpg|mpeg|m1v|wmv|bin</VIDEOEXT>
```

If your system supports any other audio or video extensions, you can add support for these file types by adding the new extensions to the end of the

MUSICEXT or VIDEOEXT nodes. Just be sure to use the same format shown in this configuration segment.

Adding Phone Support

Phone support is enabled through PhoneControl.NET (*http://www. phonecontrol.net*). CENTRAFUSE is designed to communicate directly with the PhoneControl.NET application, but before starting down this path, I recommend that you first visit *http://www.phoco.net* and see if your phone is supported. If it is (or after you've purchased a supported phone), download and install PhoneControl.NET. Once PhoneControl.NET is up and running [Hack #63], start CENTRAFUSE, enter the setup, enable support for the application, and specify the correct location to its executable file. The next time you start CENTRAFUSE, if your phone support is working properly, you will see a battery and signal meter in the top-right corner (visible in Figure 7-15). This icon indicates that CENTRAFUSE recognizes your phone, and you can now use the phone modes and screens to make calls and send SMS messages. If you place or receive a call while music is playing, CENTRAFUSE will automatically pause the music until your call is finished.

Getting Online in Your Car

CENTRAFUSE can be configured to access the Internet via your mobile phone [Hack #62], so you can surf the Web, look up weather data, and check traffic updates from your car PC. Once you are able to establish an Internet connection with your phone, you can configure your computer to use this connection as the default Internet connection under Tools → Internet Options → Connections. Enabling this feature gives CENTRAFUSE control over your Internet connectivity. Touching the Internet status bar in the top-right corner of the CENTRAFUSE display will cause it to dial and connect via the default Windows Internet connection; touch it again to disconnect.

> I implemented these features using *wininet.dll* and its methods. Your Internet connectivity status can be accessed using InternetGetconnectedState. InternetAutodial and InternetAutodialHangup provide easy methods for connecting and disconnecting via the default Internet connection. If the Internet status bar is clicked while disconnected, CENTRAFUSE will use InternetAutodial to dial the default Internet connection. If clicked while connected, it will use InternetAutodialHangup to disconnect.

Once an Internet connection is established, you can use the embedded web browser to access weather and traffic reports and surf the Web (see

Figure 7-16). However, before you begin surfing via your cell phone, make sure you contact your wireless phone provider about a data (i.e., flat-fee) plan so that you can avoid costly charges—by default, most providers charge for data by the byte.

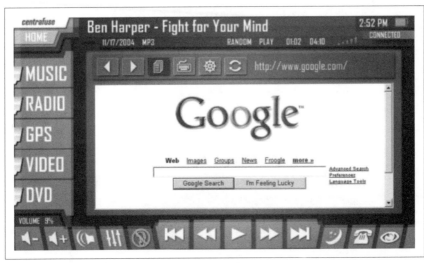

Figure 7-16. The embedded CENTRAFUSE web browser

Changing the Voice Commands

CENTRAFUSE comes with voice-activated control. To enable this feature you must install Microsoft's SAPI SDK [Hack #60], which can be found under "Downloads" at *http://www.fluxmedia.net*. Once you've downloaded and installed SAPI, you will need to enter the CENTRAFUSE setup utility and enable the voice control option. The voice commands used for CEN-TRAFUSE are fully customizable via the *grammar.xml* file located in the CENTRAFUSE system folder. The voice keyword used to tell CEN-TRAFUSE you are going to give it a voice command is located under the CID_Navigation node—the default value is *computer*. All voice commands are located under the CID_MAIN node. When performing edits to the *grammar.xml* file, *do not make any changes to the XML tags, other than altering the voice commands*. Editing any values other than the actual voice commands might disable voice support. Here's a sample *grammar.xml* file:

```
<GRAMMAR LANGID="409">
    <DEFINE>
        <ID NAME="CID_MAIN" VAL="1" />
        <ID NAME="CID_MUSIC" VAL="2" />
        <ID NAME="CID_RADIO" VAL="3" />
        <ID NAME="CID_GPS" VAL="4" />
        <ID NAME="CID_VIDEO" VAL="5" />
```

```
            <ID NAME="CID_DVD" VAL="6" />
            <ID NAME="CID_TOOLS" VAL="7" />
            <ID NAME="CID_PHONE" VAL="8" />
            <ID NAME="CID_TRAFFIC" VAL="9" />
            <ID NAME="CID_Navigation" VAL="254" />
        </DEFINE>
        <RULE ID="CID_Navigation" TOPLEVEL="ACTIVE">
            <P>
                <L>
                    <P>computer</P>
                </L>
            </P>
            <RULEREF REFID="CID_MAIN" />
        </RULE>
        <RULE ID="CID_MAIN">
            <L PROPID="CID_MAIN">
                <P VAL="CID_MUSIC">music</P>
                <P VAL="CID_RADIO">radio</P>
                <P VAL="CID_GPS">gps</P>
                <P VAL="CID_VIDEO">video</P>
                <P VAL="CID_DVD">dvd</P>
                <P VAL="CID_TOOLS">tools</P>
                <P VAL="CID_PHONE">phone</P>
                <P VAL="CID_TRAFFIC">traffic</P>
            </L>
        </RULE>
    </GRAMMAR>
```

Video Poster Images

Video poster images, which allow you to associate images with your video files, are supported in the Video Manager. This seems like a small thing, but it really improves the appearance of the video selection screen. CEN-TRAFUSE will read poster images for individual video files and for entire folders. For video files, you simply make a *.jpg* with the same name as the video file, and place it in the same directory as the video file. For example, if your movie is called *Incredibles2.avi*, your poster should be called *Incredibles2.jpg*. To make a generic graphic for everything in a folder, just create an image called *folder.jpg* inside that folder. These poster images are shown as you browse through your videos in the Video Manager.

Future Improvements

There are still a lot of things left for me to finish. Currently, I am working with some OBD-II readers [Hack #69] trying to implement cool analog gauges and sensors for the speedometer, tachometer, and so on. I also plan on diving into some XM and Sirius integration, which I have really been looking forward to. The plug-in system I am working on will allow other programmers to use my CENTRAFUSE SDK to easily integrate their own applications with mine, which will hopefully help add lots of support. I have had a great time writing this program, and I hope you enjoy using it.

—David McGowan

Use Neocar Media Center as Your Car PC #74 Frontend

Neocar Media Center is a very popular, highly customizable car PC frontend with a large European following.

A couple of years ago, I started planning my own car PC installation. I was very excited, and I thought, "In a few days I'll be playing any multimedia files I want in my car!" Assembling the hardware was easy, as there were already plenty of choices for a good car multimedia installation [Hack #52]. I just needed to find good, powerful software to manage all the new functions.

And that was the problem—nothing I found worked how I wanted it to. Some good applications were available, but none of them had all the functions I needed. So, I decided to make my own software.

This hack is about the Neocar Media Center application that I wrote (*http:// www.neocarmediacenter.com/?language=EN*). After reading it, you should have a pretty good idea of whether you want to use my software as the frontend to your car PC.

Neocar Media Center

When I started working on NMC, I had a big problem: I had only rudimentary Visual Basic skills, and I wasn't an experienced programmer. Perhaps this is what led me to really think about the design of my software before I wrote any code. Besides making a frontend application, I wanted a program that was user-configurable, because I wanted users to be able to run it they way *they* wanted. I also wanted a program that was skinnable, so that I (and other users) could change its appearance with ease. Finally, I wanted to include all the functions I wanted in one program, because I hate having to install multiple pieces of software when one could do the job.

NMC is coded to enable you to sort of build your own car PC software. That is, NMC has a lot of functions that the user can choose to use in his particular skin, or not. It's all based on different NMC modules that accomplish the main functions, such as music playing, movie playback, and image display (see Figure 7-17).

Figure 7-17. Neocar Media Center main module

Installing NMC is simple—just download the latest development version from *http://www.neocarmediacenter.com* and install it with a double-click. After installing, NMC will automatically load Neocar Manager so that you can enter the only required options: the location of your media folders for music, movies, and images. Once you've saved the configuration, all the other options will be available so that you can set up NMC how *you* want.

Neocar is comprised of three components:

Neocar Media Center (NMC)
   The frontend program itself. This is what you will interact with on a daily basis.

Neocar Skin Workshop (NSW)
   Using this, you can make a custom NMC skin design from scratch, or simply open an existing skin and modify it. You can change the fonts (color, name, size, format), button positions and sizes, text sizes, and more, all without having to redesign any image files!

Neocar Manager (NM)
   With NM, you can set all the available options, even if your skin doesn't support them. Options are ordered in categories for better readability.

NMC Features

NMC derives its functionality from several different modules. It is up to the user to select which modules to display on the main NMC window. Each module can have up to three view modes, which are fully customizable by the user. Using the view modes, you can show all the available options or just a subset, or display the module in full-screen mode. Here are brief descriptions of the currently available modules:

Main module

When you launch NMC, by default the Main module will load (see Figure 7-18). This menu displays buttons for all of the functions enabled by the skin. If you return to the main menu while audio files are playing, not only does the music continue, but NMC will also show audio controls to let you play, stop, or change the music.

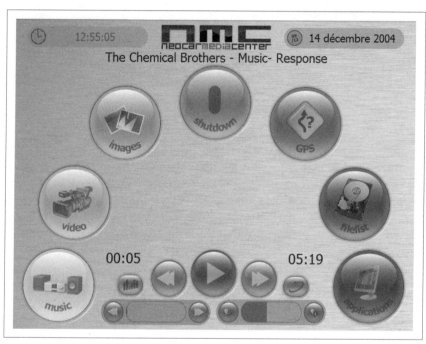

Figure 7-18. The NMC Main module (with audio controls)

Music module

This is probably the most-used part of NMC (see Figure 7-19). The Music module allows you to play audio files (naturally), but it also lets you open Winamp playlists and playlists in NMC's custom format, which allows you to include virtual folders. Once you've starting playing music, it will continue to play when you switch to other modules.

Use Neocar Media Center as Your Car PC Frontend

Figure 7-19. The NMC Music module

The Music module can play MP3, WAV, WMA, and OGG files. It also supports reading of *cue sheet* files, which are text files that prepare audio files to be burned to CD (like a summary of the included tracks, with start and end times). This feature is for those who don't want to rip individual tracks for each audio CD. It allows the whole CD to exist as a single file on the hard disk, while preserving an index of the subdivided tracks that NMC will read and display for you.

Movie module

The Movie module supports every function supported by the Music module. You can use cue sheets, use playlists to manage your playing order, go to full-screen video with an auto-hiding control bar, and so on. The Movie module can play AVI, MPEG, ASF, WMV, and MPV files.

Images module

With the Images module (Figure 7-20), you can open your image files, make automatic slideshows, and adjust the slideshow speed. The auto-hiding control bar is present, as in other modules. The Image module can display JPG, GIF, BMP, and PNG images.

External Applications module

A major feature of NMC is the External Applications module, which allows you to embed any external application as if it were part of NMC.

Figure 7-20. The NMC Images module

To use this feature, you define a list of software in the Neocar Manager that NMC will show in the External Applications module (Figure 7-21). If you click on an application in that list, you will see a brief description, and clicking another time will run it. NMC then switches to full-screen mode, showing the launched application embedded inside the NMC skin (Figure 7-22). As in the other modules, the control bar automatically hides after a configurable delay.

Keyboard module

The Keyboard module is a fully working onscreen keyboard (Figure 7-23), allowing you to enter information in NMC or in any launched external application. Like the other modules, you can design the keyboard exactly how you want it; you aren't constrained by a normal keyboard layout. NMC includes a function to let you choose the keyboard scheme to fit your language requirements.

File List module

This module (see Figure 7-24) lets you navigate through your filesystem and search for multimedia files. It can show you information about each file that can be played in NMC and will open the appropriate module for any selected file. You can also use the file list to manage audio or video playlists, by simply adding or removing tracks using dedicated buttons.

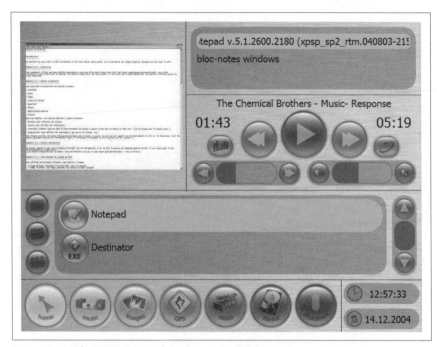

Figure 7-21. The NMC External Applications module

Figure 7-22. Full-screen navigation with control bar

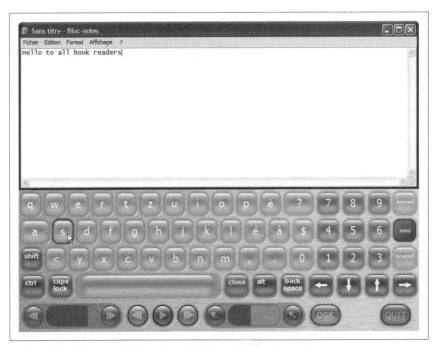

Figure 7-23. The NMC Keyboard module

Figure 7-24. The NMC File List module

Equalizer module

You can use this module to adjust sound EQ settings to your liking. You can also use it to set common levels, such as the volumes for main, WAV, line-in, audio CD, or microphone, just like the Volume Control panel in Windows.

Configuring NMC

Using skins, you can quickly customize the entire look of the application. Since skinning is an important feature to me, I wanted to make it easy to do, and I wanted to include the ability to edit the available skins and create new skins, not just apply existing ones. You can do all of this using the Neocar Skin Workshop (NSW).

The interface is similar to other image-editing software (see Figure 7-25). Using the mouse, you select a button to add to the interface, then click on the skin where you want that button to appear. NSW will then display a list of available module controls to assign to that button.

Figure 7-25. Neocar Skin Workshop

After you've created or modified a skin, NSW lets you validate it for errors. Once you've validated your creation, NSW can make an installer for your skin (using Nullsoft's NSIS installer) and upload the skin directly to *http:// www.neocarmediacenter.com*, where it will be made available for others to use.

Each skin is made from just four images:

Background image
> This is the image on which you place all other images, such as your interface buttons.

Normal buttons image
> This image combines the background image and the interface buttons in their "released" or up positions.

Pressed buttons image
> This shows the interface with the buttons in the "pressed" or down position.

Hover buttons image
> This is what the interface looks like when the mouse is hovering over each of the buttons.

The *skin.xml* file (present in the folder for each individual skin) is a file containing information about the position and size of each used control. It also contains text display properties and some skin-related options.

While loading, NMC will list the positions and sizes of each of the skin's controls and draw the buttons where you placed them. The image will then be copied from the "normal buttons" skin image, and the background will be painted on the module.

With this system, it's easy to remove a button from the skin and just let NMC use the background image to paint the module without that button. So, if NMC doesn't find a control's information, it will simply not paint or load it, so that button's commands will be unavailable.

Neocar Manager

The Neocar Manager is where you can configure all NMC-related options. You can associate files with NMC, manage your albums, manage your movies, add or remove external apps, and more. There are too many features and configuration options to describe here; the best way to get to know it is to experiment.

Future Plans

Neocar is far from finished. I'm working on several stunning new functions, including *full* GPS embedding, keyboard support, DVD support, audio CD support, character LCD support, and database-driven filesystem support, as well as lots of function improvements and general performance tuning.

The best source of feature and support information about NMC is the main web site, *http://www.neocarmediacenter.com/?language=EN*. There you can find updates on the progress of development, the to-do list, requests, bugs, and more.

—Stéphane Monnier

Use FrodoPlayer as Your Car PC Frontend

#75   FrodoPlayer is one of the most popular car PC applications, because it integrates almost every conceivable feature (and has a cool name).

FrodoPlayer started out as a way for me to tie together the many functions I wanted in a car PC. When I began my car PC project, there weren't as many programs for use with car computers and VGA touchscreens as there are now. A lot of the functions I needed just weren't easy or safe to use in a car environment, especially for drivers. I started out with a very basic media player that played only MP3s. Compare that to what FrodoPlayer is today: a system that supports music, video, DVD, CD audio, "smart" and regular playlists, XM radio, FM radio, GPS, reversing cameras, file syncing, picture slideshows, remote control, web-based control, skinning and customization, external applications, video lockout for safety and legal reasons, and ties in with external applications written specifically for the car PC market. Believe it or not, even more features are in the works, and all the existing features are constantly being improved.

As you can see, I'm quite proud of it, and I like to brag...a little.

After reading this hack, you should have a pretty good idea of whether you want to use FrodoPlayer as the frontend to your car PC.

Installing FrodoPlayer

First up, let's get the setup of FrodoPlayer out of the way. I'm going to go through some basic and intermediate aspects of setting up FrodoPlayer for the first time.

The latest version of FrodoPlayer can always be found at *http://www. frodoplayer.com*. There is also a support forum there, but more people use the forum at *http://www.mp3car.com*. This MP3Car.com web site is by far the best car PC resource in existence.

After you have downloaded FrodoPlayer and verified that you have all the prerequisites, you can install FrodoPlayer. This is straightforward and has a guided setup, so you shouldn't have any problems.

After installation, FrodoPlayer needs to scan your media collection in order to add all your music to its database. To do this, go to Settings → Database and browse to a media folder located on your non-removable hard drive. Sit back and wait a bit while the player builds your database. If you would like, you can peruse the other settings in this menu while you wait. You will only have to rebuild your database when you add media to your car PC. (A syncing function is in the works that will shorten this process considerably, but unfortunately it is not yet available.)

Okay, you have it set up now, but it might not look like you want it to. Fortunately, FrodoPlayer is completely skinnable, which means you can easily change the appearance of the entire application. Take some time to choose a skin you like from the FrodoPlayer web site.

The main interface (Figure 7-26) has Forward and Back buttons, which allow you to choose the browse modes (i.e., different ways to access your media). You can find the media you want to play by artist, genre, title, folder hierarchy, or album art, to name a few of the options. There's even a search facility that will bring up an onscreen keyboard. Before you move on, check out the full-screen mode.

Figure 7-26. FrodoPlayer's main interface

Everything on the main screen should be pretty self-explana-
tory; if it isn't, it won't take you long to figure it all out, but
you should do so before you start driving. When you drive,
you need to keep your eyes on the road, not on a new user
interface.

FrodoPlayer Features

FrodoPlayer is packed with features. When it first launches, you are presented with the media player screen and your music collection. If you press
the Menu button you'll see the screen shown in Figure 7-27, which displays
all the other functions available to you. Read the feature descriptions below,
then play around in the interface to see how the features actually work.
Experimenting like this is probably the easiest way to learn the program.

Figure 7-27. The main FrodoPlayer menu

The features available in FrodoPlayer are:

Smart playlists

Smart playlists are just database queries. These can currently be made in
the settings menus. An example smart playlist would be one that consists of only Rolling Stones songs from the '80s. Note that it is possible
to create such a playlist only if your file tags include the necessary information. To accomplish this, open the Settings menu, click on Smart
Playlists, enter in the query values, and save. It's that simple.

Import Winamp playlists

If you've spent hundreds of hours making Winamp playlists over the years, all that effort wasn't wasted. If you have Winamp playlists in *.m3u* or *.pls* format, just drop them in the playlists folder and FrodoPlayer will make use of them.

Regular playlists

Of course, FrodoPlayer supports regular playlists as well. Figure 7-28 shows the regular playlist selector.

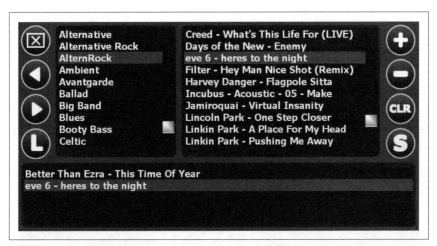

Figure 7-28. The playlist selector

Use FFDShow to post-process videos

Post-processing enhances the resolution, sharpness, and detail of digital video after it has been decompressed, compensating for some of the jagged artifacts added in the compression process. If you have a powerful enough system, you can install FFDShow (Google to find it) and use it to post-process your videos.

Add videos to the database

FrodoPlayer normally doesn't store videos in the database, but that doesn't mean you can't. Open the Settings menu, and click the Filetypes option. Add the video file types to your database, and then rebuild or sync. Just make sure your video files are located under the same main folder as your music. Now you can use the browse modes to browse your video collection. If you want to categorize your videos, just set them up in folders and use one of the directory or album art modes.

Install DVD codecs

FrodoPlayer won't play DVDs without the appropriate decoder (codec). When you install a player application such as PowerDVD or WinDVD, the appropriate codecs are installed with it [Hack #70], You don't actually have to use these programs; you just need them for their included codecs.

Install a video lockout device, or a remote camera trigger

You can buy small serial relay devices from my web site, or build your own. These devices allow FrodoPlayer to respond to input signals telling it when the car is in motion or backing up. (For wiring considerations, look at "Turn On Your Car Computer Before You Start Your Car" [Hack #46].) Installing these will allow you to disable video playback in FrodoPlayer while the car is moving, or have FrodoPlayer switch to your rearview camera when the vehicle shifts into reverse [Hack #33].

FM radio

The FM radio player (see Figure 7-29) piggybacks off a wonderful program called Radiator, which is available at *http://www.flesko.cz*. Find a supported card somewhere on the Net [Hack #19], and get it all set up and running with Radiator. Then just go to the settings page and tell FrodoPlayer where you installed Radiator.

Figure 7-29. FM radio player (picture courtesy of Konrad)

XM Radio

FrodoPlayer is XM satellite ready! To use an XM Direct receiver [Hack #19], you need a simple, cheap cable that connects the receiver to your car PC's serial port. The instructions to make this cable can be found on my site (*http://www.frodoplayer.com*) or at *http://www.mp3car.com*. You may also find vendors who provide the cables pre-made—just ask on the forums at one of the above sites.

After you have fabricated or purchased your cable, hook up your XM Direct receiver to an available serial port, or to an available USB port if you would like to use a USB-to-serial adapter. Note the port you used, and define the port in the settings. You'll now be able to tune your XM radio directly from FrodoPlayer (see Figure 7-30).

Figure 7-30. XM radio player (picture courtesy of djScript)

Automatic file syncing

File syncing can be accomplished by using an integrated third-party application called Karen's Replicator **[Hack #64]**. Karen's Replicator has been modified for touchscreen use and is available from FrodoPlayer's main menu. It supports scheduled and manual syncing. Additional information can be found at *http://www.karenware.com*. This is really useful for wireless connections between your home and car. Once your network is set up, a touch of the sync button is all that is needed to transfer your files. Optionally, you can use the Replicator's scheduling functions.

Serve up HTML or scripts to other applications

FrodoPlayer includes a small web server internally. This allows third-party tools to query and control FrodoPlayer, as well as allowing the user to write web plug-ins (FPWebins) for simple automation and control of just about anything. The web server also supports most CGI scripts, including PHP, so practically unlimited control is possible. Full programming specifications and usage instructions can be found at *http://www.frodoplayer.com*.

Remote control

FrodoPlayer can be controlled with Windows messages, which allows third-party developers to automate FrodoPlayer. This also enables users to automate FrodoPlayer by using a third-party tool such as Girder **[Hack #56]** that will allow remote controls and other hardware to control it. Complete specifications for the commands and some tutorials are available on the FrodoPlayer web site. Here is an example of how this works (you'll need a remote control, of course):

   a. Download Girder from *http://www.girder.nl*.

   b. Go to the FrodoPlayer web site, and download the sample Girder configuration file.

   c. Load the file into Girder and follow Girder's instructions for your IR receiver to get it all set up. Then click on the command in the list that you want, choose Learn, and press the desired key on your remote.

   d. After that, if Girder is running and FrodoPlayer is running, pressing the key on the remote will initiate that action. Yes, it is that simple!

Third-Party Tools

An increasing number of third-party tools can be used with FrodoPlayer. These tools are able to interoperate with FrodoPlayer as one cohesive unit.

One example is my friend Zoran Horvat's PhoneControl.NET **[Hack #63]**, which can pause and resume FrodoPlayer when you receive and terminate incoming calls. To try out PhoneControl.NET, go to *http://zoran-horvat.de/private/CarPC/default.htm*.

Another useful third-party tool, written by another friend of mine, is NaviVoice **[Hack #60]**. NaviVoice is a nice voice-activated program that will allow you to control all kinds of computer-related things. You can download the program from *http://www.whipflash.com/vamr/routisvoice.htm*. To find out more about it, go to *http://www.mp3car.com/vbulletin/forumdisplay.php?f=52* (or just search the MP3Car.com forums for NaviVoice).

Replace the Windows GUI with Frodo

You can replace the Windows XP Explorer shell (i.e., the whole Windows GUI) with FrodoPlayer. It is relatively simple to do, but it may cause instability in your OS. This will only work with a Windows XP system. Here are the steps:

1. Open the Windows Registry Editor (*regedit*).

2. Navigate to this subkey: HKEY_LOCAL_MACHINE\SOFTWARE\Microsoft\Windows NT\CurrentVersion\Winlogon.

3. Go to the Shell setting.

4. Replace explorer.exe with the full path to *FrodoPlayer.exe*.

5. Reboot.

Future Improvements

By the time you are reading this, the player will probably have changed a lot, with more features added and ease of use improved. Here's just a sampling of the features I'm working on at this writing:

* Dual screen support
* Integrated web browser, email reader, weather reporting, TV control, and radio control
* Gamma (brightness) control and relay controller support with plug-ins
* Memo recording, contact list
* File manager
* Control of FrodoPlayer from any "XM-ready" head unit
* Full Unicode support and international customization support, languages, etc.
* Safety enhancements
* Expanded GPS support

All of the things you have read about here can be found as tutorials or FAQs at *http://www.frodoplayer.com* or *http://www.mp3car.com*.

Support forums are available as well. Please check in to see what has changed and try out some of the things you find there.

—Kevin Lincecum

Index

Numbers

3G (third-generation wireless
  protocol), 255
  getting online with, 257
3ivx, 228

A

AC (alternating current), 41
  safety issues with use in cars, 44
accessory wires, 31
AC-to-DC power supply, 67
adapter outlets for cars, sources of, 30
adapters
  12V-to-5V, for DVD drive, 134
  AUX-in (see AUX-in adapters)
  choosing among, 58
  factory screens, 89
  FM radio tuner, 75
  iPod, 72
  for mounting head unit, 52
  OBD-II, 301
  RGB (video) screen, 118–120
  tape adapter, 54
Advanced Configuration Power Interface
  (ACPI), 158
Ah (amp-hours), 23
airbag system, head units and, 53
air-conditioning, piping to your in-car
  PC, 145
alarms, integration into head unit, 53
alternating current (see AC)

alternators
  deep-cycle batteries and, 39
  dual-output, 39
  upgrading, 36–37, 144
amp meter, 25
amp-hours (Ah), 23, 27
amplifiers, 48
  getting computer audio into, 60–64
    bypassing the head unit, 62–63
    PC pass-through, 63
    replacing head unit with car
      computer, 64
  inputs, 60
  passing head unit through PC
    connected to, 63
amps, 8
  calculating draw of your device, 24
  cranking amps (CAs and CCAs), 27
  determining your power needs, 14
  required by portable devices, 189
  watts vs., 22
analog audio input, adjusting volume
  of, 58
antenna connectors, 50
antennas
  car radio, routing to FM tuner, 74
  in-car TV antennas, 130
  WiFi, 258, 292
AOL Instant Messenger product
  (AIM), 278
Apple iPod (see iPod)

We'd like to hear your suggestions for improving our indexes. Send email to *index@oreilly.com*.

H

handheld remote, controlling your car
PC, 232–236
  infrared, 232
  infrared (IR) receivers, 233
  integration and compatibility, 235
  RF (radio frequency), 234
haptic (touch) interfaces, 250
hard drive spin up, 165
hard drives
  draw of amps or watts, 24
  faster, using to shorten boot
    time, 167
  minimizing shock to, 198
  portable, 268
    powering in your car, 192
hardware detection delays at boot
    time, 166
harness, 51
Haynes manual, 50
head units, 46
  aftermarket, 47
  amplifiers, 48
  bypassing by using amplifier, 62–63
  computer audio in, 54–60
    aftermarket head units, 57
    auxiliary-in adapters, using, 56
    choosing your adapter, 58
    digital inputs, 57
    FM modulators, using, 55
    input volume, adjusting, 58
    multiplexing inputs, 60
    tape adapters, using, 54
  entanglement with vehicle
    functions, 48
  installing new, 51–53
    adapters for mounting, 52
    caveats, 53
    proprietary bus connectors, 53
    standard wiring, 51
  integration with car PC, 251
  iPod integration, 72
  motorized video screen, 104–106
  option for fold-out screen, 89
  passing audio through PC and
    amplifier, 63
  removing, 49
  replacing with car computer, 64

header (WOL), 161
headliner, removing for ceiling-mounted
    screen, 107
headrest screens, 88
  installing, 92–97
    velcroing onto headrests, 95
    wiring, 96
Headunit (Linux software), 180
heat shrink, 18
"Hibernate Once, Resume Many"
    (HORM), 187
hibernation, 155, 164
  problems with SAPI, 248
  reducing system memory for faster
    boot, 166
high-definition televisions (HDTVs), 87
holes, drilling for power outlets, 30
home theater personal computer (see
    HTPC)
hotspots, WiFi, 257
  finding on the road, 289–295
    improving reception, 292
  making your car a mobile
    hotspot, 259
hours over which amp-hour ratings
    apply, 24
HTPC (home theater personal
    computer), 303
  comparisons of
    applications, 306–311
  hardware requirements, 304
  software available today, 303
  software requirements, 305
hybrid deep-cycle and starting
    batteries, 28

I

iChat, 278
iDash project, 180
iDrive, 250
iGuidance, controlling with voice
    commands, 247
IM (instant messenger) applications
  AIM, 278
  limitations of, 280
  Trillian, 279
  videoconferencing protocols, 279
In-Dash PC, 150

Colophon

Our look is the result of reader comments, our own experimentation, and feedback from distribution channels. Distinctive covers complement our distinctive approach to technical topics, breathing personality and life into potentially dry subjects.

The tool on the cover of *Car PC Hacks* is a wire cutter. Following the invention of wire came that of the wire cutter, a tool similar to pliers, with sharp-edged cutting jaws like scissors. Pliers were invented in Europe around 2000 BC to grip hot objects, principally iron. Over the centuries, many different kinds of pliers have been developed specifically for new inventions, including horseshoes, fasteners, pipes, and electrical and electronic components. Wire cutters, like other kinds of pliers, are comprised of two handles, a pivot, and a head section with gripping jaws or cutting edges. Conventional wire cutters utilize a compression-type cut in which the blade edges collide, pushing the wire out of the way. The long handles relative to the short nose of the cutters amplify the force in the hand's grip on the wire. The tool on the cover also has stripping abilities and may alternately be referred to as a wire stripper. It has an additional center notch that makes it easier to cut insulation from a wire without cutting the wire itself.

Genevieve d'Entremont was the production editor and proofreader for *Car PC Hacks*. Rachel Wheeler was the copyeditor. Mary Brady and Claire Cloutier provided quality control. Lydia Onofrei provided production assistance. Ellen Troutman-Zaig wrote the index.

Hanna Dyer designed the cover of this book, based on a series design by Edie Freedman. The cover image is a photograph from the Stockbyte Work Tools CD. Karen Montgomery produced the cover layout with Adobe InDesign CS using Adobe's Helvetica Neue and ITC Garamond fonts.

David Futato designed the interior layout. This book was converted by Keith Fahlgren to FrameMaker 5.5.6 with a format conversion tool created by Erik Ray, Jason McIntosh, Neil Walls, and Mike Sierra that uses Perl and XML technologies. The text font is Linotype Birka; the heading font is Adobe Helvetica Neue Condensed; and the code font is LucasFont's TheSans Mono Condensed. The illustrations that appear in the book were produced by Robert Romano, Jessamyn Read, and Lesley Borash using Macromedia FreeHand MX and Adobe Photoshop CS. This colophon was written by Lydia Onofrei.

Better than e-books

Buy *Car PC Hacks* and access the digital
edition FREE on Safari for 45 days.

Go to www.oreilly.com/go/safarienabled
and type in coupon code 3PJ1-S8UK-UUST-2SKT-9H5Z

Search
over 2000 top
tech books

Download
whole chapters

Cut and Paste
code examples

Find
answers fast

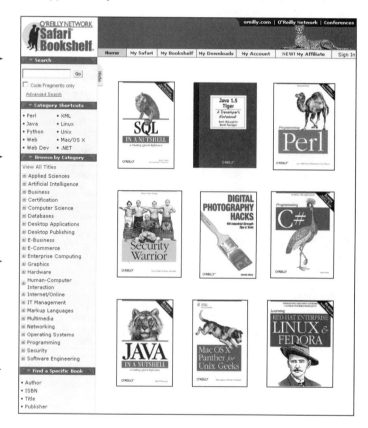

Search Safari! The premier electronic reference
library for programmers and IT professionals

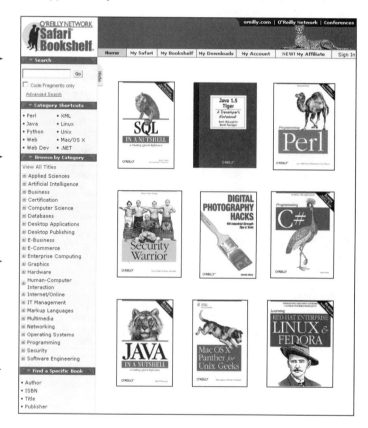

Keep in touch with O'Reilly

Download examples from our books

To find example files from a book, go to: *www.oreilly.com/catalog* select the book, and follow the "Examples" link.

Register your O'Reilly books

Register your book at *register.oreilly.com* Why register your books? Once you've registered your O'Reilly books you can:

- Win O'Reilly books, T-shirts or discount coupons in our monthly drawing.
- Get special offers available only to registered O'Reilly customers.
- Get catalogs announcing new books (US and UK only).
- Get email notification of new editions of the O'Reilly books you own.

Join our email lists

Sign up to get topic-specific email announcements of new books and conferences, special offers, and O'Reilly Network technology newsletters at:

elists.oreilly.com

It's easy to customize your free elists subscription so you'll get exactly the O'Reilly news you want.

Get the latest news, tips, and tools

www.oreilly.com

- "Top 100 Sites on the Web"—PC Magazine
- CIO Magazine's Web Business 50 Awards

Our web site contains a library of comprehensive product information (including book excerpts and tables of contents), downloadable software, background articles, interviews with technology leaders, links to relevant sites, book cover art, and more.

Work for O'Reilly

Check out our web site for current employment opportunities:

jobs.oreilly.com

Contact us

O'Reilly Media, Inc.
1005 Gravenstein Hwy North
Sebastopol, CA 95472 USA
Tel: 707-827-7000 or 800-998-9938
    (6am to 5pm PST)
Fax: 707-829-0104

Contact us by email

For answers to problems regarding your order or our products:
order@oreilly.com

To request a copy of our latest catalog:
catalog@oreilly.com

For book content technical questions or corrections: **booktech@oreilly.com**

For educational, library, government, and corporate sales: **corporate@oreilly.com**

To submit new book proposals to our editors and product managers:
proposals@oreilly.com

For information about our international distributors or translation queries:
international@oreilly.com

For information about academic use of O'Reilly books:
adoption@oreilly.com
or visit:
academic.oreilly.com

For a list of our distributors outside of North America check out:
international.oreilly.com/distributors.html

Order a book online

www.oreilly.com/order_new